CULTURE, PLACE, AND NATURE

STUDIES IN ANTHROPOLOGY AND ENVIRONMENT

Devon G. Peña and K. Sivaramakrishnan,

Series Editors

CULTURE, PLACE, AND NATURE

Centered in anthropology, the Culture, Place, and Nature
series encompasses new interdisciplinary social science
research on environmental issues, focusing on the intersection
of culture, ecology, and politics in global, national, and local
contexts. Contributors to the series view environmental
knowledge and issues from the often conflicting
perspectives of different cultural systems.

*The Kuhls of Kangra: Community-Managed
Irrigation in the Western Himalaya*, by J. Mark Baker

*The Earth's Blanket: Traditional Teachings
for Sustainable Living*, by Nancy Turner

*Property and Politics in Sabah, Malaysia: Native
Struggles over Land Rights*, by Amity A. Doolittle

THE KUHLS OF KANGRA

Community-Managed Irrigation

in the Western Himalaya

J. MARK BAKER

UNIVERSITY OF WASHINGTON PRESS

Seattle and London

THIS PUBLICATION WAS SUPPORTED IN PART
BY THE DONALD R. ELLEGOOD INTERNATIONAL
PUBLICATIONS ENDOWMENT.

© 2005 by the University of Washington Press
Design by Pamela Canell
Composition by Elevenarts, Keshav Puram, Delhi 110035
Printed in the United States of America
12 11 10 09 08 07 06 05 04 5 4 3 2 1

Published simultaneously in India by Permanent Black,
D-28 Oxford Apts., 11 IP Extension, Delhi, 110092

University of Washington Press
P.O. Box 50096, Seattle, WA 98145, U.S.A.
www.washington.edu/uwpress

Library of Congress Cataloging-in-Publication Data
can be found at the back of this book.

The paper used in this publication is acid-free and 90 percent
recycled from at least 50 percent post-consumer waste. It meets
the minimum requirements of American National Standard
for Information Sciences—Permanence of Paper for Printed
Library Materials, ANSI Z39.48-1984. ♾ ♻

FOR KIM

CONTENTS

Preface
ix

Introduction
3

ONE
An Explanatory Tapestry
20

TWO
The Dynamic Landscape of Kuhl Irrigation
51

THREE
Statemaking and Irrigation in Kangra
97

FOUR
Patterns of Change
136

FIVE
Networks of Interdependence
175

SIX
Dynamic Regimes, Enduring Flows
197

APPENDIX ONE

A Note on Methods

217

APPENDIX TWO

Two Kuhl Stories
Recounted by Shyam Lal Sharma

221

APPENDIX THREE

Summary Characteristics of Kuhl Regimes
of the Neugal Watershed

224

Notes

228

Glossary

248

References

252

Index

265

PREFACE

FOR CENTURIES, FARMERS IN KANGRA VALLEY, IN THE WESTERN HIMA-
layan state of Himachal Pradesh, India, have constructed, maintained, and
managed one of the largest networks of community-based irrigation
systems in the world. Etched into the landscape like a complex lattice, dense
networks of thousands of irrigation channels convey snowmelt and
monsoon rainwater to the hamlets and fields crowded on the alluvial plains
that slope away from the Dhaula Dhar mountains and make up Kangra
Valley. Since the initial construction of these irrigation systems—known
locally as *kuhls*—floods, droughts, and earthquakes have continually
threatened their existence. In fundamental yet historically unprecedented
ways, recent and rapid socioeconomic changes also challenge their ability
to endure. Prevailing theories of common property resource management
suggest that such conditions should lead to the demise of the kuhls. Yet
despite these shocks and changes, most kuhls in Kangra continue to brim
with snowmelt during the hot, dry, pre-monsoon season, when dependence
on irrigation for the rice crop peaks. In this book I uncover and explain
the multiple factors that together account for the durability of the kuhls
of Kangra.

The book is situated in the terrain of interdisciplinary studies. For this
project, there was no other choice. The kuhls themselves reflect and indeed
help create community, economy, political authority, and culture in Kangra.
Only an interdisciplinary lens could reveal their full complexity and
multidimensionality. Furthermore, the spatial and temporal specificity of
the many relationships that have shaped the dynamic transformations of

kuhls over the last two hundred years forced explicit consideration of the powerful effects of regionality on kuhls within a historically grounded framework. Consequently, I have woven my analysis from diverse strands of thought originating in the fields of political science, economics, history, cultural geography, and cultural anthropology.

The framework I develop for understanding patterns of change and continuity in the kuhls of Kangra establishes the importance and utility of historically informed, multidimensional analyses of regimes of natural resource management. It demonstrates the necessity of examining the regional specificities of political, economic, and social processes and institutions as they both shape and are shaped by the natural environment, in order to understand patterns of resource use and management. And it illustrates the diverse ways in which supralocal political entities can be involved in "local" resource management regimes and the effects of that involvement on configurations of state power and local social power.

This framework is especially pertinent given the current broader context of devolution and decentralization of management authority for resource management. Worldwide and across multiple resource sectors (e.g., forests, water, wildlife), state and national governments and communities are restructuring their relationships to one another and to the natural environment. This process entails reconfiguring the distribution, between state entities and communities, of rights to, responsibilities for, authority over, and benefits in natural resources. These efforts have the potential to strengthen local democratic practice, promote environmental stewardship, and improve the livelihoods of resource-dependent groups. They can also undermine local management capacities and marginalize already disenfranchised groups. By adopting a historically informed, regionally oriented, interdisciplinary approach, one can discern the contradictory outcomes associated with the trend toward devolution and illuminate the conditions under which state engagement with local resource management regimes strengthens local democratic practice or undermines it.

This story of the kuhls of Kangra unfolded over a period of years. Along the winding path that the project has taken, I have been blessed with innumerable mentors and guides, friends and colleagues. I am happy to have the opportunity to thank them here. In many key respects this book reflects the primary relationships that have enriched my life since I began my graduate studies in 1984. Indeed, the debts incurred extend farther back, to influential professors at the University of California, Santa Cruz, and Ventura Community College.

At the University of California, Berkeley, Jeff Romm, Louise Fortmann, Todd LaPorte, and David Leonard provided important guidance and insight during my doctoral studies. Jeff Romm stands out as a pillar of integrity, support, and encouragement. His commitment to the ideals of academic excellence and ethics, along with his characteristic intensity and devotion to scholarship that matters, left an indelible mark that I shall carry with pride always. His energetic engagement with this work, including a trip to Kangra to visit the kuhls, helped me do justice to the richness of the kuhls and immeasurably enhanced the quality of this work. In many ways, the book is a testament to the depth of relationship we share.

A rich set of friendships contributed much enjoyment and rigor to my time at Berkeley. Formal and informal discussions of interrelated research projects in diverse settings sustained a climate of stimulating intellectual engagement that I have found unmatched since. In particular, I would like to acknowledge the collegial support of Yvonne Everett, Madhav Ghimire, Vinay Gidwani, Kailash Govil, Jonathan Kusel, Sureerat Lakanavichian, Nick Menzies, Yashwant Negi, Marty Olson, Krisna Suryanata, and Lini Wollenberg.

This book is based on more than two years of ethnographic and archival research carried out in Kangra from December 1990 through November 1991 and from September 1992 through November 1993, with return visits in 1997 and 2002. During the fieldwork, a diverse set of relationships evolved that have enriched my life in meaningful ways; many continue to this day. In particular, I would like to honor the important roles that Krishan Kumar Sharma and his father, Shyam Lal Sharma ("Pita-ji"), played in this project and in my life in Kangra. By virtue of their knowledge and love of Kangri culture and the kuhls, they immeasurably inspired, encouraged, and supported me throughout the research. My debt to Mr. Sharma and Pita-ji extends far beyond the research endeavor. Initially Mr. Sharma translated sections of the *Riwaj-i-Abpashi* (Irrigation Customs) for me from Urdu into English. By the end of the first stage of fieldwork I had become a member of his extended family and was accorded the love, affection, and support that membership implies. Each day, upon returning from fieldwork, Pita-ji, whose increasing blindness seemed only to strengthen his powers of recollection and knowledge of the old ways in Kangra, would grill me on where I had been and what I had learned. His questions and comments sharpened and deepened my understanding; the relationship we shared will remain with me always. Mr. Sharma's nuclear family—Mata-ji, Meena,

Sanjay, Uday, and Vijay—all welcomed me into their lives, and I thank them for doing so.

I would also like to express my gratitude to the *kohlis* (watermasters) with whom I worked most closely. Shri Kishori Lal, Shri Laxman Das, Shri Ranvir Singh, Shri Dhyan Singh, Shri Kehar Singh, and Shri Jagat Ram Ohri all shared with me their deep knowledge and understanding of the kuhls. When walking the length of the kuhls they managed, some of them even slowed their characteristically fast pace to allow me to keep up. I am also grateful to the other kohlis, members of kuhl committees, and many farmers who shared with me their knowledge, opinions, and time while knowing they would receive nothing directly in return. Rajesh Thakur and Jugal Kishore provided excellent research assistance and good companionship. A note of appreciation is also due to the many district and subdistrict Revenue Department officials who granted me unfettered access to the bundles of old records, wrapped in cloth and liberally coated with the dust of decades, that enabled me to develop the historical perspective used in this study.

I would like to thank Didi Contractor for her enduring friendship, generous hospitality, and ongoing interest in this study. Her home in Kangra is a place of warmth and support as well as stimulating conversation. Heartfelt thanks are also due to Mrs. Sarla and General Korla for their warmth and generous friendship. "Korla Niwas" is still my favorite refuge in Palampur.

Anil Gupta, at the Indian Institute of Management, Ahmedabad, and T. V. Moorti, at the Himachal Pradesh Agricultural University, Palampur, were my faculty sponsors in India. Each provided valuable insights and helpful suggestions at different stages of the research process.

This project would not have been possible without the generous support of a variety of institutions. The initial field research was supported by a Fulbright-Hays Doctoral Dissertation Research Abroad grant and a Junior Fellowship from the American Institute of Indian Studies. A Ciriacy-Wantrup Post-Doctoral Fellowship at UC Berkeley gave me the opportunity to further develop the ideas presented in the dissertation, as did a Faculty Fellowship at the University of North Carolina, Asheville. Most recently, generous support from Forest Community Research has enabled me to considerably revise the final manuscript.

Portions of this book were strengthened through presentations at the University of Wisconsin, Madison's, annual South Asia Conference, October 1995, October 1996, and October 1997; at the Department of Social Sciences,

Y. S. Parmer University of Horticulture and Forestry, Solan, Himachal Pradesh, March 1995; at UC Berkeley's annual South Asia Conference, March 1995; at the meeting of the International Association for the Study of Common Property, June 1996; at the Program in Agrarian Studies, Yale University, May 1997; at the Centre for India and South Asia Research, University of British Columbia, Canada, 1997; at the meeting of the American Society for Environmental History, Tucson, April 1999; and at the Workshop in Political Theory and Policy Analysis, Indiana University, Bloomington, 1999. Portions of the book include material that appeared in an earlier form in the journal *Human Organization* (vol. 56, no. 2) and in the book *Agrarian Environments,* edited by K. Sivaramakrishnan and Arun Agrawal (Duke University Press, 2000).

At various stages in the writing of this book, I benefited from discussions with and the comments and suggestions of Kavita Phillip, Marty Olson, Vinay Gidwani, Arun Agrawal, K. Sivaramakrishnan, David Ludden, Ajay Skaria, James Scott, Elinor Ostrom, Kim Berry, and Vasant Saberwal. I am grateful to the reviewers for the University of Washington Press for their extremely helpful and perceptive comments on an earlier draft of the manuscript. Their detailed notes enabled me to strengthen and clarify many of the book's arguments and engage more directly with a variety of literatures. Lorri Hagman, acquisitions editor at the University of Washington Press, provided well-timed and helpful guidance as well as detailed comments on several key chapters. Jane Kepp's careful editing of the manuscript greatly enhanced its clarity and flow.

Last, I would like to express my enduring gratitude to my companion in life, Kim Berry, for the innumerable ways in which she made this project possible. Words are entirely inadequate to describe the continual support, personal and professional, that she has given over the years. We have together crafted wonderful life chapters—may we have the opportunity to create many more.

January 2005
Arcata, California

THE KUHLS OF KANGRA

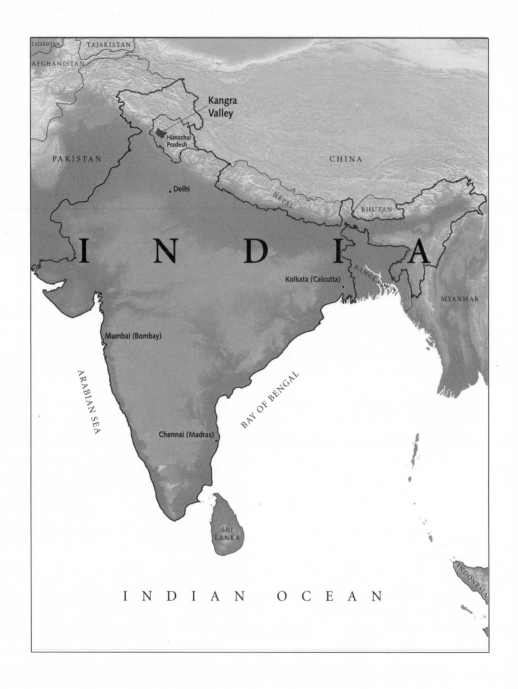

MAP 1. Location of Kangra Valley in northern India.

INTRODUCTION

ON APRIL 4, 1905, A DEVASTATING EARTHQUAKE STRUCK KANGRA VALLEY
in what is now the state of Himachal Pradesh, India. In addition to the
tragic loss of life—more than 20,000 deaths were reported (Ambraseys and
Bilham 2000)—villages were leveled, roads were destroyed, and bridges
collapsed. The earthquake also damaged the extensive networks of
community-managed, gravity-flow irrigation systems, known locally as
kuhls, that crisscrossed the valley. The timing of the earthquake, at the
beginning of the rice-planting season when dependence on irrigation water
from kuhls was greatest, could not have been worse. If the paddy crop failed,
many people in Kangra would face famine, because the region's relative
isolation from the plains to the south would make relief work difficult, if
not impossible.

The British colonial government, aware of the ramifications of interrupted
irrigation, mobilized the expertise and labor of soldiers in military engineering
units known as Sappers and Miners to rebuild and repair the destroyed
irrigation structures. By the third week of April, the chief secretary of the
Punjab government was able to cable India's Home Department secretary
that "Sappers and Miners have commenced work on [the] irrigation heads
of Baner stream" and "[a] fourth double company of Pioneers [has] arrived
Shahpur and will join the Sappers and Miners in repairing the irrigation
channels which take out of the Baner [River] in neighborhood of Kangra."[1]
With the assistance of the colonial army, the irrigation channels were
repaired and the threat of famine was averted.

Nearly 50 years later, in 1952, a different type of environmental shock struck the kuhl irrigation systems of an adjacent mountain river, the Neugal. During a torrential monsoon downpour, a landslide dammed the Neugal River in its narrow headwaters canyon, just upstream of the point where it normally flowed out across the open, sloping alluvial deltas that make up Kangra Valley.[2] Eventually the force of the rising waters burst the debris dam, sending a wall of water and debris raging down the streambed. Its force eroded large areas of fertile agricultural fields, destroyed diversion structures and main irrigation channels where they precariously traversed riverine cliffs before emerging onto the broad arable valley, and changed the course of the Neugal River itself. Two kuhls in the middle reaches of the watershed, Patnuhl and Menjha, were among those the flood destroyed. Patnuhl Kuhl, just upstream from Menjha Kuhl, was the less severely damaged of the two, and with a few weeks of joint effort, farmers from both kuhls repaired its main channel and diversion structure. For the next three years, until the diversion structure for Menjha Kuhl was successfully relocated 50 meters upstream and a new cliffside channel constructed, a water-sharing arrangement existed in which farmers from Patnuhl Kuhl diverted a portion of the water from their main channel into Menjha Kuhl.

During the last 50 years, economic and political changes in the region have further challenged farmers' ability to maintain the integrity of the kuhls on which they still depend for summer and winter crop irrigation. Though less dramatic than sharply punctuated shocks such as earthquakes and floods, the changes are pervasive. Increased household engagement with the market economy, primarily in the form of out-migration for employment, is the most significant one. Increasing nonfarm employment has differentiated people's interest in and dependence on agriculture among households in Kangra. Out-migration has created acute labor shortages for communal water-management tasks and has challenged farmers' capacities for mobilizing collective labor for annual kuhl repair and maintenance. It has also exacerbated caste- and class-based inequalities, which now stretch the conflict resolution capacities of kuhl management organizations.

Some kuhl irrigation systems failed to survive the internal tensions resulting from these changes. Their channels lie defunct. Yet at the beginning of the new millennium, most kuhl channels still brim with water during the crucial pre-monsoon irrigation season, as well as during the winter wheat growing season. The kuhl irrigation systems of Kangra continue to change and endure under conditions that theories of common property resource management suggest should lead to their demise. In this book I

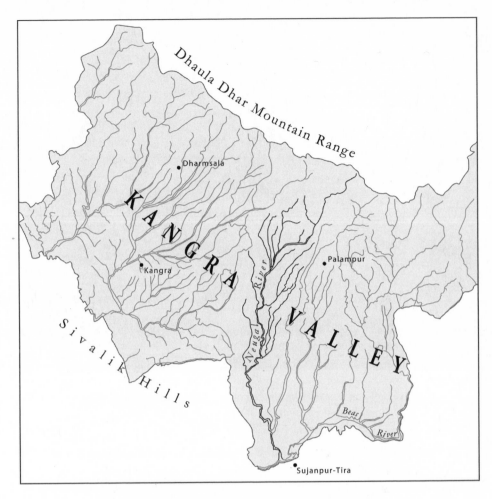

MAP 2. Kangra Valley, showing the Neugal watershed.
Adapted from the *Riwaj-i-Abpashi* (Irrigation Customs) 1918.

describe and explain the factors that have enabled them to do so. I begin the story with a brief overview of where Kangra Valley lies and what exactly kuhls are and what they do.

KANGRA VALLEY: THE SETTING

The picturesque Kangra Valley lies in the north-central portion of Kangra District, which is situated in the western part of the state of Himachal Pradesh in the western Himalayan region of India (map 1). The valley is roughly coterminous with the administrative boundaries of Kangra and

FIG. 1. Kangra Valley is composed of alluvial plains that slope gently away from the base of the Dhaula Dhar mountain range.

Palampur Tehsils (subdistricts) and is flanked by the steeply rising Dhaula Dhar mountain range on the north and the low-lying Sivalik Hills to the south (map 2). The Dhaula Dhar range, which separates Kangra District from Chamba District to the north, dominates the landscape from any point in the valley. It rises 10,000 feet above the valley floor to an average height of 14,000 feet above sea level within a distance of less than three miles. Along this escarpment, peaks exceed heights of 19,000 feet. The valley itself is a gently sloping series of forested alluvial plains and riverine terraces deposited by the mountain streams and torrents originating in the Dhaula Dhar (fig. 1). These streams, known locally as *khad*s, flow from the Dhaula Dhar south across the valley and eventually join the Beas River, which flows southwesterly through the Sivalik Hills.[3] The Sivalik Hills separate the valley from the Punjab plains to the south and west. Kangra Valley is roughly 30 miles long from west to east, and its width varies from 6 to 12 miles.

In the first regular settlement of Kangra District—a "settlement" being the registration of land for purposes of assigning tax obligations—completed

in 1855, the British settlement officer, George C. Barnes, described Kangra
Valley as follows:

> These valleys by no means present a general evenness of surface. Their
> contour is pleasantly broken by transverse ridges and numerous streams that
> descend from the mountains above. A hundred canals, filled with clear water,
> intersect the area in all directions, and convey the blessings of irrigation to
> every field. Trees and plants of opposite zones are here intermingled, and
> Alpine vegetation contends for pre-eminence with the growth of the tropics.
> The bamboo, the peepul and the mangoe attain a luxuriance not excelled in
> Bengal; while firs and dwarf oaks, the cherry, the barberry and dog-rose
> flourish in their immediate vicinity. (Barnes 1855:4)

The unusual topography of alluvial plains and river terraces dissected
by numerous perennial, snow-fed streams provides ecological conditions
suitable for some of the most extensive gravity-flow irrigation networks in
the Himalaya. The broad irrigable plains stretching out below the Dhaula
Dhar contrast sharply with the steep hillside terraces or relatively narrow
riparian fields commonly associated with Himalayan agriculture. Dense
networks of kuhl irrigation channels are embedded latticelike on the sloping
plains that constitute Kangra Valley, as Barnes observed more than 150
years ago. Each perennial, snow-fed mountain stream that flows across the
valley supplies water to as many as 40 or 50 different gravity-flow kuhl
irrigation systems before it disappears in the Sivalik Hills and eventually
joins the Beas River. All kuhls consist of a diversion structure, one or more
main channels ranging in length from less than 1 mile to more than 25
miles, numerous tertiary channels, and many (sometimes hundreds of)
named distribution points. Approximately 715 kuhls irrigate multiple
villages (some irrigate more than 40 villages), and more than 2,500 kuhls
irrigate single villages in the valley (*Riwaj-i-Abpashi* [Book of Irrigation
Customs] 1918).

Before post-independence rural electrification and the widespread
availability of piped water in most villages in the valley, kuhls provided not
only water for irrigation and, in many instances, all domestic purposes but
also hydropower for milling grain and turning potters' wheels. Although
the uses of, and consequently people's dependence on, kuhl water have
since narrowed, kuhls are still the primary sources of irrigation water. As
of 2002, they irrigated approximately 30,000 hectares in the valley.

There are two periods of peak dependence on kuhl irrigation water—

the pre-monsoon season and the months after the monsoon ends but before the onset of the winter rains. These periods correspond to the sowing seasons for *kharif* (summer) and *rabi* (winter) crops in Kangra Valley, when irrigation water is essential for preparing agricultural fields and sustaining the crops. Winter rains in the valley from December through March are complemented by snowfall in the Dhaula Dhar. During the hot, dry, pre-monsoon season from April through June, farmers divert water from streams fed by snowmelt into kuhl channels, which convey the water to agricultural fields that are flood irrigated for paddy (rice) cultivation. They divert post-monsoon streamflow for irrigating some rabi crops (primarily potatoes) from October through November. From April through June and October through November, monthly evaporation exceeds rainfall by as much as 35 and 20 millimeters, respectively (Singh et al. 1992). Thus, although average annual rainfall is relatively abundant (2,700 mm), its temporal distribution results in two water deficit periods as well as a high probability of destructive flooding during the monsoon.

The great majority of kuhls in Kangra were constructed by loosely organized collectivities of farmers or were sponsored by local elites; a few were constructed by members of the precolonial ruling Katoch lineage during the late seventeenth, eighteenth, and early nineteenth centuries. At least by the beginning of British colonial rule in Kangra in 1850, local communities were responsible for managing and repairing all the kuhls in Kangra. Local-level solutions to the collective-action challenges associated with kuhl management vary among kuhls and have changed over time in response to the stresses associated with increasing nonfarm employment.

I refer to the various institutional arrangements that have evolved to manage kuhls as the "kuhl regime," whereas "kuhl system" refers to the combination of physical infrastructure, water, and managing institutions. A central element of most kuhl regimes is the institution of *kohli* (watermaster). In the majority of kuhl regimes, the kohli supervises the annual cycle of management and repair tasks. In addition to mobilizing the communal work parties necessary for maintaining and repairing the kuhl, the kohli performs the religious ceremonies associated with kuhl management, supervises the conveyance and distribution of water in the kuhl, and resolves conflicts between farmers over water use.

In many respects kuhls are archetypal examples of the relatively small-scale, community-managed, gravity-flow irrigation systems commonly found throughout the world. However, their ability to withstand severe environmental shocks and pervasive socioeconomic stress forces us to revise the explanatory frameworks we use to understand and explain common property resource regimes. Why and how have kuhl regimes managed to maintain their physical and institutional integrity under these conditions? Framing this question requires situating kuhl regimes in the broader context of the study of irrigation and of common property resource management in particular.

KEY QUESTIONS AND EXPLANATORY THREADS

Irrigation systems have been a productive field of inquiry for scholars interested in questions ranging from the conditions under which self-organizing forms of collective action are likely to emerge and persist (Tang 1992) to the relationship between irrigation and centralized political authority (Hunt and Hunt 1976; Sidky 1996).[4] Though all irrigation systems share common tasks associated with water management and the construction, maintenance, and operation of the physical structures associated with water use (Uphoff et al. 1985), the organizational forms that have evolved to accomplish those tasks vary widely. Irrigation systems may be managed with elaborate formal institutions or have no formal organizational arrangement at all. Those that do have formal management institutions may be organized by the water users themselves ("self-organized") or by the state, they may be organized in a hierarchical or a decentralized fashion, and they may be joined with networks of other irrigation systems or managed as autonomous, independent units. They include the informally managed systems of "ordered anarchy" found in the Swiss Alps (Netting 1974) and Sri Lanka (Leach 1961), the self-organized, decentralized, nonhierarchical, autonomous systems of the hills of Nepal (Martin 1986; Yoder 1986), the self-organized, hierarchical networks of Balinese *subaks* (Lansing 1991; Lansing and Kremer 1993; Spooner 1974), and the relatively common externally organized, hierarchical, centralized irrigation systems associated with centralized political authority and large-scale agricultural production (Hunt and Hunt 1976; Whitcombe 1972; Wittfogel 1957; Worster 1985).

Self-organizing irrigation systems have long been of interest to scholars, especially interpretive anthropologists, who use their inquiries into the social organization of irrigation to understand the underlying models of society those systems embody. Some of these researchers also explicitly address questions of power and hegemony as they influence the course of events in situations in which state irrigation bureaucracies and policies collide with preexisting, community-based traditions of irrigation management (Gelles 2000; Lansing 1991; Lewis 1971). The outcomes of such interactions reveal much about the local effects of the application of development paradigms related to irrigation and modernity. These interactions are often characterized by situations in which technically driven irrigation development strategies, backed by state power, the hegemonic baggage associated with Western science, and often the authority of dominant social groups, clash with culturally embedded and enduring systems of irrigation management that are often steeped in rich local knowledge. The outcomes of these interactions vary widely. They include situations in which state irrigation officials now recognize the authority and efficacy of temple priests as water managers in Bali (Lansing 1991), less determinate outcomes in which state and local models of irrigation management continue to clash, as in the highlands of Peru (Gelles 2000), and situations in which state irrigation models have clearly replaced the preexisting system of irrigation management, as happened in southern Bihar, India (Sengupta 1980). In almost all these examples, conflict over access to and control of water constituted the terrain on which power-laden battles over meaning, knowledge, identity, and community have played out.

Self-organizing irrigation systems have also been the objects of sustained interest by other scholars, especially political scientists, who are interested in the conditions under which people act in concert to achieve, produce, or manage a collective good. Grounded in the perspective of rational choice, most theories of common property regimes explain individual participation in terms of the costs and benefits of participation, and they explain rules, sanctions, and other organizational attributes in terms of the efficiency and security of exchange between individuals within the regime (Ostrom, Gardner, and Walker 1994; White and Runge 1995). Using this framework, scholars have examined a diverse array of examples of common property resource management regimes and have derived a set of characteristics and conditions that appear to be associated with successful management of a common property resource. Self-organizing irrigation systems possess many of these characteristics, including (1) well-defined user-group and resource boundaries, (2) congruence between rules governing resource appropriation and provision, (3) the ability of resource users to modify rules, (4) the existence of monitoring, sanctioning, and conflict resolution mechanisms, (5) the political decision-making autonomy necessary for local self-organization, and (6) for larger irrigation systems, the organization of management activities into "nested" layers (Ostrom 1990; Tang 1992).

Garrett Hardin's (1968) tragedy-of-the-commons model to the contrary, classic examples of self-organizing irrigation management systems that possess these characteristics and that have persisted for centuries include the *huertas* of southeastern Spain (Maass and Anderson 1986), Balinese subaks (Geertz 1980; Lansing 1991), the *zanjeras* of Illocos Norte in the Philippines (de los Reyes 1980; Lewis 1971), and community irrigation traditions in highland Peru (Gelles 2000).

How well does this framework account for both the emergence and the durability of common property regimes under the extreme conditions of ecological stress, economic change, and social differentiation that exist in Kangra? Researchers have demonstrated that the degree of social or economic differentiation within a group of resource users and the extent of their reliance on the commonly held resource influence the likelihood of collective action for managing the resource (Bardhan 1993b; Oakerson 1986; Olson 1965; Tang 1992; Wade 1988). Furthermore, current theories predict that changes such as market expansion, migration, public sector interventions, privatization initiatives, population growth, and technological change stress common property regimes by increasing the cost of and controls over individual choices. They postulate that a regime's response to environmental change depends upon the effects of the change on individual choices and the internal regime structures that regulate them (Ostrom 1990). However, researchers cannot predict why and how a stressed regime will either persist unchanged, transform to endure, or collapse. In other words, the existing framework for explaining common property regimes is unable to account for the emergence and persistence of the kuhl regimes of Kangra. This constitutes the challenge of this book—to develop a way of understanding one set of common property regimes, the kuhls of Kangra, that explicates both their emergence and the ways they have responded to and, in most cases, endured the sorts of shocks and changes I have described.

Accounting for differential patterns of change and persistence among the kuhl regimes of Kangra requires expanding the domain of inquiry beyond that which theories of common property resource management usually consider. This entails integrating within our explanatory framework processes and influences that are generally thought to be "exogenous factors." They include the potential role of state entities in the management of a common property resource, the possibility that networks of linked common property resource management regimes help buffer individual regimes from environmental stress, and the hypothesis that the ways in which a common property resource regime reproduces salient norms, values, and social relations contribute to the persistence of the regime and cultural reproduction.

Key overarching questions help frame the new issue areas to be brought into the domain of inquiry. The first concerns the role of the state in community-based institutions for common property resource management. Under what conditions does it serve the interest of state entities to support common property regimes? Answering this question requires rethinking the relationship between state and local institutions and, indeed, our understanding of what constitutes the "state" and the "local" and how they may mutually constitute and reinforce each other.

A second question concerns the possible roles of exchange (material, symbolic, or both) between different community-based resource management systems in enabling their persistence. In what ways and under what conditions might networks of exchange among common property resource regimes further their persistence? Exploring this issue requires shifting from a microfocus on individual common property regimes to a larger, regional-scale perspective in order to first identify and then evaluate the possible effects of exchange between networked resource management regimes.

A third question focuses on the importance of the concept of regionality for understanding the persistence of common property regimes. Drawing on theories of cultural geography, one can think of regions and places as being constituted by social relations "stretched out" over space (Massey 1994) and then encoded onto and reproduced by landscapes. To what extent do kuhl regimes embody and reproduce the key social relations that compose the Kangra region? How does this perspective aid us in understanding the specific institutional forms, microlevel social relations, and ritual aspects and trajectories of change in common property regimes?

These overarching questions together incorporate multiple levels of analysis and integrate different analytical perspectives. They can be separated into four intellectual strands, each representing a different scale and set of relations. When woven together, these strands create a tapestry whose warp and weft should correspond to the transformations and rhythms of change within individual kuhl regimes.

The first strand is composed of the primarily local-level social and ecological processes that facilitate or hinder collective action—a domain of inquiry commonly addressed in theories of common property regimes. The social variables known to affect the likelihood of collective action include group size, the extent of internal differentiation such as caste and class differences, the degree of group members' dependence on the resource, the amount of variation between households in dependence on the resource, the ability of the group to exclude outside would-be resource users, and the group's rule-making and dispute arbitration capacities. Following this intellectual strand, researchers also address the characteristics of the resource that affect the potential for collective action—for example, whether or not the resource is geographically fixed or fugitive (like many fisheries)—the risk and uncertainty associated with its management, and its productivity or value.

Drawing on theories of collective action, property, risk management, and institutional economics, research on common property regimes has developed a robust foundation for understanding the relationships among these elements and the conditions under which people are likely to engage in collective action for producing, supplying, or managing a commonly held good.[5] These approaches seem less able, however, to account for the specific institutional structures—both formal and informal—that guide people's behavior as they craft and institutionalize cooperative strategies for collective benefit. They cannot explain the emergence and persistence of enduring forms of common property resource management under the sorts of stress—recurring environmental disturbance and socioeconomic change—that I have described. If we are to account for the emergence and durability under stress of common property resource management regimes, then we must broaden the scope of inquiry to include the following three strands and the pattern that they together weave.

The second strand concerns the possibility of exchange and coordination between separate but interdependent community-based natural resource management regimes and the potential effects of such exchange and coordination. This perspective broadens the scope of inquiry spatially. It points to the possible existence of latent networks that link irrigation systems within a hydraulically defined landscape unit. For example, Stephen Lansing (1991) showed how networks of subak irrigation systems in Bali, Indonesia, managed by self-organizing hierarchical religious authorities, enabled the coordination of complex agricultural activities, including irrigation management, across individual subak systems. Can such networks also help buffer individual irrigation systems from the destructive effects of recurring floods and earthquakes or the stress induced by drought? I explore this question in the context of kuhl regimes by first identifying the extent to which networks indeed link individual kuhl systems and then examining the contributions irrigation networks make to the durability of individual kuhl regimes in light of research on the roles and functions of networks from sociology and political science.

The third strand concerns relations between kuhl regimes and state entities, especially the possibility that state intervention in local resource management regimes may support their persistence. That is, the emergence and endurance of erstwhile local systems of resource management may be due, in part, to infrequent but important state involvement in them. In order to examine this type of interaction, we must tease apart the obfuscating binary opposition between state and society to reveal the complex, interconnecting relations the opposition generally masks. In the case of Kangra, I identify the specific points of, and rationale(s) for, interaction between state authority and village-based irrigation management during the precolonial, colonial, and postcolonial periods and delineate the outcomes of those interactions when they occurred.

The fourth strand concerns the importance of place and region in accounting for the forms and persistence of common property regimes. That the kuhls are in Kangra is not inconsequential to the forms that irrigation organization has assumed there or to the historical trajectory of change within kuhls. This perspective draws attention to the "Kangriness" of kuhl regimes. It enables an examination of the ways in which kuhl regimes reproduce dominant social relations in the area and the mechanisms through which those relations are encoded onto and naturalized in the landscape of Kangra. It permits identification of the informal social institutions that undergird irrigation organization and within which kuhl regimes are embedded. It allows one to address regional social formations, patterns of landownership, and wealth distribution and to show how they have informed kuhl regimes and, in turn, how kuhl regimes reinforce them.

This strand also concerns history. Kangra Valley lies on the edge of the main routes that have linked north India with Central Asia for centuries. Consequently, large numbers of men from Kangra, primarily high-caste Rajputs and Brahmans, have served in Afghan, Mughal, Sikh, British, and Indian armies. The ideas, values, norms, and modes of interaction that servicemen brought home with them influenced the historical patterns of irrigation organization in Kangra and its trajectories of change.

Weaving together the scales and sets of relationships embodied in these three strands and combining them with the domain of inquiry represented by the first strand produces an explanatory framework capable of accounting for the emergence and durability under stress of the kuhl regimes of Kangra. First, however, it is necessary to briefly situate Kangra in the broader context of transformations in land use and property rights in north India during the last 150 years.

PRIVATIZATION AND STATE CONTROL
OF THE COMMONS IN GREATER PUNJAB

Despite the widespread existence of enduring common property regimes throughout much of the world, their viability has been eroded in many cases by the multiple tensions that accompany large-scale demographic, political, and economic changes. This can result in resource degradation and a shift in property rights to either privatization or state control of the resource (Ensminger and Rutten 1991; Feeny et al. 1990; Jodha 1985; Ostrom 1990; Polanyi 1944). The dual processes of increasing privatization and state control of resources that common property theorists predict under conditions of change have occurred throughout the plains and mountains of northwestern India during the last two centuries. This area, known as the greater Punjab, included Kangra until it, along with the other Himalayan districts of old Punjab, was merged with neighboring Himachal Pradesh in 1966.

From a historical perspective, greater Punjab constitutes the broader regional context in which to situate the analysis of continuity and change of the kuhls of Kangra. The continued persistence of the communal irrigation systems of Kangra contradicts the more general trends of increasing privatization and state control of common property resources in greater Punjab. Explaining this apparent anomaly brings forth illuminating points of contrast between the social, political, and ecological characteristics of the mountains and the plains, irrigation in the hills and irrigation in the plains, and the ways in which the characteristics of particular resources and their ecological settings influence the development of forms of governance for managing them. As we will see, it also forces a more nuanced analysis of the complex, intertwined relations between the state and local communities and illustrates how the state may be involved, at some level, in the management of a common property resource.

Within greater Punjab, particularly after 1860, the rapid expansion of cultivated areas resulted in dramatic declines in village commons, especially forests and grazing land. This resulted in a massive displacement of pastoral groups as well as marginal sedentary groups for whom common land resources met important subsistence needs, especially during periods of scarcity (Chakravarty-Kaul 1996). A complex of factors fueled this process, including population growth, the colonial state's imposition of land taxes at rates that remained fixed for decades, state-sponsored capital investments in agriculture, expanding markets for commercial agriculture, and improvements in transportation networks such as roads and railroads. The British colonial administration's involvement in the codification of customary law, particularly through land settlement, facilitated this process.

The primary purpose of land settlement was to determine the nature of property rights in an area, identify rights holders, and establish tax rates and payment schedules. Although ostensibly an exercise in elucidating and recording a region's customs and laws relating to land rights, cultivation, and the distribution of agricultural surpluses, land settlements were heavily influenced by prevailing European social theories about private property, its ownership and productivity, and investment in it, by anthropological theories about social evolution, and by the successes and failures of prior settlements in other regions of India, all cloaked in the guise of debates over what constituted "local custom" (Baden-Powell 1892; Guha 1981 [1963]).

In the Punjab, the nineteenth-century land settlement process, governed by an anthropological focus on genealogy and agnatic relationships, defined village property rights in terms of blood relationships and patriarchy. This consolidated the rights to land of coparcenary (joint heirship) communities and weakened the rights of persons unable to establish a genealogical link to the original founder of the village. The rights to land held by nonagriculturalists and by women were considerably weakened during this process. And because rights to common property resources were based on ownership of agricultural land, the claims of women and nonagriculturalists to common property resources were also substantially undermined. As a result, in the imperial dialogue between colonizers and the colonized, the "native voice" that was filtered and interpreted during the codification and settlement process was a "male, patriarchal voice, the voice of the dominant proprietary body speaking against the rights of non-proprietors, females, and lower castes" (Battacharya 1996:47).

Settlement also strengthened the "community" of coparcenary landowners by making them jointly responsible for paying the assessed land tax. In exchange, landowners secured their private property rights, increased their shares in the common land, and gained authority to expand cultivation into previously uncultivated common grazing land.[6] This process occurred throughout Punjab, even in areas such as Kangra where proprietary landownership and joint responsibility for paying land taxes did not exist prior to British rule. On the plains, and to a lesser extent in the hills, the expansion of private property into the village commons "produced many local conflicts as the claims of farmers clashed with one another, as farm communities claimed the land of pastoralists and forest cultivators, and as the state, *zamindars* (landlords), tenants, and *ryots* (owner-cultivators) asserted rights to newly cultivated land" (Ludden 1999:192).

The colonial state's intimate involvement in (re)structuring property rights and facilitating the concentration of resources and power among groups that became (and still are) regionally dominant was particularly apparent among the canal colonies of the Punjab. There, the nineteenth-century imperial science of large-scale irrigation engineering was combined with social engineering to create new patterns of state power and community linked in a joint enterprise to control the environment (Gilmartin 1994). Newly constructed irrigation canals pushed agriculture into semiarid regions previously occupied by nomadic and seminomadic groups. Social engineering policies to create productive (and obedient) communities displaced these groups, and in their place, dominant caste groups were granted large tracts of newly irrigated land at relatively low rents. The same dominant caste groups played critical roles in the military, including supplying large numbers of army recruits (Ludden 1999).

The large-scale and dramatic conversion of common land to irrigated agriculture and the concomitant consolidation of power among dominant caste groups that occurred on the Punjab plains were not repeated to the same extent in the hill districts of greater Punjab, including Kangra. This was because the potential for expanding the cultivated area was much smaller in Kangra than in other regions of the Punjab. By the mid-nineteenth century, most cultivable areas had already been brought under the plow. Whereas greater Punjab had the largest proportion of uncultivated but cultivable land in British India in 1891, and by the 1920s the area of irrigated agriculture there had doubled (Chakravarty-Kaul 1996:22), in Kangra in 1855 the first district commissioner and settlement officer, George Barnes, remarked that he "did not anticipate . . . any reclamation of waste land" and that the cultivable areas "have been long since selected and reclaimed; nothing is left now, but the precipitous sides of hills, frequently encumbered with forest and brushwood" (1855:63). An examination of cultivated area in the Neugal watershed of Kangra Valley, where the research for this study was carried out, confirms Barnes's observations. Between

1851 and 1892, the cultivated area increased 8 percent, from 6,522 to 7,028 hectares. Between 1892 and 1915, the period of most rapid expansion of cultivated area in greater Punjab, the cultivated area in the Neugal watershed actually declined slightly to 6,568 hectares.[7]

Other factors also differentiate Kangra from the plains. For example, in Kangra Valley, village communities did not exist as corporate organizations with defensible entitlements to private cultivated and common uncultivated land, as they did in many parts of the plains. Instead, hamlets, often single caste, dotted the hilly landscape with little sharp demarcation of boundaries, if any, between them. Individual families held usufructory rights to cultivated areas, and these entitlements were secured through deeds (*pattah*) from the ruling Katoch lineage of hill rajas. Uncultivated areas, to the extent that they existed, were considered the property of the hill chiefs.

The narrative of privatization of the commons powerfully describes transformations on the Punjab plains during the late nineteenth and early twentieth centuries but has limited salience for the hill and mountain regions. However, the other outcome predicted by common property theorists as a response to large-scale demographic, political, and economic changes—increased state control of the resource—did occur in Kangra with regard to the "precipitous sides of hills, frequently encumbered with forest and brushwood" that Barnes referred to in 1855. Barnes, concluding that encouraging agricultural intensification was more important than forest conservation, had "given" extensive rights to the forest and wastelands of Kangra to the village communities he created in the first settlement in the early 1850s. Soon afterward, the colonial administration had second thoughts; subsequent Forest Department and (to a lesser extent) Revenue Department officers attempted to reassert state claims over forest resources, beginning with the government's 1874 revision of the first Kangra settlement.

. Thus the colonial administration commenced a long-term project of securing state control over forest access and utilization in the western Himalaya. The process through which this took place has been well analyzed (Baker 2000; Grover 1997; Guha 1989; Saberwal 1999; Singh 1998; Tucker 1983). Forest conservancy entailed many conflicts analogous to those David Ludden (1999) discussed with regard to the privatization of the commons in the plains. Conflicts over forest access and use occurred between nomadic pastoralists, known as Gaddis, and the Forest Department, between the Forest Department and the "village community," between landowners and nonlandowners, and between the Forest and Revenue Departments themselves. Out of these conflicts emerged shifting alliances such as that between the Gaddis and the Revenue Department, negotiated concessions by the Forest Department of rights of forest access and use to village communities, and new local institutional arrangements for forest management such as the Village Cooperative Forest Societies—early precursors to contemporary community forestry programs. Although certainly not uncontested, state control of forest resources in Kangra and other areas in present-day Himachal Pradesh increased dramatically during the late nineteenth and early twentieth centuries. It continues to this day.

Surrounded as community-managed irrigation regimes were by privatized common land on the plains and state-controlled forest land in the hills, their persistence in Kangra may seem anomalous. In many ways it is. Other self-organized irrigation systems in India that have been subjected to rapid political and economic changes have deteriorated or collapsed (Gordon 1994; Hardiman 1995; Mosse 1997a; Sengupta 1980). Why have the kuhls of Kangra persisted while other self-organized irrigation systems in India have not? And why were the kuhls not privatized or taken over by the state like other common property resources in greater Punjab?

Part of the answer has to do with people's continuing dependence on kuhls for irrigation in Kangra Valley. They simply have no other source of water for irrigation. Perhaps self-evidently, and in stark contrast to the nearby plains, the combination of hilly terrain and minimal scope for increased cultivation precluded the possibility of large-scale, state-sponsored canal irrigation systems and the massive capital investments, social engineering, bureaucratic technocracy, and other state simplifications (Scott 1998) they entail. The absence of large aquifers precluded the development and exploitation of groundwater for irrigation purposes, which in other regions of rural India has become one of the most important drivers of agrarian change (Dubash 2002). A full analysis of the patterns of persistence and change in the kuhl irrigation systems of Kangra, however, requires elaboration of the explanatory tapestry described earlier and its application to the empirical data derived from the field research.

1

AN EXPLANATORY TAPESTRY

HOW DO KUHL REGIMES PERSIST IN KANGRA VALLEY DESPITE RECURRING, destructive environmental disturbances and unprecedented rates of regional socioeconomic change? The answer to this question draws on theories of rational choice, social networks, state formation, and regionality. These four strands of analysis must be woven together into a single interpretive approach—an explanatory tapestry.

Theories of collective action and institutional change, grounded in rational choice theory, describe the conditions under which successful collective action is likely. They illuminate the relationship between the internal social and ecological attributes of a common property regime and its emergence and persistence. Analytical approaches to the study of the structures and functions of networks drawn from social and organizational theory point to the shock-absorbing capacities of social networks of material and symbolic exchange. This helps us develop an understanding of the potential role of exchange between interdependent regimes in promoting regime persistence despite recurring environmental shocks. When woven together, these two strands provide a partial explanation for the persistence of kuhl regimes.

The tapestry is incomplete, however, because it yields only a partial understanding of why some kuhls flourish while others decline. A robust explanation must incorporate conceptions of the state and regionality. This approach entails understanding the implications of statemaking and state formation for state involvement in resource management regimes. It acknowledges the possibility of the mutual constitution of state formation and local governance for common property resource management, and it identifies the conditions under which state involvement may facilitate the persistence of common property regimes. Last, this approach enables one to examine regional influences on the structure, function, and endurance of common property regimes. This involves exploring the extent to which the embeddedness of regimes in regional social, political, and historical formations may help to account for their form and persistence.

The resulting tapestry, developed to explicate the persistence of kuhl regimes, has broader applicability for understanding other enduring common property regimes. First, as is prevalent in current common property theory, it emphasizes local arenas as the place-based sites of collective action. But it also integrates an understanding of larger-scale influences on common property regimes—influences that tend to be underemphasized in discussions based on common property theory. This approach, for example, suggests that networks of potential exchange relations between regimes are likely to offer periodic but crucial resources that enable people to maintain the regime's integrity during times of ecological stress. Depending on where and when such stress occurs, networks provide crucial ways of managing and mitigating the risks associated with it.

Second, this approach suggests both the possibility and the importance of relations with state entities that facilitate regime persistence. If resource needs cannot be satisfied at the local level, then relations between a common property regime and the state may enable that regime to persist by providing access to required resources otherwise unavailable. Such resources may include technical assistance, conflict resolution arenas and capacities, and intensive labor inputs of limited duration.

Last, this tapestry identifies the importance of regional, culturally rooted constructions of community, authority, and identity, which constitute some of the core principles and themes that common property regimes both tap and reproduce in their formal organization. The nature of these regional formations and the degree to which they lend coherence and resilience to the more formal structures and processes of common property regimes influence both the regime's ability to persist and its trajectory of institutional change. As we will see, this is especially true during periods of rapid social, political, economic, or ecological change.

RATIONAL CHOICE AND INSTITUTIONAL CHANGE
IN COMMON PROPERTY REGIMES

Rational choice theory, the dominant theoretical lens used for explaining the evolution and persistence of institutions for common property management, rests on two assumptions: that individuals make choices that maximize their own benefits or utility and that collective behavior is best understood as the aggregate of choices made at the individual level. Within the constraints of these assumptions, rational choice theorists attempt to explain the evolution of cooperation between individuals. The challenge of doing so is illustrated by the prisoners' dilemma game, which demonstrates how individually rational decisions can generate collectively irrational results.

The prisoners' dilemma game is a two-person, noncooperative, nonrepetitive game. In it, two people are held in separate jail cells, unable to communicate with each other. Their jailer knows they are guilty but has too little evidence to convict them. He has told them that if they both confess, they will receive severe but less than maximum sentences. If both refuse to confess, then most of the charges will be dropped. However, if only one confesses but not the other, then the confessor will receive the lightest possible sentence while the other will get the maximum sentence. Clearly, in light of these choices the optimal *collective* strategy is for neither prisoner to confess. But because they cannot communicate with each other and so have no assurance that the other will not confess, it is rational for each to confess and thus produce an outcome that is disadvantageous to them both.

This classic model of how individual rationality can lead to collectively detrimental outcomes was popularized by Garrett Hardin (1968), who used it to explain the logic behind the "tragedy of the commons." In the context of communal grazing land, Hardin showed why individual herders—using the same logic as the individual prisoner who confesses—would augment their own herd size in order to maximize individual profit, even though they knew the resource was limited. Other herders, not wanting to restrict their use while others profited, would increase their herd sizes, too. In this model, overgrazing and the "tragedy of the commons" result from such individually rational decisions.[1] Situations like these are vulnerable to a general class of problems associated with free riding, in which an individual benefits from the use of a common resource but does not contribute to its provision and hence undermines the collective will required to steward the resource.

Conceptual space for resolving many of the dilemmas associated with free riding can be created by acknowledging that unlike the prisoners in the dilemma, most people are not in jail and therefore are not subject to the same constraints as those assumed in the prisoners' dilemma game, such as nonrepetitive interactions with no communication among the players. As we have learned from the many successful examples of common property resource management, people can devise rules, contracts, and organizations that provide some degree of security regarding the strategies others will choose. Doing so gives them the necessary assurance to be able to choose strategies that avoid the prisoners' dilemma outcome. This is the domain of transactions-cost economics (e.g., North 1986; Williamson 1975), which integrates the basic tenets of rational choice theory with an approach that emphasizes the informational and organizational costs that collective action entails. Institutions develop in order to minimize those costs.[2] Individuals form contracts with others specifying the terms of exchange and thereby minimize the costs of negotiating subsequent exchanges. When a number of individual contracts are grouped under a general, overall contract, they constitute an organization. In this view, organizations as group contracts minimize the transaction and production costs that would otherwise be incurred if the exchanges that occur within them were negotiated individually in the marketplace.

The transactions-cost approach emphasizes the costs of measuring the attributes of the goods and services that are exchanged and the costs of evaluating the performance of individuals who contribute to the provision of the good or service. In theory, the difficulties associated with measuring these attributes lead to the development of monitoring and enforcement of contracts. Enforcement costs are reduced to the extent that exchange is personal and repetitive. Hence the advantage of forming the relatively stable, long-term contracts that characterize organizations (North 1986).

While institutional economists seek to explain all institutions in terms of transaction costs, other theorists focus on a subset of institutions whose purpose is the provision of collective goods. They seek to specify the conditions under which rational, self-interested individuals will or will not engage in collective action to provide collective goods. For example, Mancur Olson (1965) focused on the internal characteristics of the organizing group, the nature of the collective good, and the extent to which selective benefits accrued to group members in order to explain the emergence of sustained collective action. Elinor Ostrom (1990), drawing on the work of Olson and others, analyzed the conditions under which collective action for common property resource management was likely to occur.[3] These authors argued, if they did not also "prove," that under some conditions, rational, self-interested individuals will engage in collective action for a common good and thereby avoid a tragedy of the commons.

Their research has demonstrated the importance of communication among players in the context of repeated games. Face-to-face communication enhances players' payoffs in noncooperative games, even in the absence of binding agreements and sanctioning.[4] Communication beyond that necessary to develop an agreement and a strategy should not, according to game theory, influence the game's outcome, but it does. As Ostrom and others suggest, this is because "mere jawboning" serves to establish trust among the players and to signal their reaction to players tempted to violate the agreement (Ostrom, Gardner, and Walker 1994:197). Others, using an evolutionary model of decision-making, note the positive effect of communication on game theory outcomes (Schotter and Sopher 2003). In the case of intergenerational games, communication, in the form of word-of-mouth advice-giving and learning from one generation to the next, is important in forming conventions. Social conventions establish norms of behavior that guide subsequent actions in ways that reinforce past decisions.

A focus on repeated games and evolutionary dynamics is also evident in Peyton Young's analysis of the ways in which social conventions emerge through "the gradual accretion of precedent" (1996:106). In his analysis, past actions influence current expectations, which determine actions in the present, which in turn set up future precedents. The equilibria thus created appear stable against small, recurring, random shocks, which are essentially deviations from the norm or convention. Not only does Young carry forward the implications of communication in the repeated or evolutionary settings described by Ostrom, Gardner, and Walker (1994), but he also echoes the argument that in situations where communication exists, deviations from the preferred strategy are best addressed through a "measured reaction heuristic" (as discussed in Ostrom, Gardner, and Walker 1994:199). Small deviations are met with mild reactions and sanctioning behavior, rather than by immediately resorting to the more extreme "grim trigger" strategy that game theory would predict. The measured reaction thereby preserves the overall integrity of the strategy against small shocks or perturbations. These observations are consistent with the ways in which monetary fines are levied against Kangra Valley households that do not contribute labor for the repair and maintenance of kuhl channels. That is, small and infrequent infractions go unremarked, and only households that are "very" absent are sanctioned.[5]

The use of evolutionary explanations has led to a focus on the importance of reputation and the incentives to maintain reputation as a significant force in the persistence of conventions. For example, the desire to maintain one's reputation as defined through "traditional codes of behavior" leads individuals to support social conventions even though those conventions might be disadvantageous to them (Akerloff 1984:72). Partial deviance from the rule does not necessarily lead to the unraveling of the rule or convention if a significant proportion of people still support it and thus continue to associate reputation maintenance with rule or convention compliance (Akerloff 1984:77). The maintenance of reputation is especially important in the development and continuation of social conventions that may be inconsistent with utility-maximizing behavior (see also Axelrod 1986; Bicchieri 1990). As we will see, this view of the relationship between reputation maintenance and adherence to social convention helps illuminate the rationale for interkuhl water-sharing arrangements in which the kohli of an upstream kuhl agrees to share water with an adjacent downstream kuhl, either during periods of water scarcity or following a destructive flood or earthquake.

How can these theoretical approaches help us understand institutional change in common property resource regimes? Let us explore the rational choice approach to understanding institutional change by using an example from the kuhls of Kangra. Within a rational choice framework, institutional change consists of changes in the rules that make up an institution.[6] Rule changes occur when a quorum of franchised members supports the proposed change (Ostrom 1990). The main drivers of institutional change are "fundamental and persistent changes in relative prices" of the goods and services that are exchanged through the group contracts that institutions represent (North 1986:234).[7] Because people value the goods and services that an institution provides in ways that reflect their own unique sets of preferences, changes in prices will affect them differently. The tensions created by such changes may lead individuals to attempt to alter the contract or to leave the organization altogether. A person will support a rule change when, for that person, the expected benefits exceed the expected costs as filtered through his or her own set of norms and alternative opportunities. When the expected costs exceed the expected benefits, an individual may choose no longer to contribute to the provision and management of the common property resource. However, the free rider problem and the large number of people involved constitute sources of institutional "stickiness" that may prevent institutional change even when the relative benefits and costs of membership have shifted dramatically (Akerloff 1984; North 1986).

People evaluate the expected benefits and costs of a proposed rule change according to their internal norms, opportunity costs, and discount rates. Opportunity costs are the costs associated with giving up A in order to acquire B. The opportunity costs of contributing labor for kuhl repair and maintenance are the other tasks that could not be accomplished—or the income foregone, in the case of nonfarm employment—because labor was instead devoted to the kuhl. Discount rates refer to the present value of a future benefit and the rate at which the value of that benefit is discounted back to the present. Opportunity costs and discount rates affect valuation of the kuhl regime's benefits relative to other opportunities that are foregone for the sake of participating in the kuhl regime.

In Kangra, opportunity costs and discount rates vary substantially among individuals and groups, especially between households with and without access to nonfarm employment and remittance income. Relative to households without access to nonfarm employment, households that do enjoy such employment have higher opportunity costs because of the income they would forego by choosing to participate in communal kuhl work instead of nonfarm employment. They also have relatively higher discount rates because their increasing reliance on the market economy tends to result in declining future valuations of kuhl irrigation water for the household economy. Together, these factors diminish incentives for contributing the labor necessary for kuhl maintenance and repair. On the other hand, the fewer the alternative opportunities, the lower the opportunity costs and discount rates and the greater the household's dependence on kuhl water. In the narrow sense, dependence on kuhl water is related to the availability of alternative water sources for irrigation. In the broader sense, it concerns a household's dependence on agriculture and the extent to which participation in the local or regional economy through nonfarm employment simultaneously reduces dependence on kuhl water for agriculture and labor availability for collective water management tasks.

A rule change concerning labor mobilization that has been adopted in some kuhl regimes illustrates one of the institutional changes that have resulted from the interplay of increasingly differentiated discount rates and opportunity costs among the irrigators of a kuhl. Mobilizing labor for channel cleaning has become increasingly difficult since the late 1970s because of the expansion of off-farm employment opportunities. Declining dependence on agriculture has reduced some households' interest in contributing labor for the maintenance and repair of kuhl systems. As rates of absenteeism on the days appointed for channel cleaning increase, the farmers who do come have to contribute more and more labor in order to maintain the kuhl. The inequalities this introduces can eventually threaten the integrity of the whole kuhl regime and lead to a tragedy of the commons. Members of some kuhl regimes have responded to this problem by changing the operational rules that govern resource mobilization. These regimes substituted monetary contributions based on cultivated area for the previous system of contributing one's own labor. The money collected is used to hire wage labor to clean and repair the kuhl under the kohli's supervision.

In assessing the expected benefits of shifting from a labor- to a monetary-based system of resource mobilization, an Ostrom-like argument would hold that a farmer would need to be able to anticipate how the change would affect the quantity, variability, quality, and sustainability of resource flows as well as the degree and nature of conflict within the regime. Determining the effects of a rule change along these parameters requires information about the size of the user group and the resource system, the variability and current condition of the resource, market values for resource units, past conflict levels, and the present and proposed rules (Ostrom 1990:196).

In order for a farmer to assess the expected benefits of contributing money instead of labor for kuhl maintenance, he or she would need to know how the change would improve water flow relative to current levels and how it might reduce conflict between regime members. Both assessments require knowledge about water flows when the channels were well maintained and about previous conflict levels, prior to the increase in off-farm employment opportunities. Still, this information will not enable estimation of the benefits of the rule change until it is integrated within a causal framework that attributes reduced water flows and increased conflict levels to more people working off the farm. Only then could a farmer anticipate the outcome of changing the resource mobilization currency from time to money.

The costs entailed in considering whether or not to substitute money for labor for accomplishing kuhl maintenance and repair tasks are influenced by the number of individuals involved, the heterogeneity of their interests, the decision-making rules for changing rules, and the asset distribution of the members. Although the likelihood of collective action necessary for a successful rule change is negatively related to group size and group heterogeneity, some inequality in asset distribution fosters collective action (Baker 1998). As Ostrom noted (1990:198–202), the nature of the proposed rule, the history of change within the regime, and the autonomy to make and enforce rule changes also affect the costs of considering a rule change. This suggests that the costs of evaluating the substitution of monetary payments for labor contributions for kuhl maintenance will be least in smaller, homogeneous regimes characterized by some asset inequality that have previously implemented changes and that have the autonomy to implement further changes.

The costs of implementing a land-based tax for kuhl maintenance include compiling a list of the cultivated area of every regime member, collecting the tax at an annual meeting, developing and implementing enforcement mechanisms, maintaining written accounts, and supervising kuhl maintenance using paid labor. An individual considering whether or not to support the substitution of monetary payments for labor contributions for kuhl maintenance would compare the costs associated with changing and implementing the new rule with the costs of continuing to monitor and enforce the labor-based system.

Internalized social norms and individual discount rates influence the way in which an individual values the expected benefits and costs of a proposed institutional change. A kuhl regime member for whom the expected improvements in water flows resulting from the rule change matter little because he or she has an off-farm job and no longer relies on subsistence agriculture may nevertheless support the change because it provides an inexpensive way to fulfill a social obligation, maintain his or her reputation, and avoid negative social sanctions. A regime member with a low discount rate—that is, one without outside employment—will likely support the change because of the expected improvement in water flows and consequent reductions in the risk of crop failure due to water scarcity. Thus, both discount rates and social norms influence how a farmer will evaluate the shift from labor to monetary contributions for system maintenance. The cumulative impact of such individual decisions will influence whether or not institutional change takes place.

Rational choice theories help us understand the conditions under which collective action is likely to occur and the microlevel processes associated with institutional change in a common property regime. Although rigorous within the confines of the assumptions associated with rational choice, this formulation does not fully account for the specific and diverse institutional forms that have evolved for managing kuhl irrigation systems or for their dynamic persistence over time. There are several reasons for this. First, the rational choice framework precludes analysis of the potential role of extralocal political forces in creating, supporting, or strengthening these systems. As we will see, in Kangra, state systems and the processes related to statemaking are related to the persistence of kuhl regimes.

Second, despite the contributions of evolutionary and repeated game theory, rational choice approaches tend to adopt an ahistorical perspective that provides little analytical traction for understanding how and why individual kuhl regimes have changed over time. This is because locality-specific social constructions of community and social identity, structures of power, and belief systems are external to the framework, yet these socially and historically rooted phenomena affect the nature and forms that institutional arrangements for common property resource management assume.

Third, in modeling the decision-making behavior of actors as a set of strategic calculations designed to maximize an individual's payoff, the rational choice perspective tends to focus on the specific decision-making context itself, thus underemphasizing the ways in which resource management institutions function as arenas for the reproduction of community, hierarchy, and status. The motivation underlying actions that may not appear "rational" in the context of an individual kuhl regime may become clear when interpreted as an "emergent property of the social structure within which actors are embedded" (Uzzi 1997:61). Last, the natural environment itself imposes specific constraints and possibilities that bear on the potential and limits of gravity-flow irrigation in Kangra Valley and that in turn influence the development of water management institutions.

Clearly, by itself the rational choice perspective is narrow and its assumptions constraining. In order to fully comprehend the rationality underlying Kangri farmers' decisions, as well as the institutional structures for water management that have emerged and their trajectories of change, we must address issues not encompassed by the rational choice perspective. These include, for example, the potential role of networks of interkuhl relations in buffering individual kuhl regimes from risk and uncertainty, the role of statemaking and state formation in the emergence and persistence of some kuhl regimes, and the effects on kuhls of the cultural and historical context of irrigation in Kangra. In order to understand these relationships, we need to explicitly incorporate other strands of thought into our explanatory framework. The next strand concerns the possibility that interkuhl networks may enhance the ability of individual kuhl regimes to maintain their integrity despite recurring destructive shocks.

NETWORKS FOR MANAGING ENVIRONMENTAL UNCERTAINTY

Coordination and resource pooling among hydrologically linked irrigation systems may reduce the risks associated with damaging floods, earthquakes, and droughts. Such coordination can facilitate labor mobilization to repair the system following floods and earthquakes and the provision of water flows during the period of repair as well as during drought. The paucity of research on risk-reducing coordination among common property regimes might be thought to reflect the paucity of risk to be reduced. This seems unlikely, however, because many common property regimes, irrigation and otherwise, exist in settings characterized by significant ecological disturbances or resource scarcity. It more likely reflects the fact that ephemeral forms of intersystem coordination are relatively difficult to observe, because of their infrequent manifestation and the tendency of researchers to concentrate primarily on individual resource management regimes rather than on the broader patterns of resource management discernible at larger scales of analysis such as the regional or watershed level.

Despite this trend, some researchers, particularly in irrigation studies, have addressed aspects of intersystem coordination. They include Stephen Lansing (1991), with his work on the role of religious authority and water temples in coordinating water deliveries, water management, and agricultural cycles across large networks of subak irrigation systems in Bali. In a similar vein, John Ambler (1989) discussed the coordination of crop planting to reduce peak water demands across irrigation systems in West Sumatra, Indonesia. David Mosse (1997b:475) argued that tank irrigation systems in south India composed interlinked chains or "cascades" associated neither with autonomous "village republics" nor with a centralized hydraulic state but linked with decentralized or segmentary forms of political organization. More recently, Ostrom and colleagues have begun examining irrigation systems as examples of complex, linked, "social-ecological systems" to determine the possible contribution of intersystem linkages to the robustness of individual units in the network (Ostrom, Anderies, and Janssen 2003). To what extent might these forms of intersystem linkage contribute to the persistence of individual common property resource regimes?

Let me begin by developing an analytical view of the role of networks in enabling individual common property regimes to manage risk and uncertainty. Organizational theory, particularly in its focus on relations between organizations, provides a useful vantage point from which to explore these themes. To use it, we must think of a kuhl regime as a type of formal organization. We can then draw on theories of interorganizational relations, especially resource dependence theory, to explore the possibility that coordination between interconnected kuhl regimes can be an effective strategy for mobilizing resources and buffering environmental shocks.

The underlying assumptions of resource dependence theory are that organizations depend on their environments for critical resources and that as these resources become scarce, organizations survive and prosper to the extent that they can successfully secure access to them (Aldrich 1976:420; Galaskiewicz 1985:282). To a great extent, the nature of uncertainty regarding a critical resource determines the degree to which it constitutes an environmental contingency that the organization must find a way to manage. James Thompson (1967:30), following Richard Emerson's work on power and dependence (1962), argued that an organization's dependence on an element in its environment was directly related to the organization's need for the resource the element provided and inversely related to the presence of alternative sources of that element.[8] Organizations depend on material and exchange resources. Material resources are the primary inputs such as raw materials or budget allocations that organizations require to survive. Exchange resources are the relationships through which an organization obtains the material resources it requires.[9] Organizations use negotiated arrangements to manage relations with those elements of their environment on which they depend (Thompson 1967:34).

Although most kuhl systems in Kangra Valley are highly dependent on river water, managers of kuhls have no exchange resources available to them (other than ritual; see chapter 2) through which they can directly manage the unpredictability of water supply due to floods and earthquakes.[10] According to resource dependence theory, an organization, in order to manage environmental contingencies, will attempt to gain power by trading on its ability to reduce the constraints and contingencies other organizations face in their environments (Thompson 1967:34). While this formulation suggests that exchange resources can be deployed indirectly to reduce an organization's dependence on an element in its environment, it maintains the theory's focus on a single organization and on dyadic exchanges between it and other organizations. In order to account for the extensive coordination among kuhl regimes under conditions of common environmental vulnerability, high environmental dependence, and uncertain resource supply, it appears necessary to shift the level of inquiry from the individual organization to the organizational field—in this case, to the network of kuhl regimes within a watershed. This expanded focus enables examination of relations among kuhls, of the extent to which a network of interkuhl relations exists, and of the degree to which such networks may contribute to reductions in environmental uncertainties.[11]

Jeffrey Pfeffer and Gerald Salancik (1978:70) drew a useful distinction between a set of organizations that transact with each other (the organizational field) and the larger social context in which the set of transacting organizations is embedded. They suggested that the environment of an organizational field has three main structural characteristics: the degree of interconnectedness among the organizations, the degree of resource scarcity, and the distribution of power and authority. They argued that when interconnectedness and resource scarcity among organizations were high and the concentration of power and authority low, interdependence, conflict, and uncertainty for individual organizations would increase. Interconnectedness, thus understood, was a liability because it led to increasingly uncertain and unstable environments.

The image that Pfeffer and Salancik portrayed of "organizational environments as loosely coupled networks of clusters of organizations which are themselves more closely interconnected" (1978:70) provides a useful lens through which to examine the possible roles and importance of relations among interconnected kuhl regimes vis-à-vis the risk and uncertainty that periodic environmental shocks represent for individual kuhls. In the case of loosely coupled networks of kuhl regimes, however, the assumption that interconnectedness is a liability seems not to hold. Rather than heightened competition for scarce resources, interdependence provides the basis for cooperative interorganizational coordination. Thus, although competition for water among kuhl regimes does exist, interdependence also provides the basis for extensive interkuhl water-sharing arrangements that emerge during periods of water scarcity and following destructive floods and earthquakes.

The "collective-action" view within organizational theory provides one way of thinking about organizational interdependence in a manner that does not presume that it leads to conflict. This view emphasizes the collective survival of organizations. It suggests that interorganizational networks play important roles in enabling organizations to construct "a regulated and controlled social environment that mediates the effects of the natural environment" (Astley and Van de Ven 1983:250–51). Thus, for example, loosely coupled kuhl networks might enable kuhl regimes, through exchange relations, to regulate and reduce the risks associated with environmental disturbances. Normative frameworks of expectations pertaining to codes of conduct and rights and responsibilities govern these exchange relations (Astley and Van de Ven 1983). The normative framework enables the network to make, as a unit, collective decisions that meet its collective interests as well as those of its individual member organizations. This approach suggests that interdependence may lead to symbiotic coordination among kuhl regimes.[12] Examples of such coordination include resource sharing, coordinated decision-making among multiple kuhl regimes, and collective action to influence state policies that bear upon kuhl management.

In his research on the structure and functions of embedded networks of interorganizational relations, Brian Uzzi (1996, 1997) elaborated on the potential coordinating functions and other beneficial aspects of organizational networks. Drawing on Mark Granovetter's earlier (1985) arguments concerning the effects of embeddedness on economic action, Uzzi's detailed empirical analysis of embeddedness and organization networks is relevant for understanding the potential ways in which networks of interkuhl relations might facilitate their persistence. Defining embeddedness as the effects of social ties on economic action, Uzzi sought to account for the specific ways in which embeddedness and the structure of networks affected economic behavior. On the basis of qualitative and quantitative data, he demonstrated the ways in which embedded networks of interorganizational relations enhanced resource mobilization, cooperation between individual organizations, and coordinated adaptation (1996:675). These positive attributes existed because of the trust, detailed information transfers, and collaborative problem-solving arrangements that characterized the behavior of exchange partners in embedded networks (1997:42). As we will see, these positive attributes also characterize key elements of relations among networked kuhl regimes in Kangra.

In his analysis of the rationale that guides decision-making processes in interorganizational networks, Uzzi argued that rather than employing the strategic, atomistic, interest-maximizing calculus assumed by transactions-cost economics, agency theory, and game theory, individuals in networks of social relations adopted a "heuristic-based" decision-making rationale. That is, they based their decisions on trust and an altruistic commitment to maintaining the integrity of the network, even if this meant sometimes acting in a manner contrary to their short-term economic interests. In this regard he noted that "trust is a governance structure that resides in the social relationship between and among individuals and cognitively is based on heuristic rather than calculative processing" (Uzzi 1997:45). The social relationships of which trust can be an emergent property both constitute the network and extend beyond it into other spheres of social action. Because of the positive effects of embedded networks, organizations within them have a greater chance of enduring over time than do organizations engaged in primarily arm's-length, marketlike forms of exchange.

A PARTIAL MODEL OF KUHL REGIME
RESPONSE TO CHANGE AND SHOCKS

The first two strands of the explanatory tapestry—rational choice frameworks for understanding common property resource institutions and organizational theories of networks and interdependence—can be woven together and used to help discern and explain patterns of similarity and differences between kuhls that have persisted in Kangra Valley and those that have not. Rational choice models of transactions-cost economics and game theory suggest that persistence is more likely in regimes with relatively small, homogeneous user groups with a slightly unequal wealth distribution who depend on the benefits the regime provides. Internal regime stress arises when members' opportunity costs for participating in the regime begin to diversify—for example, when different households participate to varying degrees in the market economy. This can dramatically alter the distribution of dependence on and interest in the collective benefits the regime provides. Under conditions of rapid political, economic, or social change, regimes are better able to persist when the change does not diversify members' opportunity costs or when it affects their interests in the same manner. Regimes are less able to persist when contextual changes alter the distribution of interest in regime benefits among members. A change that results in an increasingly skewed distribution of incentive—for example, high incentive among some members, low among others—creates tensions within the regime that manifest as higher rates of absenteeism, increasing conflict, and rule infractions. These tensions are exacerbated when they coincide with other inequalities between regime members. The extent of these tensions increases with the degree of coordination necessary for regime management.

Regime stress and conflict caused by increasingly differentiated individual discount rates, together with members' ability to manage stress and conflict, are directly related to the size and diversity of the resource, the number and diversity of the regime members, and the degree of inequality among members. The extent to which regime benefits are essential to members' household economies and the degree to which members depend on regime benefits influence the physical scale—for example, the command area of an irrigation system, the size of a community forest, the extent of common grazing lands—at which common property regimes can persist in a context of rapid economic change. Regimes that provide benefits that are essential to the household economy (or to the economy of any other social unit, such as a hamlet or village) are able to persist at larger scales than are regimes that provide inessential benefits, because the value of the regime's benefit is directly related to people's willingness to contribute to its provision.[13] And if alternative sources of regime benefits are readily available, then the scale at which a regime can persist will be smaller than it would be if alternative sources were absent.

The degree of interdependence among regimes—that is, their network density—also influences the scale at which common property regimes can persist in the face of floods, droughts, and earthquakes. Kuhl regimes engaged in relatively dense networks have greater capacities for exchange and greater potentials for developing cooperative water-sharing arrangements with each other than do isolated regimes or regimes in "sparse" networks. The ability of regimes to coordinate among themselves in response to periodic, short-duration disasters such as floods and earthquakes, without formal or hierarchical structures, is an organizationally inexpensive but effective response to environmental shocks. More interdependent regimes should be able to persist at higher scales than less interdependent regimes.

When taken together, the extent to which regime benefits are essential, the degree of dependence on regime benefits, and network density generate a set of expectations regarding the ability of common property regimes to persist despite recurring environmental shocks and economic changes that diversify opportunity costs. The factors may be measured as high or low and combined to create a two-by-two-by-two cube producing eight possible combinations of essentialness, dependence, and interdependence (fig. 2). Rational choice and network theories suggest that under conditions of economic change and severe environmental disturbances, interdependent regimes that provide high-value essential benefits for which alternative supplies are unavailable will be able to persist at relatively large scales (cell A). Interdependent regimes that do not provide particularly high-value essential benefits and for which alternative sources of benefits are available will be able to manage environmental shocks through cooperative exchange networks but will be less able to manage the internal conflicts resulting

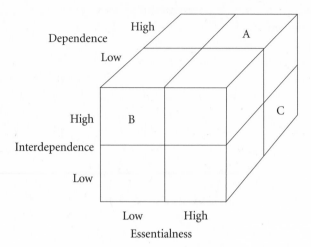

FIG. 2. A cube indicating the predicted relationship between values of the variables "essentialness," "dependence," and "interdependence" and a common property regime's capacity to persist despite environmental shocks, economic change, or both. Regimes in cell *A* are expected to persist despite shocks and change; those in cell *B*, to persist despite shocks but not change; and those in cell *C*, to persist despite change but not shocks.

from the differentiation of members' opportunity costs (cell *B*). Regimes that are not interdependent but do provide high-value essential benefits for which alternatives are unavailable should be able to manage conflicts associated with economic change but are vulnerable to the destructive forces of environmental shocks (cell *C*).

The three factors—essentialness, dependence, and interdependence—are general in effect but vary in form. What characteristics of kuhl regimes in Kangra might be used as indicators of these factors? An excellent measure of the essentialness of the benefits a kuhl regime provides is the distinction that farmers in Kangra make between areas of different agricultural productivity. The low-lying fertile fields on riverine terraces adjacent to the streams that flow from the Dhaula Dar range are referred to as *har*. These are the prime irrigated rice- and wheat-growing areas. Rising above the har fields are gently sloping, plateaulike areas—the upper shoulders of the alluvial fans that make up Kangra Valley. These areas, drier and less fertile than har fields, are known as *larh*. Larh fields are used primarily to cultivate maize in the kharif (summer) season and wheat in the rabi (winter) season. Given the greater productivity of har over larh fields, returns to labor are higher in har than in larh, and consequently, kuhl irrigation water has a higher value in har fields. Additionally and not insignificantly, the distance water must be conveyed to reach har fields is always much shorter than the distances involved in conveying water to the higher larh fields. Therefore, a kuhl that irrigates har fields is more "essential" than one that irrigates larh fields. The ratio of har to larh fields may thus be used to compare kuhl regimes in terms of how essential they are.

The availability of alternative sources of water affects people's degree of dependence on kuhl regimes. In Kangra, seasonal creeks that flow after the onset of the monsoon provide alternative supplies of water to some kuhls. For these kuhl regimes, this obviates the need to rebuild the labor-intensive headworks, diversion structure, and upper channel sections after every monsoon cloudburst and flood. The presence of seasonal creeks whose water may be diverted into downstream, tertiary irrigation channels significantly reduces farmers' dependence on the kuhl system. The introduction of piped water and electric-powered mills further weakens the web of dependency on kuhl water, because kuhls formerly provided water for home gardens and livestock and power for mills.

The measure used for the interdependence of a kuhl is the ratio of the number of other kuhls that irrigate each of the villages it irrigates to the number of villages the kuhl itself irrigates. This is a rough quantitative approximation of the density of irrigation networks and therefore of the potential for interkuhl coordination and exchange.

In figure 2, I partially classify the ability of kuhl regimes to persist despite socioeconomic change and environmental shocks. The measures of essentialness, dependence, and network density make it possible to identify kuhl regimes with different combinations of these factors. However, the explanatory tapestry remains incomplete. The frameworks used to create figure 2 do not encompass the ways in which regionality shapes the persistence of kuhl regimes, informs their organizational structures, constitutes normative expectations that help mold interkuhl relations, and influences authority and conflict resolution capacities. Furthermore, the potential relationship between statemaking and state involvement in kuhl regimes and their effects on regime durability remain to be examined. In short, although figure 2 may be internally coherent, it provides only a partial explanation. In order to develop a more complete explanation, we need to expand the tapestry to assess the possible mutual constitution of state entities and communities in common property regimes and the effects of regionality on regime endurance.

STATE INVOLVEMENT IN COMMON PROPERTY REGIMES

Recall that following the destructive 1905 earthquake in Kangra the colonial administration mobilized military expertise and labor to rebuild the irrigation channels and headworks. The image of military engineers and enlisted soldiers working to rebuild villagers' damaged irrigation structures belies dominant views of the relationship between community-based resource management institutions and state authority, in which state systems erode traditional resource management systems. As Mosse (1997b) noted, this view of the state—in which supralocal political authority at best provides the neutral political space necessary for local organizations to flourish and more often promulgates policies that undermine local capacities for resource management—is associated with both the "rational choice" and the "moral economy" schools of thought regarding community-based collective action. Neither of these perspectives generally admits the possibility that structures of state political authority may, under some conditions, support the persistence of common property regimes. Yet as we will see, the mobilization of military resources for kuhl repair is only one example in a long history of interaction between state institutions and kuhl regimes in Kangra that spans the precolonial, colonial, and postcolonial periods.

To understand the nature and purpose of this interaction and its effects on the persistence of kuhl regimes, we must develop a view of the state that encompasses the mutually constituting relationship between state institutions and civil society. For the state does not comprise a monolithic, undifferentiated social formation, nor do state and civil society exist in isolation or opposition to each other. Rather, the state is more appropriately understood as being composed of a set of differentiated institutions, riven horizontally and vertically by internal fractures, with sometimes competing agendas and mandates, each seeking to acquire, maintain, and strengthen its own legitimacy, power, and influence (Mitchell 1999). The pursuit of legitimacy, power, and influence takes different forms in different contexts. In some cases it may have to do with controlling territory or people; in others it may focus on generating revenue. To achieve their goals, state institutions develop strategic negotiations and alliances with different sectors of society. By doing so, they strengthen the position and power of those very sectors—in effect creating certain kinds of communities and specific configurations of state power.

For north India, David Gilmartin (1994) and David Ludden (1999) analyzed this process with respect to nineteenth-century, state-sponsored, large-scale canal irrigation projects and the creation of new farm communities dependent on canal irrigation. Colonial policies designed to increase agricultural production by granting large farm plots at low rents to loyal, dominant caste groups in newly irrigated areas of the Punjab simultaneously expanded governmental authority into new territory and solidified state legitimacy. For the Kumaon Hills of the western Himalayan state of Uttaranchal, Arun Agrawal (2001) has shown how village-based forest management institutions (*van panchayats*) that were created by the British colonial government in 1931 constitute vehicles for the interdependent processes of extending state authority into new places and strengthening the local power and authority of dominant caste groups and men.

Vasant Saberwal (1999) further explored the mutual imbrication of state systems and local communities in the western Himalaya in his discussion of the long-running competition between the colonial Revenue and Forest Departments in Kangra District over the control of forest land and the power to regulate local practices in forests. Saberwal showed how, during the postcolonial period, the transhumant Gaddi shepherds of Kangra entered into strategic alliances with elected legislative representatives. These alliances secured the Gaddi community's access to Forest Department–controlled grazing areas. The differentiated nature of state involvement in local practices can be even more dramatic in its effects on local resource management regimes. In Kangra during the latter half of the nineteenth century, the same colonial administration that curtailed local rights of forest access and use simultaneously supported the expansion of irrigated agriculture and local capacities for kuhl management (Baker 2000).

To understand the motivations and agendas behind such diverse policy initiatives, we must expand the scope of analysis to include broader political concerns and issues in their historical context. Incorporating a historicized understanding of state involvement in agriculture and forestry in Himachal Pradesh, for example, enables an explication of the shift in the colonial administration's priorities from agricultural expansion in the interest of food security to, later in the nineteenth century, forest conservation in order to secure timber supplies for rapidly expanding rail networks. Similarly, Haripriya Rangan (2000) has shown how, contrary to conventional wisdom, the history of colonial state involvement in forests in Uttarakhand (formerly part of Uttar Pradesh, now in Uttaranchal) did not consist of the steady application of scientific forestry policy and state appropriation of forest resources but rather proceeded through a series of distinct phases, each connected to a larger set of colonial concerns.

Positing a less monolithic, more nuanced and contingent understanding of the state and of the negotiated nature of the relations between state and society also enables an analysis of the different types of relationships and experiences that obtain between state institutions and society, including the possibility that strategic alliances may evolve between local elites and state agents. In the context of irrigation management in south India, Robert Wade (1988) discussed the importance of local elites' ability to negotiate with officials in the state irrigation bureaucracy in order to secure water deliveries for their villages. With regard to forest protection in India, ShivSharan Someshwar (1995), Arun Agrawal (2001), and Shubhra Gururani (2000) showed how the enforcement of rules regulating forest access and control and the imposition of fines for rule infractions varied by gender, caste, and social position. Even the experience of citizenship can vary by class, caste, and gender, as Akhil Gupta (1998) showed for contemporary development programs and bureaucracies in Uttar Pradesh.

In order to understand the state's roles in local irrigation management in Kangra, as well as the effects of state involvement on local irrigation organization, we must view the state as an internally fractured set of institutions competing with one another, connected to a wider set of policy concerns and directives, and entering into strategic alliances and negotiations with local groups in a manner that both strengthens state authority and benefits segments of the local "community." State involvement in kuhl irrigation management in Kangra is related to the process of statemaking and state formation in a variety of ways. In his study of statemaking and forestry in West Bengal, K. Sivaramakrishnan (1999:5) argued that statemaking was "fundamentally about defining the forms and legitimations of government and governmentality." Statemaking involves the production of civil society through microlevel negotiations between state agents and local elites, even as it enables the expansion of "the ideological and organizational power of the central government to penetrate society, exact compliance, and invoke commitment" (1999:5).

By linking statemaking to governmentality, Sivaramakrishnan invoked Michel Foucault (1991), who used the term *governmentality* to refer to the third formation of modern power, the other two being sovereignty and discipline. Governmentality, though hard to define in a nutshell, concerns the "arts and rationalities of governing" (Bratich, Packer, and McCarthy 2003:4). It refers to the variety of techniques, technologies, coordinating strategies, and programs that mediate the relationship between the governed and the state and through which the governed consent to governance. The notion of governmentality, developed and generally applied in the context of the liberal state, takes on dramatic new meanings in the context of colonial states, which lacked any semblance of democratic practice or the development of a civil society empowered to consent to be governed— both of which are hallmarks of the liberal state. The colonial state in India was forced to pursue the goals of governmentality (legitimacy in the eyes of the colonized) through cloaked structures of imperial domination (Prakash 1999). The result was a powerful process, in many respects unparalleled in Western societies, of "bureaucratic expansion and rationalization under which the population's economic, demographic, and epidemiological properties were surveyed, enumerated, measured and reconstituted" (Prakash 1999:126). The exercise of governmentality and the pursuit of statemaking in colonial India thus required imperial domination to masquerade as the arts and rationalities of governing.

In the context of Kangra and kuhl irrigation, a focus on statemaking draws attention to the manner in which relations between state institutions and social groups are negotiated and renegotiated over time, with a particular emphasis on the resulting constellations of local and state power. Closely related to statemaking is state formation, the "creation of institutions and knowledges that systematize practices . . . and the creation of state-sanctioned authority that is recognized as legitimate by citizens" (Agrawal 2001:35). The contingency of the negotiations that take place between state entities and local groups, when combined with a focus on the systematization of institutions and knowledge at the local level, creates a powerful lens for understanding the logic of state involvement in local resource management regimes. The processes through which state institutions secure legitimacy and revenue and expand into new spaces are mediated by the negotiations through which social groups define and create the conditions under which they consent to be governed. The delicate balance between central government authority and local control, a hallmark in particular of British colonial rule in India, was subject to frequent assessment and revision. The resulting iterative negotiations that obtained between state institutions and social groups shaped and influenced the character of both and have been carried forward into the postcolonial era.

Advancing this strand of the explanatory tapestry is essentially to argue for bringing the state into the study of common property resource management. Hardin's distinction between state, private, and common property regimes contains an implicit assumption that the state is heavily involved in the first but not the last two. Although it is self-evident that the state is a dominant player in the context of state or public property regimes, such as forest management in greater Punjab, the state also plays pivotal roles in private and common property regimes. Minoti Chakravarty-Kaul (1996:22) criticized what she called "the Property Rights School" for espousing a view of the role of the state that was conceptually too narrow because it was restricted to the allocation of rights over scarce resources. She argued that in the Punjab, the colonial administration played an intimate role in "establishing and altering the constraints within which property rights were established." This included the creation of new types of rights as well as communities of rights holders. In return, the state secured its own legitimacy and authority. The specific nature of this sort of negotiated exchange of entitlement for political authority is historically, ecologically, and culturally conditioned, but it almost always affects private and common property regimes. The example of the canal colonies in the Punjab, where government investment in large-scale irrigation and transportation networks facilitated the consolidation of power and authority among influential caste groups, illustrates this point with regard to private property.

Within common property resource management regimes, the state almost always plays a more active role than that of simply allocating property rights. Many, if not most, common property regimes are imbricated in the processes of statemaking and state formation as sites for contesting or strengthening the legitimacy of state rule and for reinforcing or transforming differences among locally situated actors. In few instances, if any, does the state simply provide the neutral political space for a common property resource management regime to flourish. Indeed, when the state provides resources that the regime requires but that would otherwise be unavailable (i.e., capital, technology, labor or its coordination, and conflict resolution capacities), without undermining local capacities for collective action, it may play a role in enhancing regime durability and strengthening the social relations that inhere within the regime. The effect of such state involvement on regime durability may be especially important in contexts where common property regimes have relatively high coordination requirements and operate in diverse social and ecological conditions or when they are subjected to frequent and intense environmental disturbances. Analyses of common property regimes, whether enduring, declining, growing, or stagnating, may well be incomplete without incorporating an analysis of the role of the state into the understanding of regime dynamics.

REGIONALITY'S IMPRINT ON COMMON PROPERTY REGIMES

The fourth strand of the explanatory tapestry extends the analysis to include the influence of Kangra as a historically, politically, socially, and ecologically constituted region on the development and persistence of kuhl irrigation systems. Considering Kangra as a region composed of dynamic and differentiated social relations "stretched out" over space (Massey 1994:2) provides analytical traction not only for examining the ways in which kuhl regimes are influenced by the relations that constitute Kangra but also for exploring the ways in which kuhl regimes are themselves arenas in which those relations are reproduced and contested. By this I mean the multiple ways in which kuhl regimes simultaneously reproduce Kangri cultural systems of meaning, identity, community, and place and constitute sites for the renegotiation of some elements of those systems, particularly in the context of rapid regional socioeconomic change. Thus kuhl regimes are themselves vehicles for the symbolic production of locality in Kangra (Appadurai 1996). Their persistence reflects the ways in which kuhl regimes are valued because of their symbolic and cultural meanings and are enmeshed in networks of material and symbolic exchanges; persistence is not simply a function of rational calculations about the material value of water.

Examining the relationship between kuhl regimes and their social, historical, and ecological setting expands the scope of analysis from formal kuhl irrigation organizations to the broader set of social and political relationships in which they are embedded. This entails examining the influence of Kangri notions of fairness, norms of reciprocity, and the importance of reputation on farmers' willingness to participate in the management and distribution of kuhl water. It also involves analysis of the myriad ways in which hierarchical relations based on caste differences are naturalized, reproduced, and contested within kuhl regimes. With respect to understanding the emergence of interkuhl water transfer arrangements during droughts or following destructive floods, this perspective incorporates the influence of Kangri notions of generalized reciprocity, the importance of acting in accordance with the principle of *bhai bundi se* ("through brotherhood"), and reputation maintenance.

Moreover, this focus on regionality enables analysis of the production of symbolic as well as material capital with regard to kuhl regimes. It suggests the ways in which state authorities can parlay material capital into symbolic capital (Bourdieu 1990 [1980])—for example, by sponsoring the construction of kuhls and in some cases redirecting tax revenues from irrigated agriculture to support temples.[14] In this manner, precolonial, colonial, and post-independence Indian state authority was created and maintained through state involvement in kuhl irrigation management. Similarly, the annual religious rituals performed by the kohli following the repair and maintenance of the kuhl (rituals that involve all those who participate in the multiday work parties) are critical aspects of kuhl persistence because the ritual itself produces community. Kuhls also contribute to the production of a particular and unique Kangri *pahari* (mountain) identity. Kangri oral traditions are replete with stories recounting the difficulties associated with surveying and constructing certain kuhls. Some of these stories encode the environmental knowledge possessed by different social groups, others reinforce caste privilege, and yet others incorporate social values related to gender- and kin-based differences in the status of household members. Thus, kuhl regimes that provide irrigation water during the dry pre-monsoon season are also sites for the inscription of social relations based on gender, kinship, caste, and other social differences.

Room must also be made in the analysis for the imperative of nature as it influences kuhl regimes and kuhl organization. Mosse (1997b:473), expanding on Edmund Leach's (1961) observation that hydrology affects social structure, pointed out that social structures have "ecological and territorial dimensions." So, for example, the possibility that ruling lineages in Kangra could generate symbolic political capital by sponsoring the construction of some of the longest kuhls in Kangra Valley was in turn enabled by the local topography, which divides the landscape into fertile riverine terraces and less fertile plateau-top cultivated areas. That the distinction between the two types of land is culturally and ecologically important is suggested both by indigenous soil type categories that encode the differences between them and by the very different trajectories of change within kuhl regimes that irrigate primarily one or the other soil type. Watershed topography strongly influences the possibility for water transfers between separate kuhl regimes through the ways it shapes the network of adjacent kuhl channels. In Kangra Valley itself, some watersheds are relatively steep and narrow, with less arable land, whereas others are broader and have greater scope for irrigated agriculture. Kuhl regimes in the former class of watershed tend to irrigate smaller areas of hydrologically isolated arable land and thus offer fewer opportunities for interkuhl water exchanges than do kuhls that irrigate large expanses of contiguous arable land.

Ecology and social relations themselves interact in numerous ways. Topography affects settlement patterns; Rajput and Brahman hamlets in Kangra tend to be located at higher elevations than lower-caste hamlets. This means that often in kuhl regimes, high-caste privilege and authority reinforce the inherent advantages of being upstream. Thus, social power and topography together compound the difficulties low-caste farmers from downstream hamlets encounter regarding water supply and the unequal distribution of the burden of kuhl maintenance and repair between upstream and downstream irrigators. In some cases, the only effective way for downstream groups to challenge such caste- and locationally derived inequalities has been to withdraw from the kuhl regime altogether. In others, downstream groups have employed a variety of tactics, including oral accounts, to legitimate and naturalize their claims against competing, upstream, high-caste claims. More recently, new institutional arrangements have given some downstream groups increased leverage to counter both caste- and location-based inequalities.

The imperative of nature also dramatically influenced the colonial state's involvement in irrigation in Kangra. Unlike the relatively flat, fertile, Punjab plains to the south of the hills, the relatively enclosed and undulating Kangra Valley held no place for the imperial science of large-scale canal irrigation and the modernizing projects of which it was a part. This meant that the conjunction of state knowledge and state power that was prevalent throughout most of the British Raj—a conjunction that, in the forms of scientific forestry and irrigation engineering, was a core element in the process of statemaking—was not applied in Kangra with regard to irrigation technologies. Consequently, there was little or no opportunity for "modern" irrigation technologies to undermine and supplant indigenous systems of irrigation, as occurred in Bali, the Philippines, and elsewhere.

Instead, British colonial administrators, once the colonial army wrested control of the region from the Lahore-based Sikh government during the second Sikh war of 1846, played a very different role in irrigation development, but one that still involved statemaking. Prevented by ecology from large-scale irrigation development and concerned about food security and revenue generation, colonial administrators embarked on a series of interventions that in many ways represented a continuation of the role of the precolonial state in kuhl management. These interventions included providing occasional subsidies for kuhl repair, sponsoring the construction of some new kuhls, adjudicating conflicts over water rights, and codifying customary irrigation rights. Although these activities did not involve the application of imperial science and the development of a large technocratic bureaucracy, they did entail the systematization of knowledge and expansion of state authority into new areas, and in doing so they furthered statemaking and state formation in Kangra.

To understand the role of kuhl regimes in the "production of locality," we need to employ a social theory of action (derived, for example, from Bourdieu 1977 [1972], 1990; Douglas 1986; and Giddens 1976, 1984, 1986) that extends neoclassical economic assumptions of rational and utility-maximizing behavior and narrower (as in Parsonian) theories of action. For example, Anthony Giddens's emphasis on the routine in social life and his cognitive theory of individual commitment to socially constructed roles and behavior complement and extend Parsonian notions of norms and sanctions as the basis of commitment. His theory of *structuration*—the continual reproduction in everyday life of social structure through individual action and interaction—suggests a way of expanding the focus of inquiry from individuals' calculations of the costs and benefits of contributing labor to get water to the broader relationship between kuhl regimes and the social structures in which they are embedded.

A similar inference can be drawn from Pierre Bourdieu's notion of *habitus*, defined as "systems of durable, transposable dispositions, . . . principles which generate and organize practices and representations that can be objectively adapted to their outcomes without presupposing a conscious aiming at ends or an express mastery of the operations necessary in order to attain them" (Bourdieu 1990 [1980]:53). The dispositions that compose the habitus are the "cognitive and motivating structures" (1990:53) that people with common histories share. These produce internalized regularities in patterns of thought, aspiration, and strategies of action (Powell and DiMaggio 1991). Internalized at the cognitive, affective, and evaluative levels, these regularities are daily reproduced through individual and collective action. They constitute a powerful, locally rooted "grammar"—a means of communicating in meaningful ways—that informs the evolution and development of collective action and the institutional forms such action assumes.

The legitimacy of local institutions and practices is further enhanced through "naturalizing analogies"—that is, behavioral conventions that have a "parallel cognitive convention to sustain" them within the broader social structure (Douglas 1986:50). An institution or practice that persists over a long time is naturalized by incorporating into it parallel structures of interaction from the larger, historically and socially constituted setting.

These parallel structures of interaction both precede the institution or practice and are ceded authority in the process of their reproduction in an institution or practice.

Naturalizing analogies and the social grammar of the habitus also constitute the building blocks for structures of cultural hegemony—the culturally mediated relationship between consent and coercion (Gramsci 1971). The shared social reality constructed through naturalizing analogies and the institutionalized expressions of habitus serve to reinforce preexisting patterns of domination and resource use within a social group. They reinforce, for example, the dominant position of high-caste groups within kuhl regimes as well as the authority of the kohli. Naturalizing analogies can strengthen the ideological underpinnings of hierarchical, caste-based social divisions as well as gender-based inequalities within households. Dominant groups employ naturalizing analogies such as stories, myths, and rituals to help manufacture consent to the prevailing social order. For example, in the context of village forest management councils in Kumaon, Agrawal (2001:31) has shown how prevailing social norms influence the unequal application and enforcement of formal rules governing resource use and access in a manner that reinforces local power structures and reflects the "structured deprivation of power" to which women and low-caste members are subject.

But because habitus constitutes a grammar and not a script, subordinate groups can attempt to contest the prevailing social order by advancing reconfigurations of it. This is especially true under conditions of social and economic change such as currently prevail in Kangra. Instances of such reconfigurations include the case of a kuhl committee that is led by a woman, cases in which the rules governing contributions for kuhl maintenance are changed to substitute water usage for status as the measure of expected labor contribution, and cases in which people simply exit the kuhl regime altogether and shift to rain-fed agriculture—a move possible only if those exiting have alternative sources of income such as nonfarm employment. These reconfigurations challenge some of the patterns of social power and resource use prevalent in the region while, for the most part, maintaining the overall integrity of kuhl regimes. They constitute microchallenges and renegotiations of the patterns of cultural hegemony in Kangra.

Regime institutionalization—the extent to which a kuhl regime incorporates and reproduces social practices and relations embodied in the broader social and cultural context—may buffer the impacts of shocks and changes on regime persistence. During the process of institutionalization, "the moral becomes factual," and once institutionalized, the factual becomes cognitive (Zucker 1991:83). Once institutionalized, the practice or institution has an objective existence as part of socially constructed reality. It can be transmitted from one individual to another as part of that shared social reality.

Cultural persistence is directly related to institutionalization. A "strong" institutional environment may reduce the degree of elaborateness and the amount of organizational structure required, because "cultural controls can substitute for structural controls" (Scott 1991:181). Similarly, the habitus, which is a product of history and which generates social practices consistent with that history, guarantees the consistency over time of social practices "more reliably than all formal rules and explicit norms" (Bourdieu 1990 [1980]:54). Thus, when symbols and beliefs are shared, categories common, and procedures accepted as routine, the need for them to be formally encoded within an organization declines. As institutionalization declines, external formal rules and sanctions must substitute for the declining salience of naturalizing analogies.

This suggests that an institutionalized irrigation organization—for example, one with well-developed naturalizing analogies that embodies key elements of the Kangri habitus—should be more persistent than a less institutionalized regime. Furthermore, an institutionalized regime will likely have fewer formal rules, sanctions, and enforcement mechanisms than one that is less institutionalized. Or, as Mary Douglas (1986) might argue, the latter may have less legitimacy because it is not well supported by "naturalizing analogies" within the broader social context. An increase in rule formalization might therefore signify a loss of organizational legitimacy and itself constitute an organizational response to the stresses resulting from challenges to the naturalization of inequality and dominant patterns of cultural hegemony in Kangra. It might also be related to increased interaction with state systems that impose their own forms of naturalizing analogies on regimes.

Within this framework, the specific organizational structure of kuhl regimes, the forms of authority and practices they encode, and their persistence can be explained partly by the ways in which they incorporate and reproduce institutionalized elements of social structure that are central to Kangri culture. Four of these elements are norms of reciprocity, role specialization, religious beliefs, and local conceptualizations of prestige and honor (*izzat*). The relatively high degree of institutionalization of the kuhls in Kangra may partially account for their ability to persist at the scales they have despite recurring environmental disturbances and rapid regional socioeconomic change.

Unlike institutional economics, in which institutional change is attributed to "fundamental and persistent changes in relative prices" (North 1986:234), a focus on regionality suggests that institutional change arises from the development of contradictions, the force of exogenous environmental shocks, or other factors such as procedural rationality. Contradictions can develop between an institution and its environment, between it and other institutions, or between basic forms of social behavior (Jepperson 1991). Such contradictions—or environmental shocks—prevent an institution from reproducing itself, thus forcing it to change or disappear. For example, kuhl regimes encounter contradictions between their reliance on norms of reciprocity and the decline of those norms as an institutional form in Kangri culture. Without the "naturalizing analogy" of this norm in the broader social structure, its legitimacy in kuhl regimes becomes open to question, challenge, and renegotiation. Kuhl regimes respond to this contradiction by formalizing rules and sanctions, changing the basis of resource mobilization for system maintenance, or both. In this manner, contextual changes of long duration and broad spatial effect, such as changes in regional political economy, generally lead to permanent changes in regime structure that manifest as increased formalization. In many cases, kuhl regimes have undergone radical changes in their formal organization. These changes were direct responses to the legitimation of rational bureaucratic organizational models within state structures of authority, particularly those that provide assistance (financial, technical, or otherwise) to kuhl regimes.

The explanatory tapestry created by weaving together the four strands of analysis discussed in this chapter will guide our exploration of how kuhl regimes in Kangra Valley have, for the most part, maintained their integrity in a context of environmental shocks and socioeconomic changes. It is an eclectic tapestry, one that draws upon multiple frameworks and theories, some of which presume quite different models of human behavior. Compare, for example, the atomistic, instrumentalist logic of the calculating, self-interested individual with that of the person engaged in multiple networks of exchange whose motivation is an emergent property of the social structure in which he or she is embedded. These different logics of exchange are not mutually exclusive but complementary; they are employed to different degrees and in different combinations in different social settings. Other strands of the tapestry incorporate quite different phenomena.

Compare, for example, the emphasis on the potential role of state systems and statemaking in community-based resource management institutions with the focus on the imperatives of nature and reproduction of locality within kuhl regimes. Only such a multifaceted approach can adequately account for the differential persistence of the kuhls of Kangra. Having readied the tools of analysis, it is time to return to the story of the kuhls, beginning with a look at the setting of kuhl irrigation.

2

THE DYNAMIC LANDSCAPE OF KUHL IRRIGATION

A VARIETY OF PLACE-SPECIFIC ECOLOGICAL AND SOCIAL FACTORS CON-
join in Kangra Valley to create unique and diverse opportunities for
agriculture and gravity-flow irrigation. Ecological conditions that have
enabled relatively large-scale irrigation systems to develop also damage kuhls
and threaten their long-term persistence. Variations in proximity to
perennial streams and in soil fertility, often a function of local topography,
create stark spatial discrepancies between adjacent kuhls in terms of the
labor demands for irrigation and the returns on labor investments. Social
and cultural characteristics of the region, such as norms of hierarchy and
exchange, patterns of land distribution and settlement, and local
constructions and reproductions of community, make up the broader social
context of kuhl irrigation. Their spatialized configurations influence the
persistence of kuhl regimes.

Diverse social relations and material and cultural exchanges also connect
Kangra Valley in myriad ways with other regions and places. These
connecting relations and exchanges include, for example, flows of labor
from Kangra to other regions on the plains of north India (historically for
military service but now for other forms of employment as well), the
currency in Kangra of notions of political authority and constructions of
community that draw on extraregional referents, and strong linkages
between the villages of semisedentary, pastoral Gaddis in Kangra and the
Gaddi "homeland" of Chamba District, to the north of Kangra.

The collective articulation of these diverse ecological, social, political,
and economic factors—some contained within Kangra Valley and others

extending beyond it—together make up Kangra as a region. Conceiving of Kangra as an internally differentiated region composed of dynamic social relations "stretched out" over space (Massey 1994:2) enables us to identify the factors that account for the diverse ways in which kuhl regimes have evolved and changed over time. Each kuhl regime embodies, as it were, a slightly different articulation of spatialized social relations and ecological conditions. Thus, one way of thinking about the landscape of Kangra is as the collective embodiment of social relations and ecological conditions represented by the valleywide network of kuhl regimes. This dynamic landscape, a product of the interaction of spatialized social relations and ecological possibilities and constraints, both encodes information (Duncan 1990) about the social relations that have helped to constitute it (Mitchell 2000:103) and functions as the spatially differentiated terrain upon which the effects of regional political-economic changes manifest themselves and are responded to.

The most dramatic of these changes is the recent transformation of a primarily agrarian economy into one in which nonfarm income is increasingly important. Although remittance income has always been a part of the area's economy, the scale of the current nonfarm employment sector is historically unprecedented. This increase in nonfarm employment has dramatically changed the pattern of household dependence on kuhl irrigation water and hence willingness to contribute to its provision. Reduced willingness to contribute manifests itself in a variety of ways that are strongly conditioned by spatialized social relations (often related to the degree of inequality within a kuhl regime) and ecological conditions (often related to variations in soil fertility and the proximity of fields to a perennial stream) encoded in the Kangri landscape. In addition to a nuanced reading of this landscape, comprehending the full extent of the challenges that increasing nonfarm employment poses for the maintenance of kuhl integrity requires understanding the annual rhythms of labor demands and management tasks associated with kuhls.

REGIONAL ECOLOGY: OPPORTUNITIES
AND CHALLENGES FOR KUHL IRRIGATION

The topography of Kangra Valley—riverine terraces and alluvial plains that slope away from the base of the Dhaula Dhar massif—provides opportunities for extensive gravity-flow irrigation. At the same time, the combination of extreme monsoon rains and the steep, narrow canyons that flank the Dhaula Dhar is conducive to destructive monsoon floods. The topographical distinction between riverine terraces and the agricultural areas on the tops of the sloping alluvial plains further marks important, topographically derived differences in soil fertility, agricultural productivity, and labor requirements for irrigation. These differences manifest in important ways within the context of rapid socioeconomic change.

The spatio-temporal distribution of rainfall in Kangra Valley creates alternating periods of water scarcity and surplus. Seventy-five percent of the valley's average annual rainfall of 2,700 millimeters falls during the monsoon season, from mid-June through the third week of September. Monsoon rains can be extraordinarily intense. During one 24-hour period in July 1976, for example, more than 53 millimeters of rainfall were recorded at the Palampur weather station. Such rains can transform the small rivers draining the Dhaula Dhar into roaring torrents that transport huge boulders and wield tremendous destructive power. In extreme cases a mudslide in a narrow upstream canyon creates a temporary dam that eventually bursts, sending a wall of water, boulders, and trees hurtling downstream. Such floods remove all signs of the kuhls that lie in their path, often carry away large sections of agricultural land, and usually change the course of the river. Village elders who remember past floods (like those that occurred on the Neugal in 1944 and 1952) describe the deafening roar of the water and the thundering sounds of boulders crashing against one another as the engorged river hurled them downstream. It is common knowledge that when a river's flow suddenly slows during a monsoon storm, a flood threatens and people should leave the channel area. Periodic floods pose a serious danger to the long-term stability of kuhls. Repairing a damaged kuhl takes months or years, and in some cases a kuhl's diversion structure and upstream channel may never be repaired. Instead, a permanent water-sharing arrangement may be negotiated with the next upstream kuhl.

Because of the bifurcation of the local topography into riverine terraces (*har*) and higher fields on top of the alluvial fans (*larh*; fig. 3), most villages in Kangra Valley engage with multiple kuhls. Short kuhls (less than one kilometer) and the upstream portions of longer kuhls irrigate the fertile har fields on the riverine terraces immediately adjacent to a perennial stream. A village's larh fields are irrigated by the middle and tail-end portions of longer kuhls, which must begin many miles upstream in order to bring water to these higher fields. In addition to the greater labor input necessary to convey irrigation water to larh fields, larh areas tend to be less fertile than har areas. The spatial differentiation of the command areas of

FIG. 3. *Har* and *larh* areas. Har fields are immediately adjacent to the Neugal River (center middle ground), whereas larh fields are located on the tops of the plateaulike areas farther from the river (left background)

many kuhls into har and larh areas has important implications for tracing the effects of increasing nonfarm employment and concomitant increasing labor scarcity. Local topography thus creates opportunities for extensive gravity-flow irrigation, fosters conditions that promote networks of overlapping short and long kuhls, and begins to suggest the spatial distribution of the fault lines that will emerge as nonfarm employment increases.

DISPERSED SETTLEMENT PATTERNS

Unlike the nucleated villages commonly found on the plains, in Kangra Valley the settlement pattern consists of numerous small hamlets, often inhabited by the descendants of a founding ancestor. Known as *tikas*, they are the smallest units of local administrative organization. Tikas consist of one or more house clusters and areas of cultivable, forest, and grazing land. The house clusters that make up a tika are generally scattered along ridge tops or on upland plateaus away from the more productive, irrigated agricultural fields. George C. Barnes (1855:4), the first British settlement officer in Kangra, described the settlement pattern this way:

The dwellings of the people are seldom grouped together, but lie sprinkled in isolated spots over the whole valley. Every house is encircled by a hedge of bamboos, fruit trees and other timber useful for domestic wants. Sometimes a cluster of five or six houses occurs, and here a grain-dealer's shop and extensive groves denote the headquarters of the township. These scattered homesteads, the pictures of sylvan elegance and comfort, relieve the monotonous expanse of cultivation, and lend an additional charm to the landscape.

Tikas vary tremendously in size, from as few as 10 to more than 200 households. Smaller tikas are generally single-caste settlements. Larger tikas tend to be multicaste. As we will see, whether a tika is single- or multicaste influences conflict levels in kuhl regimes and thus has an important bearing on members' ability to effectively resolve the tensions stemming from increased nonfarm employment. The fields that the inhabitants of one tika cultivate (and the kuhls that irrigate them) are likely to be distributed across those of several adjacent tikas within one or two *mauzas*. Mauzas, or "revenue villages," are groups of tikas that made up the old fiscal units the precolonial rajas used for revenue collection.

The smallest spatial unit is the house cluster (*narar*). A house cluster is a tightly concentrated group of homes, usually from 2 to 20, sometimes sharing adjacent walls but almost always connected by interlocking courtyards. Partitions of the joint family, combined with patrilocal marriage, over time produced the house cluster. It has no administrative status or corporate property, but it holds great significance for social relations because its members tend to be of the same lineage, descended from a common ancestor who founded the settlement. In Kangra, blood ties and residential proximity lead to frequent interaction and generate joint interests (Parry 1979:136–39). At election time, the entire subclan often forms a political faction, or a subunit of a faction composed of the whole clan, and votes as a block. Members of the same house cluster attend the important life-cycle rituals at each other's households and occasionally share in the preparations required for them; at these occasions house cluster members engage in reciprocal exchanges of gifts of cloth and money.[1] All the households in a cluster will be invited to send a representative to join the marriage party of a groom of the clan when it leaves to bring the bride to the groom's natal village. After the death of a member of the house cluster, all households are expected to observe some degree of mourning restrictions. The norms of reciprocity that characterize relations between residents of a house cluster are replicated throughout other spheres of life in Kangra, including the management of the kuhls, communal cleaning of village wells, and labor exchanges.

There is a vague correlation between altitude and status. Although exceptions abound, high-caste house clusters and tikas tend to be situated on the ridges and hill slopes above lower-caste clusters. This does not imply that caste distribution follows an upstream-downstream gradient. Rather, at any point along the rivers flowing from the Dhaula Dhar south across Kangra Valley, a transect extending perpendicular to the river across the agricultural terraces, up hill slopes to ridges, and sometimes to a higher series of terraces will be somewhat correlated with the status of the house clusters it intersects. At a larger spatial scale, Rajput hamlets tend to be more prevalent near the southern edge of Kangra Valley, where it merges with the Rajput-dominated Changar region to the south; the primarily agricultural castes such as Girths and Rathis generally reside in settlements near the edges of the fertile, low-lying valleys they cultivate; and transhumant Gaddi households are concentrated in villages at the base of the Dhaula Dhar, which separates Kangra Valley from the Gaddi ancestral homeland of Chamba District to the north. The spatial differentiation of caste and settlement patterns, in addition to the topographic considerations mentioned earlier, suggests some of the regional heterogeneity to be found in Kangra Valley.

INCREASING NONFARM EMPLOYMENT

Although the magnitude of the nonfarm employment sector in the last decade of the twentieth century (and the concomitant diversification of dependence on and interest in kuhl irrigation) was historically unprecedented, the subsistence agriculture economy of Kangra has long been supplemented by nonfarm income. As far back as 1874, the settlement officer James B. Lyall, noting the importance of nonfarm sources of income, remarked that "subdivision has . . . reached its lowest point; if all these people relied on their land only for a livelihood, numbers would be starved" (1874:85). During the precolonial period, men, especially Rajputs, left their villages to fight as mercenaries in the Mughal, Sikh, and local Katoch armies.[2] Often one male from each family was employed in this manner. Throughout Kangra, a portion of the land tax was cancelled in exchange for military service.

The tradition of out-migration for military service extended through the colonial period and continues to this day. A contingent of Dogras—a

term applied to Rajputs, Rathis, Thakurs, and Brahmans from the hills—
raised primarily from Kangra District fought on the side of the British
during the 1857 revolt. By the early 1900s Dogras from Kangra made up 3
regiments, 9 squadrons, and 39 companies of infantry in the Indian army
(Punjab District Gazetteer 1909:243). Kangra District supplied about 70
percent of all Dogras. Records show that 17,113 men from Kangra District
served in the First World War, and by 1921 approximately 40,000 Kangra
men were serving in the military (Punjab District Gazetteer 1926:125, 465).
Because of this heavy out-migration for military service, it is not
uncommon, while walking the narrow footpaths that connect hamlets in
Kangra, to meet a military pensioner who may have served in places as far
off as the Mediterranean region during the Second World War or, more
recently, in one of the wars with neighboring Pakistan. The life trajectories
of the many people who have served in the military outside Kangra
constitute links between Kangra and other regions; they act as conduits for
the transfer of ideas about hierarchy and organization that manifest in the
more recent organizational transformations of some kuhl regimes.

Tea estates, first introduced in Palampur and Kangra Tehsils (subdistricts)
by the British in 1849, also provided nonfarm employment. By 1902, 4,615
hectares had been planted to tea. Its cultivation employed almost 5,000
persons (Punjab District Gazetteer 1909:123). Many laborers came from
the Changar region, south of the valley. Early tea planters complained of a
labor shortage during their busiest season, which they attributed to the
demand for recruits from local villages for military service and to
agricultural intensification resulting from the construction of roads,
improved market access, and rising grain prices.[3] Lower-caste men and
women were generally employed on the tea estates. Lower-caste men also
migrated to the plains, where they worked as unskilled and skilled laborers,
and to Simla (the summer capital of the colonial administration and now
the capital of Himachal Pradesh) to work as coolies and rickshaw pullers
(Parry 1979:42).

Although the historic pattern of out-migration in search of work
continues apace, recently some people have migrated to Kangra in search
of work. Men, as well as some women, have come to Kangra from Nepal to
work the approximately 3,000 hectares of tea plantations. Poor families
from Rajasthan come to Kangra to do labor-intensive work in construction
and road building. The continuing flow of people out of Kangra in search
of employment, when matched with inflows of low-paid, unskilled workers,
speaks to the relative economic well-being of Kangra as a region.

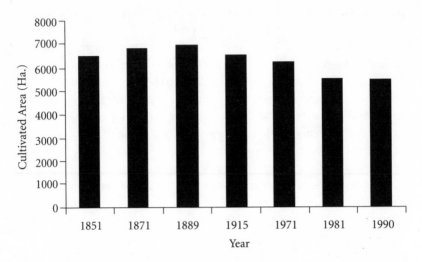

FIG. 4. Cultivated area in the Neugal watershed, 1851–1990. Unpublished *tika* (hamlet) assessment notes prepared for the land settlements of 1851, 1871, 1889, 1915; Government of India 1971, 1981, 1990.

The expansion of the nonfarm employment sector during British rule was accompanied by long-term changes in area under cultivation. Figure 4 shows changes in the cultivated area of the Neugal watershed from 1851 to 1990.[4] After an initial increase between 1851 and 1889, the cultivated area fell from 7,028 to 5,450 hectares between 1889 and 1990, a decline of 22.5 percent. More importantly, half of the abandonment occurred during the 10 years between 1971 and 1981. Much of this land is now used as *banjar*, that is, for grass production for livestock fodder.

While the cultivated area was decreasing, the population of Kangra was steadily increasing. Between 1901 and 2001, the total population of the district increased threefold, from 478,364 to 1,339,030. At the local level, between 1951 and 2001 the population of the kuhl-irrigated portion of the Neugal watershed rose from 29,309 to 69,844 (fig. 5). Coupled with the rise in population and the decrease in cultivated area was the rise in nonfarm employment. Between 1961 and 2001, the number of males in the Neugal watershed engaged in full-time nonfarm employment increased from 2,095 to 9,046 (fig. 6). Between 1961 and 1981—a period of rapidly increasing nonfarm employment—the number of males engaged in agricultural work dropped, presumably because men left agriculture for nonfarm wage employment. Since 1981, however, the overall number of males in agriculture

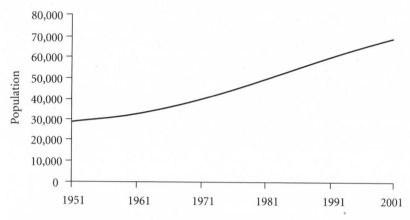

FIG. 5. Population of the Neugal watershed, 1951–2001. Source: Government of India 1951, 1961, 1971, 1981, 1991, 2001.

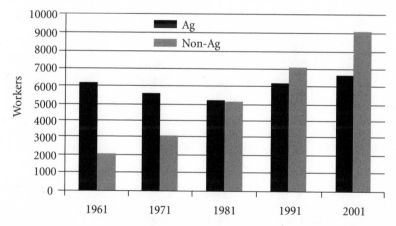

FIG. 6. Agricultural and nonagricultural male workers in the Neugal watershed, 1961–2001. Source: Government of India 1961, 1971, 1981, 1991, 2001.

has increased to just above the 1961 level. The 2001 census shows that two-thirds of those males engaged in agriculture were "marginal workers," meaning they worked in agriculture less than six months of the year prior to the census enumeration. These data suggest that many of these workers were underemployed in agriculture, a point confirmed by numerous conversations throughout my fieldwork in which men expressed their frustration at their inability to secure a nonfarm job. Although consistent with historical trends in nonfarm employment, the size of the male work force engaged in wage labor, either locally or outside the district, far exceeds prior levels.[5]

The nature of nonfarm employment varies greatly, often by a person's educational status. Private-sector jobs in transport, commerce, and small businesses are found in the few regional economic centers in the district. Private-sector jobs in industry and other large businesses are found in the larger economic centers of Pathankot, Ludhiana, and Jallundhar in the neighboring state of Punjab, and in Chandigarh and Delhi. The military remains the largest public-sector source of employment. Other public-sector employers include the Revenue, Forest, Irrigation and Public Health, and Public Works Departments.

The expansion of the nonagricultural workforce has been accompanied by changes, primarily among the younger generation, in attitudes toward farming. The majority of youths complete what is roughly equivalent to a high school education in the United States, and many continue with postgraduate studies. Almost every young man or woman who has this much education would prefer a job as a government clerk or even a less secure daily wage job in the private sector over farming. With the expansion of primary and secondary schools throughout most of the district has come a general devaluation of manual labor and farming.

As the remittance component of the economy has increased, reliance on subsistence agriculture has correspondingly decreased among some segments of the population. The declining dependence on agriculture is tempered by the strong local bias against buying food grains and the high value attached to self-sufficiency, at least as far as grains are concerned. It is hard to overestimate the importance of the subsistence food ethic. It is rooted in deeply held beliefs that relate health and well-being to the consumption of one's own grains. There is also a strong preference for the taste of home-grown grains, and many a Kangri song and proverb extol the sweetness of Kangra basmati rice. Nevertheless, the increases in nonfarm employment have dramatically affected the interest and ability of households with access to nonfarm remittances to contribute scarce labor for the repair, maintenance, and management of kuhl systems on which they depend less and less. This phenomenon, as refracted through the spatialized social relations that influence equity and conflict levels (such as caste heterogeneity within hamlets) and through ecological conditions that influence returns to agricultural labor and incentives for dispute resolution (such as proximity to perennial streams and larh-to-har ratios), constitutes the driving force behind the current transformation, persistence, and, in some instances, demise of the kuhls of Kangra.

LANDOWNERSHIP PATTERNS

Relative to dominant land distribution patterns throughout most of the grainbelt regions of the Indo-Gangetic plains, patterns in hilly regions tend toward more equitable distributions of agricultural land, less concentrated landholdings, and lower rates of landlessness. In this respect, Himachal Pradesh, including Kangra, is no exception. It has the third most equitable distribution of land and wealth of any state in India (Greenberg 1997:86). It also has the smallest average landholding size in India—only 1.3–1.6 hectares. Tenancy and sharecropping are less pervasive in Kangra than on the plains, and landlessness is almost nonexistent. According to the 1950 district census, approximately 90 percent of all cultivators partially or wholly owned the land they worked, 8 percent of all farmers were tenants or sharecroppers, and only 1 percent of landholders were noncultivating landowners (Vashishta 1951:130–31, cited in Greenberg 1997:87).

Landholdings in Kangra have historically been quite small; even "large" holdings are small compared with those in other regions of India. In Palampur Tehsil of Kangra Valley, only 58 holdings exceeded 10 acres of cultivable land, and more than half of the holdings greater than 5 acres were less than 8 acres (Parry 1979:36). Table 1 gives the district-level figures for 1976–77. The table indicates that at the district level, 64 percent of landholdings were one hectare or less, and fewer than 7 percent were greater than four hectares.

TABLE 1. Number and Percentage of Landholdings by Size Class,
Kangra District, 1976–1977

Landholding Size (ha)	Number of Holdings	Percentage of Holdings
< 0.5	59,531	44.3
0.5–1.0	26,586	19.8
1.0–2.0	24,430	18.2
2.0–4.0	14,934	11.1
> 4.0	8,979	6.7

SOURCE: Government of Himachal Pradesh 1979.

The lack of skewed landownership and the absence of a politically powerful and entrenched noncultivating landowning elite are two reasons why land reform legislation was passed in Himachal Pradesh and why it was at least partially implemented. Land reform in Himachal Pradesh consisted primarily of land ceiling and tenant rights legislation. The Himachal Pradesh Abolition of Big Landed Estates and Land Reform Act of 1953 established land ceilings of 18, 27, and 72 acres for irrigated double-cropped, irrigated single-cropped, and other types of land, respectively. The 1972 Tenancy and Land Reforms Act further restricted the ceilings to 10, 15, and 30 acres. This bill also directed that all occupancy tenants were to become owners of the land they cultivated, subject to specific conditions controlling the circumstances under which an owner could reassume leased land. The 1951 Himachal Pradesh Tenants Security of Tenure Act, the 1952 Punjab Tenancy Act, and the 1971 Tenant Protection of Rights Act, along with the 1972 Tenancy and Land Reforms Act, were developed to protect security of tenure for tenants by governing the conditions under which eviction was permissible and to govern the amount a landowner could claim in rent by establishing a ceiling of one-fourth of the produce (Singh 1985, cited in Greenberg 1997:93).

Although implementation of these laws has in some cases been lax, one of the outcomes of the land reform legislation, which has exacerbated the push for nonfarm employment, is that while all households now have some land, many have too little for food-grain self-sufficiency. From this phenomenon, in combination with population increases, has resulted a common pattern in which one brother stays home to manage the agricultural responsibilities while the other brothers (with or without their families) leave the area for nonfarm jobs.

Yashwant Negi (1993) analyzed changes in landholding patterns at the state and regional levels in Himachal Pradesh from 1970 to 1986. He showed that holdings in the size class greater than four hectares declined by 9 percent between 1976–77 and 1980–81 and by another 18 percent between 1980–81 and 1985–86. During the same two periods, holdings of less than one hectare increased by 2 and 37 percent, respectively, and average holding size decreased by 15 percent. Although at the state level the area cultivated increased, for the two districts he surveyed in the middle and low hills (Una and Solan), he reported a slight decline in cultivated area and a 30 percent increase in the number of small farms (1–2 hectares). He suggested that land fragmentation due to inheritance patterns, the weakening of the bonds of joint families, and land reform legislation explained why there were more small farms and fewer large farms.[6]

Although land distribution patterns do differ among kuhl regimes in Kangra Valley, and although they do influence conflict levels within kuhl regimes, the absence of skewed land distribution patterns there relative to other regions of India has promoted the persistence of kuhl regimes by forging a shared interest in kuhl water for irrigation and by muting the class- and caste-based tensions more commonly present on the plains. The absence of large absentee landlords, a noncultivating elite, and landed estates in Kangra, coupled with the fact that many landowners are also tenants and vice versa, has supported the historical development of a base of common interest in irrigation. To some extent, increasing nonfarm employment opportunities have disrupted this shared interest. Conflict running along the fault lines of caste and landownership differences has also erupted. However, continuing reliance on kuhls also provides some of the necessary incentive for farmers to search for institutional mechanisms for managing increasing conflict and to sustain the collective action necessary for kuhl maintenance, repair, and management.

IRRIGATION'S INFLUENCE ON CROPPING PATTERNS

The availability of kuhl irrigation water is the most important determinant of cropping patterns in Kangra District. In Kangra Valley and other parts of the district where kuhl irrigation water is available, the dominant cropping system is paddy (rice) in the kharif (summer) season and wheat in the rabi (winter) season. In those parts of Kangra Valley (primarily larh areas) and Kangra District where kuhl irrigation is not available, the dominant cropping system is maize-wheat. Together, paddy, maize, and wheat accounted for 90 percent of the total cropped area in the district in 1985–86. Figures 7 and 8 show the cropping patterns for the 1989–90 kharif and rabi seasons for Kangra District and the Neugal watershed.

The smaller area sown to maize in the Neugal watershed relative to the rest of the district reflects the greater availability of kuhl irrigation water there. In villages with irrigation, maize is sown only in the unirrigated larh areas along the ridgelines and in the upland terraces. The cropping patterns for Kangra Valley as a whole are similar to those for the Neugal watershed. Often, barley and wheat are sown together, or either may be sown with gram. In unirrigated areas, mustard is often intercropped with wheat, and a pulse

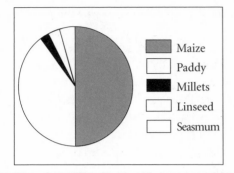
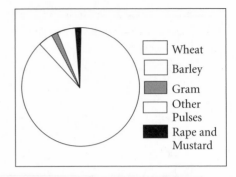

FIG. 7. Proportion of cultivated area sown to different crops in Kangra District, 1989–90. Left: the *kharif* cropping pattern; right: the *rabi* cropping pattern. Source: Government of India 1991.

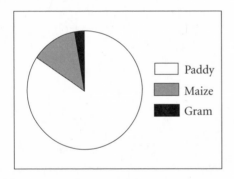
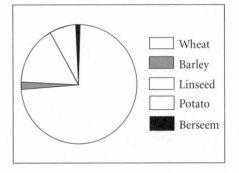

FIG. 8. Proportion of cultivated area sown to different crops in the Neugal watershed, 1989–90. Left: the kharif (summer) cropping pattern; right: the rabi (winter) cropping pattern. Source: Government of India 1991.

such as gram may be sown with maize. *Berseem* (*Trifolium alexandrinum*), also known as Egyptian clover, and linseed are two important rabi crops. The former provides fodder during the annual period of fodder scarcity from January through March. Linseed is sown as a cover crop; it improves the yield of the next paddy crop but it is no longer pressed for its oil.

THE ECONOMIC MARGINALITY OF AGRICULTURE

Not surprisingly, kuhl irrigation dramatically increases agricultural yields. This is good, because even with the increased yields associated with irrigation, farming in Kangra is only marginally viable from an economic standpoint. Crop yields have been compared for irrigated and rain-fed conditions at Palampur by the Himachal Pradesh Agricultural University using the recommended package of practices regarding date of sowing, spacing, depth, varieties, fertilizer application, and so forth. Table 2 summarizes the results of the trials. It clearly indicates the dramatic increases in crop yields resulting from irrigation and, by implication, demonstrates the important role of kuhl irrigation in the local cropping system. As a reality check, Table 3 gives the actual average yields of the major crops in Kangra District for 1988–89. Although these average figures mask important variations between irrigated and unirrigated crops and do not reflect local variations in soil fertility and productivity or yield differences between farms with different levels of inputs (field preparation, weeding), they do suggest the range of yields under actual field conditions.

On kuhl-irrigated farms, maize and dry-sown paddy yield a negative net return of 750 rupees per hectare; irrigated wheat yields only 350 rupees per hectare; and high-yielding varieties of paddy sown by the *mach* (sprouted seed) method yield 810 rupees per hectare (Sharma 1990: Appendix 5.7). Low returns from hill agriculture have been reported for Uttar Pradesh as well. Annual returns of only 239 to 460 rupees per capita have been calculated for *guhl* irrigated farms in Almora District of Uttar Pradesh.[7] The per-hectare estimate of net returns ranged from 3,600 to

TABLE 2. Irrigated and Rain-Fed Crop Yields (Quintals per Hectare), Palampur

Type of Crop	Rice	Maize	Wheat	Gram	Potato
Irrigated	22.5	25.0	34.0	6.1	100
Rain-fed	15.4	18.3	26.0	2.0	29

SOURCE: Singh et al. 1992.

TABLE 3. Average Yields of Major Crops (Quintals per Hectare),
Kangra District, 1988–1989

Crop	Yield
Rice	8.6
Maize	10.9
Wheat	15.3
Gram	4.5

SOURCE: Government of Himachal Pradesh 1990:64.

5,700 rupees (Pande 1991:95). However, the labor provided by family members was not included in the cost estimation. This explains the high per-hectare return, relative to Kangra District, the figures for which include the labor contributions of family members.

The marginal profitability of agriculture in Kangra underscores several points. The first is that households approach grain and pulse production not as an economic activity but as a subsistence activity. During fieldwork, I found no households that sold either grains or pulses. Given the use of draft power in Kangri agriculture and the labor-intensive methods of cultivation, neither grains nor pulses can compete on the market with green revolution grains produced in the Punjab and sold in provision shops in Kangra. However, green revolution rice and wheat, though cheaper than that produced in Kangra, is believed to be inferior in flavor, quality, and nourishment than locally grown grain. This partly accounts for the pervasive and deep-seated preference for eating one's own grains and pulses rather than store-bought ones.

The strong local subsistence ethic favoring self-sufficiency in grain production may also be a holdover from earlier periods when self-sufficiency was a partial hedge against crop failure due to floods, frost, hailstorms, and other calamities. Extreme weather events still periodically disrupt local agricultural production. Stories that describe the distribution of surplus grains to avert famine during crop failures in the past and local sayings that describe the special qualities of millet, which resists insect and other damage for several seasons and can therefore be stored and used for famine relief, attest to the reality of localized food shortages and underscore the importance of self-sufficiency.

Some cash crops are grown in Kangra. The primary ones are potatoes, mangos, and lichees; orchards of the last two have been planted in larh areas since the early 1980s. A short-lived wave of export-oriented flower production passed through the district in the 1980s but proved to be uneconomical due to transport, market linkage, and other problems. Some farmers are experimenting with organic farming, such as organic potato production, but for a variety of reasons this practice has yet to become widespread. The overall marginal economic viability of agriculture in Kangra partially accounts for the drive to find nonfarm employment. When household members do have nonfarm jobs, the resulting high opportunity cost of labor acts as a disincentive to allocate labor for labor-intensive subsistence crop cultivation and for the maintenance and repair of kuhls. The effects, in terms of both cropping patterns and kuhl management, are discussed in subsequent chapters. In order to interpret and discuss those effects, we must first explore the organization and structure of irrigation management in Kangra.

KUHLS IN KANGRA: LARGE NUMBERS AND DENSE NETWORKS

Historically, kuhls were the only source of irrigation in Kangra. In 1897 they accounted for 100 percent of the irrigated land in the district (Anderson 1897:8), and they still account for 95 percent of the net irrigated area there. The majority of irrigated land in the district lies in Kangra and Palampur Tehsils, which together make up Kangra Valley. Much of the rest of the district lies in the dry Changar region, where the absence of perennial snow-fed streams and broad irrigable valleys precludes the development of kuhl irrigation.

The kuhls of Kangra Valley constitute a dense, interlocking network of irrigation systems. Approximately 715 major kuhls and more than 2,500 minor ones irrigate more than 30,000 hectares in the valley.[8] Kuhls range in size from command areas of only a few hectares to single systems that irrigate more than four thousand hectares. As command areas vary, so do the number of tikas that fall within a single kuhl's command area, from 1 to more than 50. Similarly, their lengths vary, from less than 100 yards to more than 25 miles. The institutional arrangements that exist for managing these systems run the gamut from simple collective arrangements among farmers with little or no role specialization to elaborate and refined organizations with several designated kohlis and sophisticated methods for measuring water flow.

The distinction between har and larh areas is important for understanding the interlocking kuhl networks in many of the watersheds in Kangra Valley. Recall that har areas are the lower agricultural fields; they lie just above the riverine cliffs, 10 to 50 meters above the river. Larh areas are the upper fields on top of the alluvial fans, generally 50 to 100 meters above the river and usually separated from the har areas by a steep hill slope.[9] Because of the elevational differences between har and larh, the kuhls that irrigate larh areas must begin 5 to 15 miles upstream from those that irrigate fields in the lower har areas. Often, a kuhl that irrigates larh areas in village B irrigates the har areas of upstream village A; another kuhl that irrigates the har areas in village B also irrigates the larh area of downstream village C; and so on. At the watershed level, the pattern of multivillage kuhls and multikuhl villages creates a network of interdependence between upstream and downstream kuhl regimes. The pattern of overlapping kuhls flowing downhill on either side of a perennial river is not entirely unbroken. In the lower reaches of the irrigated portion of the Neugal watershed, some villages do not have larh areas. In the lowest reaches, where the Neugal River cuts deeply through the sedimentary conglomerate of the Sivalik Hills, villages have no har areas. Where they exist, however, overlapping kuhl networks create opportunities for interkuhl cooperation and exchange.

THE *KOHLI:* INTEGRATOR OF LOCAL KNOWLEDGE AND GOVERNANCE AUTHORITY

The hereditary position of kohli is central to the management of most kuhls.[10] The kohli organizes and supervises the communal tasks related to kuhl maintenance and repair. He conducts the religious rituals associated with kuhl management. He oversees water distribution, especially during March, April, May, and June, when, prior to the onset of the monsoon, peak demands for water coincide with the lowest stream flows of the year. During these periods the kohli resolves conflicts between farmers regarding water utilization and decides whether or not to install water measuring devices or, when water scarcity is particularly severe, to shift the kuhl from continuous to rotational flow. If drought combined with upstream diversions reduces the river's flow to a trickle, or if the kuhl is destroyed by a flood, then the kohli is responsible for negotiating water-sharing arrangements with the kohli(s) of the next upstream kuhl(s).

In return for his services, the kohli receives a fixed proportion of both the kharif and rabi crops at the time of harvest. Besides their subsistence value, the grain payments farmers give the kohli are material and symbolic representations of the community's support for him. They reinforce the social relations of resource management. Similarly, reluctance to give the kohli his share of the harvest—where and when it exists—represents an implicit challenge to those relations and reflects the changing patterns of authority associated with kuhl management.

The origin of the right to be kohli (a position previously valued highly for both its social prestige and its material benefit) seems to have derived, in at least some cases, from a person's performing a public service relating to the construction or repair of a kuhl. This might have included the donation of land or the provision of labor for constructing a kuhl or repairing it after a flood or earthquake. During the precolonial period, the kohli might have been appointed by an agent of the ruler or by the raja himself (Barnes n.d.; Coward 1990).

Oral tradition and the ways in which it reproduces core social formations reinforce the kohli's decision-making authority. For example, stories abound that tell of kohlis in the past who commanded respect and a certain amount of fear. They describe kohlis who had the ability to draw on the power of local deities to bring water to their kuhl during times of drought and to control destructive floodwaters and infestations of pests. One such story, recounted to me by Shyam Lal Sharma ("Pita-ji," patriarch of the family with whom I stayed during part of my fieldwork), describes the destruction wrought by floods upon a kuhl in divine retribution against a farmer who had struck the kohli during an altercation (see Appendix 2). Through the kohli's successful appeal to the kuhl's deity to mete out a just punishment, the story naturalizes the kohli's power and helps generate a divine sanction for his authority. Such stories invariably include references to named places in Kangra Valley where the events described in them took place. The act of telling these stories serves to inscribe the landscape with the social power of the kohli and thus to help reproduce the power and salience of the institution. In this manner, the Kangri landscape can function as a site for "social integration" (Mitchell 2000:141) and the reproduction of a key institution related to kuhl management.

The institution of kohli also reproduces many of Kangra's core cultural practices and reinforces key social formations, thus lending it legitimacy and staying power. Because it incorporates hereditary role specialization and the exchange of services for in-kind payments, the institution of kohli reproduces hallmark characteristics of the caste system. *Warisi,* the word used to describe the inheritable right to be a kohli, also referred to the inherited right to cultivate land and to claim other inherited village posts during the precolonial and colonial periods. As an ascribed role, the institution of kohli parallels the ascription of status and role by birth within the caste system. It also derives support from the long tradition of military service in Kangra. The emphasis on hierarchical authority and the concentration of decision-making and conflict resolution authority in military culture resonates with and supports the roles and functions of the kohli. This is especially evident in the behavior, commitment to principle, meticulous attention to detailed record-keeping, and conflict resolution style of kohlis who have served in the military.

In recent decades, as households in Kangra have participated more fully in the market economy and as the centrality of agriculture and the institutions that support it diminish (and notwithstanding the efficacy of narratives that naturalize the kohli's authority), the status of being kohli has declined. Consequently, the decision-making authority of most kohlis has decreased, and the respect previously accorded them has diminished. As discussed in chapter 4, the declining authority of the kohli and attempts to reinforce it are some of the main drivers of contemporary institutional change in kuhl regimes.

THE MOBILIZATION OF LABOR AND ORGANIZATION OF WORK IN KUHL REGIMES

At the end of March or in early April, when the winter wheat is ripening, there is a lull in the agricultural cycle. Farmers use it to spend several days reconditioning their kuhls in preparation for the pre-monsoon hot season, when reliance on kuhl irrigation water peaks. The local word for this work is *khana*. Organized into work parties by the kohli, farmers remove accumulated sediment and vegetation from the channel bottom and sides, reconstruct the small dams that carry kuhl water across seasonal streambeds and narrow gullies, reinforce weak sections of the channel bank, and rebuild the diversion structure (*danga*) at the head of the kuhl, which diverts water from the river into the channel.[11] Because most households cultivate land in har and larh areas, irrigated by different kuhls, farmers generally contribute to the maintenance of multiple kuhls.

The Organization of Khana

The organization of khana varies from kuhl to kuhl; it appears to vary directly with the amount of work necessary to maintain the kuhl.[12] Kuhls with relatively short channel lengths (1 km or less) and relatively small command areas generally do not have kohlis. In these kuhl regimes, small groups of farmers informally organize kuhl maintenance tasks among themselves. In most cases, smaller kuhls can be readied for water in one day. A day or two prior to the first irrigation of the kharif season, two or three farmers walk the length of the kuhl, removing sediment and vegetation as they go. At the head of the kuhl they construct a small dam of river stones. If water is distributed rotationally, then the farmer whose fields are irrigated at a given time is responsible for maintaining the kuhl at that time. If farmers distribute water continuously to the whole command area, then farmers receiving inadequate water (generally, those in the downstream portion of the kuhl's command area) will clean the channel and strengthen the danga until the flow is adequate to flood their fields continuously.

Kuhl maintenance tasks can be organized informally when command areas are small because farmers who cultivate contiguous plots in a relatively small area almost always live in the same hamlet and often in the same house cluster. The interests members of a house cluster share are usually strong enough to provide an adequate basis for the collective efforts that maintaining smaller kuhls require. In these systems, conflicts stemming from water use are likely to be mild. Because one individual can, in a matter of hours, substantially increase the flow of water, the stakes involved seldom warrant acrimony. When conflict over water use does escalate, it often stems from friction in another arena, such as a feud over the division of a joint estate or accusations of encroachment on each other's land, which spills over into water management.

Khana is formally organized in kuhls that have one or more kohlis. Although the tasks are relatively consistent across all kuhls, the organization of work varies among them. Different kuhl regimes employ different rules to determine each household's contribution for khana, the sequence in which sections of the kuhl are cleaned, and the distinction between communal and private responsibility for channel maintenance. The rules for mobilizing resources for khana are the same for tenant and owner cultivators.

In all kuhls that have kohlis, in late March or early April the kohli determines and announces the day on which the annual cleaning of the kuhl will begin. Because of the increasing prevalence of nonfarm employment, which generally occupies people Monday through Saturday, many kohlis have begun scheduling some of the most important workdays on Sundays in order to maximize the chances of a good turnout. On the morning of the chosen day, the kohli, wearing a white turban to symbolize his authority (fig. 9) and usually carrying a stout stick for balancing on narrow channel embankments, measuring water depth, and encouraging laggard workers, walks through the hamlets within the kuhl's command area, calling loudly for each household to send a laborer to begin khana.

From 8 to 20 or 30 men gather at the work site and usually divide themselves into two groups. One group, using the *kudal,* a short-handled implement with a blade similar to that of a heavy spade, scrapes accumulated sediment from the channel sides and bottom into piles. The second group follows, lifting the sediment out of the channel and removing

FIG. 9. Laxman Das, kohli for Sapruhl Kuhl, supervising *khana*.

vegetation using the ubiquitous, general-purpose, hand-held sickle (*drati*). It is difficult, back-straining work (fig. 10). Often the kohli tries to maintain the pace by building and playing on rivalry between the two groups. With taunts and threats, he challenges the second group to catch up with the first, which, if this begins to happen, responds by increasing its own pace. As the two groups move along the channel, the kohli ensures that the work is of adequate quality to enable the kuhl to operate at full flow without spilling over its banks.

Except for short breaks for water and tea, the work continues throughout the day until early evening. At the end of the day the kohli records in his notebook the names of all present. Sometimes he also notes whether a household sent a small boy instead of a grown man or whether someone came late, worked especially hard, or was slothful. Kohlis who have retired from military service seem to pay particular attention to these forms of record-keeping and are keen to note the quality of work each farmer contributed.

FIG. 10. Shoveling accumulated sediment from the channel, Sapruhl Kuhl.

Record-keeping, however, is a relatively recent phenomenon. Until about 1960, no rosters were maintained of who did and did not show up for khana. The kohli kept a mental tally of who had not sent a household member or a laborer for khana. Farmers who did not participate in khana had low priority for water, in terms of both timing and quantity of water delivered. Both before and since the advent of record keeping, some types of households have been allowed to skip the labor contributions demanded by the kohli. For example, woman-headed households with no sons present are excused from khana because of the cultural norms related to family honor and the control of women that govern where women can go and with whom they may be seen in public. These norms prevent women (especially young, unmarried women) from participating in the communal work associated with kuhl management.[13] Households in which men are unable to do khana because of illness are also excused, as are noncultivating landowners such as shopkeepers and artisans.

At present, khana is formally organized in 20 of the 39 kuhls in the

Neugal watershed. In 13 kuhls, every household is expected to send one male member each day khana is done.[14] Households that do not send a member are expected to pay for a laborer to go in their stead. In six kuhls, labor contributions are calculated as a function of the area of kuhl-irrigated land the household owns.[15] In one kuhl (Samruhl Kuhl), monetary contributions based on irrigated area have replaced labor contributions. Irrigators formed committees in 14 kuhls. One of the functions of kuhl committees is to enforce the formal rules governing labor contributions for khana that have been developed since the mid-1950s. The formalization of kuhl management, examples of which include the establishing of rules and sanctions governing labor contributions, the creation of kuhl committees, and the substitution of paid labor for voluntary labor in some kuhls, is a relatively recent phenomenon. It is emblematic of the sorts of responses kuhl regimes have developed to the regional economic transformations described earlier.

In all kuhls with organized khana, the construction of the headworks and diversion dam (danga) and the cleaning and repair of the main channel from the danga down to the most upstream diversion point (*tup*) are organized communally. The communally maintained portion of the main channel ranges from 1 to 15 miles long. It generally traverses the vertical riverside cliffs and often crosses smaller streams and gullies. Its repair is onerous and time consuming. Channel maintenance below the top tup is organized in a number of different ways. The most common method, observed in eight kuhls, is to divide the channel into sections bounded by tups and to allocate responsibility to farmers who share a tup for maintaining the main channel from that tup to the next one upstream.[16] The kohli does not supervise this work but does inspect it and on occasion requests that it be redone. Another common method for organizing khana along the main channel below the first tup is for the kohli to supervise small groups of farmers along different sections of the main channel. This occurs in five kuhls.[17] Without exception, responsibility for cleaning the subsidiary channels that carry water from the main channel to the terraced fields lies with the household or households whose fields the channel irrigates.

The amount of work required to maintain either a main or secondary channel influences whether or not the kohli supervises it. If the distance between tups is relatively short and no labor-intensive repairs are required, then in most cases the kohli simply inspects the work done without his direct supervision. If the distance between tups is relatively long—greater than 50 meters—then in most cases he supervises work parties responsible for different sections of the kuhl. Farmers sharing tail-end tups work together to maintain the lower reaches of the main channel, those sharing mid-reach tups maintain the central sections of the channel, and so on to the top tup.

For multivillage kuhls, the downstream village is responsible for khana on the main channel between it and the next upstream village. In cases where two or more villages are adjacent to each other and a long stretch of main channel (0.5–5.0 miles) separates them from the next upstream village, then khana is generally divided such that each village is responsible for an agreed-upon section of the main channel. Larger kuhls that irrigate 30 to 40 villages have four or five main channels. Responsibility for each of them is divided among the villages sharing the channel.

The amount of time required for khana differs dramatically among kuhls. Khana for smaller kuhls that irrigate one or two villages can be completed in two or three days. Maintaining the larger kuhls with multiple main channels is more time consuming, and their kohlis call farmers for khana 25 to 35 days each year. After damage by monsoon rains, channel repairs require further labor contributions.

Khana for the longest kuhls in Kangra (whose numerous main channels range from 10 to 25 miles long) used to take three weeks or longer. Because of the great distances these kuhls traveled, farmers used to cook, eat, and sleep next to the kuhl where each day's work ended. After three weeks or more of continuous channel maintenance, the work parties from each main branch would converge at the common channel leading to the danga. As recounted to me many times during fieldwork, more than 200 men would congregate to repair and maintain the main channel, construct the danga, and participate in the religious ceremony the kohlis performed. No doubt such gatherings also provided ample opportunities to discuss the outlook for the coming agricultural season, arrange marriages, and deal with other topics of mutual interest.

These large gatherings no longer take place. With the post-independence increase in nonfarm employment and the availability of piped water for domestic purposes, it became increasingly difficult to mobilize the large numbers of laborers necessary to maintain these systems. Attuned to their electoral clout, village *panchayats* (elected village councils) in the command areas of these kuhls petitioned their political representatives (members of the Legislative Assembly of the state of Himachal Pradesh) to have the state

FIG. 11. Carrying loads of sod (*cheb*) alongside the cliffside section of Raniya Kuhl.

government manage these long kuhls. Consequently, their management was taken over in the 1970s by the state's Irrigation and Public Health Department, whose paid staff now maintains them.

For all kuhls, one of the most difficult sections of the channel to maintain is that between the top tup and the danga, which traverses the steep riverine cliffs created by the downcutting action of the river. Just getting repair materials to the site requires handing rocks and sod (*cheb*) from person to person from the river's edge to wherever they are needed to reinforce the channel sides and plug leaks (figs. 11, 12). A leak at this point soon becomes a waterfall that can quickly destroy a whole section of the channel. To minimize the risk of channel collapse due to its carrying too much water, many kuhls have one or two spillways just downstream of the danga through which excess water can be returned to the river. After monsoon cloudbursts, the spillways are opened to regulate the kuhl's flow and prevent water from spilling over the channel sides. If the kohli lives near the danga, he controls the kuhl's water flow using the spillway. If he lives away from the danga, he designates a farmer to do this who lives near the head of the kuhl and who generally uses water from the top tup.

FIG. 12. Using sod to repair a damaged section of the channel of Raniya Kuhl.

This farmer, known as the *maloli*, receives no formal compensation for performing this task.

Constructing the Diversion Structure

After the completion of khana, collective attention is turned to the danga. Stones, cheb, sticks, sand, and bunches of pine needles are used to build the diversion structure from the stony riverbank into the current (fig. 13). Rules specifying that the dangas of upstream kuhls must be more permeable than those of downstream kuhls attempt to ensure a somewhat egalitarian distribution of water between upstream and downstream kuhls.[18] Thus, only stones may be used to construct the danga of the most upstream kuhl, to enable the greatest amount of water to pass through it. Farther downstream, needles and branches of the *chir* pine (*Pinus longifolia*) may be added (fig. 14). Below this, other riverine vegetation may be used, and by about midway through the watershed, cheb, the sodlike mixture of earth and grass excellent for plugging the spaces between stones, is added to the repertoire of permitted danga construction materials.

FIG. 13. Constructing the diversion structure (*danga*) for Pangwan Kuhl.

FIG. 14. A portion of the danga for Raniya Kuhl. Because it is located in the upper reaches of the watershed, customary rules specify that only stones and branches (not sod) may be used to build it, in order to ensure that some water passes through for downstream kuhls to divert.

My observations of the relationship between a danga's position along the watershed and materials used in its construction confirmed that farmers followed these rules. Like stories about kohlis that are inscribed onto the Kangra landscape, the physical forms of the diversion structures as they vary from upstream to downstream encode on the landscape an ethic of access to water that recognizes the validity of downstream water supply claims. The annual reenactment of this norm through reconstruction of the danga serves to reproduce and reinforce the norm itself. This helps to provide the social basis for the interkuhl water-sharing arrangements that emerge following destructive floods and earthquakes and during droughts.

After the danga is completed, the kuhl will operate at full flow. In many kuhls, the volume of discharge is gauged just downstream of the danga by observing the water level of the channel against a customary depth marker, often a large boulder. The kohli judges the kuhl to be at full flow when the water level in the channel reaches a spot on the boulder that, from past experience, he knows indicates full capacity. For most kuhls, the next khana will take place one year later, but for some kuhls, a secondary khana is carried out prior to field preparation for the rabi crop in early autumn.

PUJA: THE SYMBOLIC CONSTRUCTION OF COMMUNITY

In the mid-nineteenth century, George Barnes described a ritual held for a kuhl in the western part of Kangra District that irrigated 15 villages. He noted that "on the 1st Sawun [the Hindu month corresponding to parts of July and August] a grand procession takes place to the canal head." There, "a sort of fair is held, and five 'bulees' or heads are offered in sacrifice— one buffalo, one goat, one sheep, one cock and one pitcher of wine" (Barnes 1855:23). To have warranted such a large sacrifice of "heads," this must have been an important kuhl indeed—or perhaps an unnamed temple stood adjacent to the canal head and its worship was integrated into the ritual and fair. Alternatively, it might be that during the last 150 years both sacrifice and the use of wine in rituals have simply disappeared from a region where they were once common. Today, at least, animal sacrifice is exceedingly rare in Kangra, and nothing resembling a fair is associated with kuhl rituals.

Whatever the reasons for the apparent transformation in the form of *puja* (ritual), it is still an integral part of the annual cycle of water management in Kangra. Puja serves primarily to help ensure that adequate water will flow into the kuhl during the dry season before the onset of the monsoon. The object of devotion in this case is the kuhl's *mata-ji,* the

FIG. 15. Ranvir Singh, kohli for Pangwan Kuhl, preparing the offering for the deity during *puja*.

FIG. 16. Presenting the offering of cloth to Sonia Kuhl's feminine deity.

FIG. 17. Ranvir Singh distributing *prasaad* after the puja, Pangwan Kuhl.

mother of the kuhl, the feminine deity that inhabits the kuhl itself. In some kuhls the object of the puja is more personalized. In the case of Raniya Kuhl (queen's kuhl), irrigators propitiate the local hill queen who provided the funds for constructing the kuhl in the late eighteenth century. Irrigators of Sapruhl Kuhl, where the man who sponsored its construction sacrificed his daughter-in-law at the canal head in order to make the kuhl flow (so the story and song go), have built a small shrine in her honor and worship her every year as part of the cycle of kuhl ritual.

Invariably, the kohli conducts the puja (fig. 15). He generally does this immediately after completing spring khana, when most of the kuhl's irrigators are present. During the puja the kohli, at the danga or a nearby designated boulder, invokes the feminine spirit of the kuhl, presents an offering of cloth, and asks her to bless the farmers with her presence in the upcoming dry season (fig. 16). After offering *prasaad* (any offering of food to a deity, in this case a cooked sweet dish made from semolina) to the goddess, he shares it among all those present (fig. 17).

In several downstream kuhls, a red flag attached to a pole is positioned in the kuhl's danga, and cloth representing two items of clothing called a *chadre* and a *choli* is placed under a rock in the river. Until the beginning of the twentieth century, women in Kangra wore the chadre and choli. The choli was a sort of blouse, but without a back, that had long sleeves, embroidery on the front piece, and strings that tied around the back to hold it in place. The chadre, a type of light shawl, was draped over the woman's head and flowed down her back to below the knees. Women wore these two garments with the *ghagra*, a type of skirt, and a *sothan*, similar to long trousers. Although the Punjabi *salwar kamiz*, or loose-fitting pants and knee-length blouse, supplanted the chadre and choli in the early twentieth century (as part of the more general import of attributes of plains culture into Kangra), placing pieces of cloth representing a chadre and choli in front of a feminine deity remains a common part of puja in the area today. For Sapruhl Kuhl, the kohli offers a complete set of bride's clothing at the temple of the sacrificed daughter-in-law. To cover the cost of the prasaad and cloth, farmers make a small contribution (two to five rupees and one or two kilograms of grain) to the kohli.

The kohli usually performs puja once a year. If water scarcity threatens the paddy crop due to a late or weak monsoon, he will organize a second puja to the kuhl's deity at the danga. Although I never saw this happen, I was told that rather than a sweet dish's being offered as a prasaad, a goat would be sacrificed, offered to the deity, and cooked and distributed to those present. The kuhl's irrigators would contribute to cover the cost of the goat. Stories abound of past kohlis with unusual powers who, during times of great water scarcity, were able to bring more water into their kuhls after performing this puja.

Puja to the kuhl's feminine deity helps to ensure adequate water flow before the monsoon rains begin. Too much water, however, can also be a problem, especially when it arrives as destructive floods. To ward off floods, the kohli also does puja to Quaja Pir, whom farmers in Kangra describe as a local deity who can control, guide, and calm the flooded river. Interestingly, in the Islamic culture of South Asia, *pir* is an Urdu term with Persian roots that refers to a Muslim or Sufi deity; *quaja*, too, is an Urdu term with Persian referents. The worship of a deity with Islamic referents in a region that has never had a large Muslim population points to the interactions between inhabitants of Kangra Valley and the Muslim peoples and cultures of Central Asia. Puja to Quaja Pir involves supplicating the deity to spare the kuhl from the flood's destructive fury. The kohli usually worships Quaja Pir when he does puja for the kuhl's deity. He offers prasaad to Quaja Pir and then distributes it to all those present. Sometimes the puja is performed separately from that of the kuhl's deity and closer to the coming of the rains in July.

The ritualistic elements of kuhl management that puja embodies strengthen and reproduce the group of irrigators as a community. Offering prasaad to the deity and then distributing, sharing, and consuming the blessed offering marks all those who participate as community members. While walking home after performing the puja, the kohli continues to distribute prasaad to everyone he meets on the way. The symbols, actions, and relationships that kuhl puja encompasses are repeated in daily domestic rituals, on every trip to a shrine or temple, and at all life-cycle ceremonies. During life-cycle ceremonies, members of the household sponsoring the ritual walk to every other household in the house cluster or tika and distribute prasaad to each of them. Each household must be given a small amount of prasaad—to miss a household is not taken lightly and may symbolize the cutting off of social relations or a feud. Accepting prasaad signifies relationship. In this manner the distribution of prasaad identifies the community with which one enjoys reciprocal relations. Analogously, when the kohli distributes prasaad to all the irrigators of a common channel or kuhl, he is simultaneously marking, making, and strengthening community among those individuals.

FIELD PREPARATION FOR PADDY: INTENSIVE LABOR AND HIGH DEPENDENCE ON KUHL WATER

After completing khana for the one or more kuhls that irrigate their fields, farmers turn their attention to harvesting wheat and potatoes, the two main rabi (winter) crops of the area. Harvesting of both these crops usually takes place from the last week of April through the first week of May. Immediately afterward, field preparation for paddy sowing begins.

Kangri farmers use any of three types of plowing, depending on the land use of the previous growing season and the degree of difficulty of breaking up the soil. Fields that were either fallowed or sown to oilseeds during the rabi season are usually dry and hard by May. The plowing of these fields, known as *ghuhar*, is quite difficult for both the driver and the two bullocks pulling the single-furrow wooden plowshare. After the plowing, women swing long-handled, malletlike wooden implements known as *bhataan* to break up the large clods left behind. A second, lighter plowing, known as *jel*, follows the ghuhar plowing (I describe the third kind later). Fields sown to wheat during the rabi season are not so difficult to plow, and their plowing is also called jel. After the completion of jel, men use the spadelike kudal to cultivate the edges of the irregularly shaped terraces that the plow could not reach. They also use the kudal to shave off the sides of the terrace walls, or bunds, to make them smooth and slightly outward sloping, thereby maximizing the cultivable area.

The method of paddy sowing employed determines the next stages of field preparation. There are two main methods: *battar* (dry seed sowing) and *mach* (sprouted seed sowing). Transplanting seedlings from a nursery field to the flooded terraces, a practice known as *oor*, is rarely done. The two most frequently stated reasons for not transplanting paddy are labor constraints and the view that output from oor is only marginally higher than that from mach.

Farmers prefer mach over battar because sowing sprouted seeds gives the seedlings a head start, produces more at harvest time than dry sown seeds (primarily due to increased tillering), and enables an earlier harvest, thus minimizing the risk of crop damage from early autumn hailstorms.[19] On kuhl-irrigated farms, yields for dry seed and sprouted seed paddy sowing average 14.7 and 18.1 quintals per hectare, respectively, for local varieties, and 23.9 and 32.1 quintals per hectare for high-yielding varieties (Sharma 1990:147). However, farmers realize the advantages of mach only if they have an assured supply of water, for mach requires a constantly flooded field. If, after the sprouted seeds are sown, kuhl water is inadequate to keep the field flooded, then the seedlings will die and the dry and hardened soil must be plowed and sown again.

Unlike mach, battar does not require a constant flow of kuhl water, and therein lies its advantage over mach and its attraction to farmers. After the dry seeds are sown, they will not sprout until the monsoon rains begin, at which point there is little risk of the fields drying out during the life cycle of the paddy. The advantage of reducing dependence on kuhl water and minimizing the risk of damage to crops from water scarcity that battar provides comes at the price of reduced yields and increased vulnerability to hailstorms because of a later harvest. The choice of paddy sowing method for a field reflects the farmer's confidence in the availability of kuhl water. Whereas previously the areas sown using the mach and battar methods were quite constant (indeed, during the colonial period settlement officers used the method of paddy seed sowing to distinguish between first-class cultivated areas with assured water supplies and second-class areas with uncertain water supplies and assessed revenue rates accordingly [Middleton 1919:15]), now, in portions of the command areas of some kuhls, water supply and availability have become increasingly uncertain and farmers have switched from mach to battar. The method of sowing paddy constitutes a spatial indicator of security of water supply.

Fields to be sown by the mach method will be given one flooding from the kuhl after completion of jel (fig. 18). Generally, one or two days are required for adequate saturation. Farmers then level the flooded field with a horizontal plank drawn by two bullocks and weighted with a large stone and the driver (fig. 19). After leveling, men and women wade through the mud, smoothing out any remaining clods and removing clumps of grass (fig. 20). They adjust the flow of water from one field to the next by making cuts (*chanu*) in the terrace wall (bund) leading to the next downstream field. Farmers control the water level, which is maintained at about three inches deep, by adjusting the depth of the cut. Depending on local topography, from one to several chanu may be cut into the bund of one plot, each leading to separate plots or to different sections of the same one. When plots are fertilized with manure, the farmer dumps the head-carried load of manure under the flow of water from the upstream chanu. The moving water facilitates the distribution of organic matter across the plot. Men and women farmers monitor and adjust water levels as necessary to maintain standing water in the paddy fields until the paddy crop matures.

Six days before sowing mach, farmers place the rice grains to be sown in a burlap sack and submerge it in water. After three days they remove the sack from the water, close it tightly to keep out air, and place it in a dark room. After the flooded field has been leveled and prepared, they bring the burlap sack, bulging with sprouted paddy seeds, to the field. The farmer places the sprouted seeds, known as *lung*, in a flat basket and separates them by hand to prevent their clumping. With the basket tucked against his waist, he wades through the field. With three to five quick flicks of the wrist per handful, he broadcasts sprays of sprouted seeds throughout the plot (fig. 21). After two to three days the seeds send out shoots, and the root, sprouted while in the sack, grows down into the mud. After five to six days the rice seedlings already stand one to three inches above the water level.

Weeds, as well as root clumps from the previous wheat crop, grow quickly along with the paddy seedlings in the flooded fields. The rice seedlings themselves are somewhat unevenly distributed, growing in clumps in some areas and not at all in others. To remove the weeds and sprouted wheat rootstalks and to thin out and evenly distribute the rice seedlings, male farmers do a third type of plowing, known as *hod*, approximately 21 days after sowing the sprouted seed. They run the plow lightly just underneath the layer of water, mud, and seedlings (fig. 22). Men and women follow behind, throwing the weeds and wheat stalks onto the terrace bund and distributing the rice seedlings from areas of high density to those of low density. Hod is an operation that combines weeding, thinning, and transplanting. After completing hod, men and women farmers carry out

FIG. 18. The initial rotational flood irrigation
carried out before *mach*, or sprouted seed sowing.

FIG. 19. Leveling the flooded fields for mach.

FIG. 20. Preparing the flooded fields for mach.

FIG. 21. Sowing sprouted rice seed, or *lung*.

FIG. 22. The combined weeding, thinning,
and transplanting operation known as *hod.*

the remaining tasks associated with paddy cultivation until the crop ripens. They maintain adequate water levels in each plot, weed (usually twice), and apply fertilizer (organic as well as inorganic).

Fields sown using the battar method are not flooded, nor is the hod operation carried out in them. The fields are plowed as described previously and then leveled with the horizontal plank. The dry leveling operation is known as *mai.* After leveling, the dry seeds are broadcast by hand, the field is replowed, and the mai operation is repeated. The dry seeds remain dormant in the fields until the monsoon rains begin.

WATER DISTRIBUTION IN THE *KHARIF* SEASON

During the kharif season, the kohli distributes water to each tup, although the manner of water distribution varies from kuhl to kuhl. The period when farmers first flood the dry fields just prior to mach is the time of most intensive water use. During this time, farmers and the kohli invariably follow a rotational system of water delivery throughout the kuhl's command area. No kuhl has the capacity to flood irrigate its whole command area simultaneously. In some kuhls, water deliveries move from downstream to upstream tups, and in others the sequence is reversed. In yet others, farmers take turns, village by village, and reverse the order of turns every year to help ensure equity. The de facto order in which farmers receive water results from the interplay between the rules in use and which fields are ready for flooding—that is, in which fields farmers have completed ghuhar and jel plowing. If a farmer has not finished plowing before his turn comes up, then he will miss his turn. The kohli will redivert water to that farmer's tup only after others have received their turns.

Water stealing is a real threat during this time of intensive water use. It occurs at canal heads when irrigators from downstream kuhls (usually under cover of darkness and in good numbers) dismantle the danga and block the water flowing into upstream kuhls, thereby increasing the flow of water into their (downstream) kuhls. It also occurs along the main channel when farmers divert water into their tups out of turn, when a farmer with no rights to a kuhl's water makes a break in the channel to take water to his fields, and when the main channels of two kuhls are adjacent to each other for a stretch and the irrigators from the downstream kuhl surreptitiously divert water from the upstream kuhl into theirs.

Organized guarding against water stealing is called *honda*. Responsibility for doing honda shifts among the collectivity, the individual irrigator, and the kohli. During the period of rotational flooding, the person whose fields are flooded is responsible for doing honda. This presents the difficult situation of the farmer's having to protect his share of water from illicit upstream use and simultaneously control and direct the flow of water from plot to plot. A common solution to the problem of needing to be in two places at once is to create an informal arrangement with an adjacent farmer such that each will do honda for the other.

During this period the kohli also makes frequent trips to the canal head, usually with an assistant or two, to prevent illicit water use and to make small repairs where leaks appear. If an illegal diversion has been made, it will be blocked, and the person benefiting from the diverted water may be reported to the kuhl committee. If the kohli catches someone in the act of stealing water, he will be at least loudly chastised on the spot and possibly allotted less water when his turn comes up. If culprits are stealing water to divert into another kuhl, there are many possible outcomes, depending partially on the strength of the two parties. In most cases the culprits retreat quickly, hastened by threats and blows of the bamboo staff that everyone doing honda carries. At other times the offender may be thrown into the main channel. If the conflict is a recurring one, the kohli may ask the kuhl committee to help resolve it. If the conflict cannot be resolved at the local level, then a case may be lodged with the subdistrict judiciary.

Once the initial flooding of the fields and sowing of mach has been accomplished, the pattern of water distribution shifts from rotational to continuous flow to each of the main channels, secondary channels, and tups in the kuhl. The rule used to allocate water is area-based and does not vary by kuhl, by position in the kuhl, or by soil type. For every four *kanals* (0.16 ha) of land, one finger of continuous flowing water is allotted (one finger of water is a stream of water one finger wide and two fingers deep).[20]

The kohli knows how many fingers of water should be allotted to each division within the kuhl, whether between two main channels, a main and a secondary channel, or a secondary channel and a tup. This knowledge is based on the area irrigated downstream of each fork. Although the records of the *patwari* (village Revenue Department officer) contain this information, the kohli rarely consults them. He knows by memory the number of fingers of water to which each channel is entitled. Walking the length of the kuhl, the kohli is able to rattle off the name and water duty of every tup and channel. Through their association with cultivated areas, place-names themselves encode information about water distribution and thus represent a spatial mapping of water flows within a kuhl.

Measuring water flow precisely, however, is time consuming and costly. The kohli makes the decision to install and monitor measuring devices only when the total volume of water flowing in the kuhl from the canal head approaches the minimum required to irrigate the kuhl's command area. If the danga can be kept in good repair, leakage minimized, and illicit water use effectively guarded against, then more often than not precise water measurements are unnecessary. Under such conditions the kohli controls water flow to each branch by placing stones known as *chakotli* at the point of division and packing them with cheb, the soil and grass mixture used for plugging leaks. In some cases, where main channels divide, concrete structures have replaced the chakotli-and-cheb method of distributing water to the two branches.

If, prior to the onset of the monsoon rains, water flow in the Neugal Khad and other streams draining the Dhaula Dhar diminishes to the extent that scarcity threatens, then the kohli (or the kuhl committee, if present) may decide to install the flow regulating devices known as *thellu*. To construct them, the kohli calls one or two local carpenters (*tarkhan*). The thellu consists of a piece of bamboo placed horizontally at the bottom of the channel whose flow will be regulated. Under the kohli's close supervision, the carpenter cuts two notches into the top side of the bamboo. The distance between the notches corresponds exactly to the number of fingers of water required to irrigate the fields below the tup. The carpenter jams vertical uprights into each notch. The carpenter and kohli install the thellu by placing it in the bottom of the channel and packing stones and cheb on the bank side of each upright, as well as underneath the horizontal bamboo, thereby restricting water flow to between the two uprights (fig. 23). They install thellu at every division point in the kuhl. Smaller kuhls require 20 to 30 thellu; larger kuhls need as many as 300 to 400. Often, one thellu regulates water flow into multiple channels, depending on the number of subsidiary channels that simultaneously diverge from the main channel. For every channel a thellu regulates, two carefully positioned uprights control the amount of water that flows into it. Thus, a thellu that regulates flow into two channels has four uprights (fig. 24), a three-channel thellu has six, and so on.

It takes the kohli from one to three days to arrange for the installation of all the thellu in a kuhl. The kohli, the carpenter, and the farmers who receive water from the branch being regulated are present at the placement of each thellu. The kohli never partially regulates a kuhl: either he regulates the flow through every tup or no tup is regulated. The carpenter, in exchange for constructing the thellu for all the division points in a kuhl, is absolved of his responsibility for doing khana. In some cases he also receives payment on a per thellu basis.

After overseeing the placement of all the thellu, the kohli walks the length of the kuhl every day or two to check their placement, to guard against water thieving, and to repair breaks in the channel banks and danga. Farmers, under cover of darkness, sometimes dig underneath the bamboo horizontal of the thellu. This increases their water supply by allowing water to flow under the bamboo piece as well as between the two uprights. To the casual observer, such illicit water use is difficult to spot, even in daylight. The kohli must therefore examine each thellu carefully and regularly to prevent water stealing and ensure adequate water delivery at each diversion point.

Dol is a special form of water allocation in which most or all of the water in a kuhl is allocated to one village for a predetermined and limited number of days and nights. Farmers in a village with dol rights to a kuhl use this one-time water delivery to carry out the operation known as *sag battar,* the flooding of dry land in preparation for plowing and dry seed sowing. In some cases, dol begins on a set date each year. In others, the

FIG. 23. A *thellu* with two uprights,
regulating flow into a single channel. Sonia Kuhl.

FIG. 24. A thellu with four uprights,
regulating flow into two channels. Sonia Kuhl.

village with dol rights asks the kohli of the concerned kuhl to start its dol on a day of its choosing. A village with dol rights has no legitimate claim on the water of that kuhl other than for the number of specified days. Neither is it responsible for helping do khana or kuhl repair work. Members of the village are, however, responsible for water guarding on the days they receive water.

Farmers rely on kuhl water as the only source of irrigation from the time of sowing until the onset of the monsoon rains. Once the rains begin in late June or July, reliance on kuhl water diminishes in areas through which ephemeral streams flow. When possible, farmers divert water from these nearby rain-fed streams into the kuhl's channel, thus obviating the need to repair and maintain the danga and upstream sections of the kuhl. In command areas that do not constitute microwatersheds for ephemeral streams, farmers must irrigate using kuhl water conveyed from the canal head throughout the paddy season. Each time the river reaches flood stage it damages the danga and sometimes the upstream portion of the kuhl. In some seasons the danga must be rebuilt as many as four or five times. Depending on the severity of the damage, the kohli either repairs it with the help of a few farmers from the upstream sections of the kuhl or calls for help from each household in much the same way he mobilizes labor for khana.

Depending on weather and crop variety, farmers harvest paddy from three and one-half months to four months after sowing. The kohli receives payment at the time of harvest at the rate of one *thimbi* of paddy for every four kanals of land under paddy cultivation.[21] Previously the kohli received one thimbi of paddy for every six kanals of land under paddy cultivation.

RABI-SEASON CROPS AND WATER DISTRIBUTION

The paddy harvest extends from October through the beginning of November. Immediately following the paddy harvest and threshing, field preparation for the rabi season begins. The primary rabi crops are wheat and oilseeds (fig. 25). In the upper and middle reaches of the Neugal watershed, farmers also cultivate potatoes. Often, farmers sow oilseeds in with the ripening paddy crop; at the time of the paddy harvest the seeds are just beginning to germinate. Field preparation for wheat closely resembles that for paddy. After men plow, men and women break the remaining clods by hand, and then men level the field with the mai drawn by two bullocks. They sow the wheat seed by hand in the same way as dry seed paddy sowing. Wheat seed sowing takes place from mid-November through early

FIG. 25. The maturing wheat crop.
Rabi crops require less irrigation that kharif crops.

December. Potatoes, a relatively recent crop, are sown in December and early January.[22]

Rabi crops do not require continuous standing water at any point in their growth cycle. Furthermore, winter rains from December through early March contribute to the maintenance of adequate soil moisture. Thus, farmers need significantly less water during the rabi season than they do for the kharif season. They do use kuhl water to flood the fields once, after the kharif harvest and before rabi-season field preparation, in order to make plowing easier. Following rabi crop sowing, kuhl water may be used to provide intermittent irrigation if the winter rains are late or if a dry period of three or four weeks results in inadequate soil moisture. Wheat and oilseeds often receive no kuhl water throughout their growth cycle. However, farmers usually irrigate potatoes three times by channeling water down a deep, central furrow, from which it flows into shallower furrows between the rows of potato plants.

Kuhl management during the rabi season is, predictably, less formalized than that during the kharif season. In many kuhls, though not all, farmers do khana to remove the grass, sediment, and other debris that accumulated during the kharif season. If water flow is adequate without doing khana, then it is left until the following spring. When it is necessary, autumn khana is generally less intensive and thorough than spring khana. Not every household contributes labor; rather, labor is mobilized on a voluntary basis, with those expecting to sow potatoes contributing the most. In some cases, an ephemeral stream bisecting the kuhl's channel downstream of the danga has enough water flow to meet the water requirements for rabi crop irrigation. In such cases, autumn khana is done as far as the ephemeral stream.

Because of the low demand for kuhl water during the rabi season, the kohli's responsibilities are less than they are during the kharif season. If khana is to be done, then the kohli is responsible for organizing labor and overseeing the work. If an unusually severe winter storm damages the kuhl's danga, then he is responsible for mobilizing labor for its repair. When farmers require water for a one-time irrigation prior to plowing, they ask the kohli to direct water through the main channel to their tup. The kohli is also responsible for directing water as and when required for the potato crop. Because there is no need for continuous flow irrigation during the rabi season, water measurement and flow regulation devices are never used then. Water guarding is generally not practiced at this time. Farmers may walk the length of the kuhl when receiving water for pre-plowing irrigation, but this is more to check for leaks and breaks in the channel than to prevent water theft. Also, because of the low demand for kuhl water during this season, conflicts over water are rare. This further lightens the kohli's burden of duties. At rabi harvest time, the kohli receives half of what he receives at the kharif harvest. Prior to the rabi crop harvest, the kohli assesses the amount of work that will be required for khana for the upcoming kharif season and organizes khana as described earlier. This completes the annual cycle of water management activities.

A DYNAMIC LANDSCAPE

Recurring environmental shocks and dramatic changes in the regional economy characterize the context of kuhl irrigation in Kangra Valley more than does the stereotypical stability often attributed to traditional village India. In addition to the ecological shocks of floods, droughts, and earthquakes, a variety of other changes have affected kuhl regimes. After 1850, extensive land transfers, shifts in average landholding sizes, and expansion of irrigated agriculture resulted in increased investment in and expansion of kuhl networks. More recently, a declining cultivated area, increasing population, and expansion of nonfarm employment have severely stressed kuhl regimes. These trends suggest the dynamic interplay among social, political, and economic forces that characterizes the regional context of kuhl irrigation.

Throughout its history, Kangra Valley has experienced fundamental changes that belie notions of village stability and continuity. The reproduction of core organizing principles such as reciprocity, hierarchy, and duty within kuhl regimes, and in some cases their inscription onto the Kangri landscape, helps to account for the persistence of kuhls despite the social, political, and economic transformations that have occurred. The incorporation of core cultural practices and relations into kuhl regime management activities promotes regime persistence by increasing the degree of regime institutionalization. Examples of this include the practices and relations incorporated into the institution of kohli and the ways in which kuhl puja helps to create community. As we will see in chapter 4, the specific effects of these contextual dynamics on individual kuhl regimes are heterogeneous, inflected by local social as well as ecological parameters. The spatial and temporal heterogeneity of trajectories of change within individual kuhl regimes also includes diverse relationships with supralocal political entities during the precolonial and colonial period—the theme to which I turn next.

3

STATEMAKING AND IRRIGATION IN KANGRA

A PREVAILING VIEW OF THE ROLE OF THE STATE IN COMMON PROPERTY
resource management is that it either provides the necessary "neutral"
political space for communities to manage resources collectively or it
undermines the viability of that space by actively promoting privatization
of the resource or asserting state control over it. This perspective
underestimates the local effects of state action and draws attention away
from the ways in which common property resource regimes can constitute
arenas for contesting or constructing specific constellations of community
and state power. Taking the prevailing view, we may fail to appreciate the
ways in which the legitimation of a particular regime of common property
rights is itself a productive process. By this I mean that state involvement
in common property resource regimes produces specific types of
communities and particular institutional structures and expressions of state
power and authority.

State support, whether for common, private, or public forms of property
regimes, invariably reinforces a specific array of power relations at the local
level, thus helping to forge specific types of communities. The colonial state
in Kangra, for example, through policy mechanisms such as the assessment
and collection of taxes on land, influenced the structure of village
communities and the distribution of resource rights and access within them.
In some cases, the state may actively intervene in determining the nature
of communal rights to a resource, including the specification of who
possesses rights of access and under what conditions. In greater Punjab,
including Kangra, this occurred during the colonial settlements (land

registrations) of the late nineteenth century, when rights of access to and use of common land were restricted to tax-paying landowners, thus weakening the entitlements of nonlandowning groups to these resources. In this case, because of the linkage between ownership of private cultivated land and access to common uncultivated land, the colonial state strongly influenced the nature of rights in common land resources.

State involvement in common property resource management regimes not only affects local power relations and systems of property rights but also contributes to the project of statemaking. To draw again on the example of greater Punjab, state interventions that consolidated access to resources and power among landowning elites simultaneously strengthened the colonial state. Alliances between dominant clans, castes, and lineages and the colonial administration fostered the political support of powerful groups for the colonial state. Granting authority to the "community" of landowners to expand cultivation into previously unenclosed common land encouraged dramatic increases in the cultivated area in the Punjab during the later decades of the nineteenth century. Concurrent state-led efforts in Punjab to create canal colonies by distributing newly irrigated land to dominant clans and lineages bolstered support for the colonial regime and strengthened local social power.[1] These efforts also increased the revenue the administration received in areas where variable settlements had been implemented.

The notions of negotiation and exchange, often used to describe the basis of political authority in precolonial India, may also be used to illuminate a key dynamic that obtains between the state and local communities with regard to common property resources. In an exchangelike transaction, the state may, under some conditions, legitimate or help create a particular constellation of rights and in return receive legitimacy and support from the local (and strengthened) communities who benefit from those rights.[2] Describing the relationship between the state and local groups in terms of exchange and negotiation avoids the pitfall of reifying the state-local dichotomy. It forces investigation into which local groups and which branches, departments, or agencies of the state are actually engaged in the negotiation and exchange process and with what effects. This approach, while "bringing the state back in" (Evans, Rueschemeyer, and Skocpol 1985) to the study of common property institutions, avoids the conceptual and empirical pitfalls associated with attempts to define the state as an autonomous entity and to distinguish it from "society."[3] Rather than trying to define the ever-elusive boundary between state and society, we must examine the various modalities of exchange and relation that simultaneously bind them together and contribute to their mutual constitution.

Thus, kuhl regimes can function as vehicles for the production of state power and the consolidation or realignment of local power differentials. They are sites for the production of symbolic political capital as well as material capital that benefits state entities and local communities. Acquisition of these benefits has motivated precolonial, colonial, and postcolonial state engagement with kuhl regimes. The precise forms this engagement has assumed over time have varied with the basis of state authority, changing systems of property rights, the broader policy context—especially with regard to colonial agricultural expansion and forest conservation policy agendas—and, beginning with the colonial period, rivalries between governmental departments such as the Revenue and Forest Departments. Though primarily locally managed and maintained, almost all kuhl irrigation systems articulate with the state in some way. This articulation simultaneously contributes to the solidification of local patterns of social power and strengthens the legitimacy of state structures of authority. It has also produced extremely varied forms of state involvement in the management of kuhl regimes.

THE PRECOLONIAL PERIOD: EXCHANGE OF REVENUE FOR SOVEREIGNTY

A brief discussion of the precolonial political history of Kangra illustrates the various ways in which the hill rajas of Kangra adopted "technologies of power" (Ludden 1999:77) developed by the Gupta empire in the fourth century C.E., something that occurred in all the major agrarian regions of South Asia. The primary Gupta-era technology of power was the institution of giving land to temples and Brahman priests in order to sanctify and solidify political authority. Such grants were also made to strengthen political alliances and in some cases to transform potential rivals into allies. Gift-giving solidified the link between agrarian social power and state institutions throughout many regions of South Asia, including Kangra, where it was used to establish and maintain territorial political authority. The granting of rights to revenue from a particular area (known as a *jagir*) in exchange for political support was one of the most common mechanisms state leaders used to solidify their authority and secure the support of potential adversaries.[4] In his discussion of medieval kingship in India, David Ludden (1999:80) noted that "a [state] donation to Brahmans, monasteries, monks, or temples represented an investment in agrarian territoriality." In Kangra, the idiom of exchange as the basis for political authority included state sponsorship of the largest kuhl systems in the Neugal watershed and, in at least one case, explicit links with temple patronage.

Kangra, far from being an isolated mountain valley, was intimately engaged with regional political processes and events. Hill Rajputs from Kangra, for example, fought in Mughal armies in Central Asia, and Katoch rulers from Kangra at times paid tribute to Mughal rulers in Delhi or Sikh rulers in Lahore and were thus involved in negotiated exchanges with higher-order regional political systems. These forms of engagement were important vehicles through which ideas about political authority, hierarchy, and duty (dharma) arrived in Kangra, took root, and filtered through village institutions, including kuhl regimes. Such engagement also contributed to the pattern of periodic migration, primarily during the nonagricultural season, of upper-caste men to join the armies on the plains of South and Central Asia. The mobility of segments of Kangra's population established what was to become a hallmark of life in Kangra—seasonal out-migration.

Finally, precolonial political history shows that there has been a long tradition of extralocal political involvement in the kuhls of Kangra. Although kuhls have been and still are primarily local systems, their articulation with extralocal political regimes is an important part of the explanatory tapestry that accounts for their persistence.

Negotiation of Political Autonomy by the Katoch Rulers

Before the emergence of the Rajput-ruled hill kingdoms in the foothills of the western Himalaya during the first millennium C.E., local rulers known as *ranas* or *thakurs* functioned as small, independent chieftains (Hutchison and Vogel 1933:13). Their origins are difficult to identify, but they and their clan members probably displaced earlier Buddhist settlements that can be dated back to the second century C.E. Because many of the ruling families of present-day Rajasthan use the titles rana and thakur, there probably was an early connection between the chieftains and that region. The founders of the hill states, who reduced the ranas and thakurs to tributaries, also came either directly from the plains or from families that traced their origins to the plains. That many of the ruling lineages came from Rajasthan via the plains of north India illustrates the cultural and political linkages between the western Himalayan hill states and the Indo-Gangetic plains to the south.[5]

Little is known about the prehistory of Kangra or the origins of its ruling Katoch lineage.[6] However, the wide dispersion of the Katoch lineage throughout the hills of the western Himalaya, the numerous smaller independent states founded by its offshoots, references to the "Katooch mountain kings" by chroniclers who accompanied Alexander the Great to the region, and the descriptions of Trigarta (an early appellation for Kangra) provided by the Chinese pilgrim Xuan Zang in the fifth century all attest to the lineage's antiquity.[7] From an analysis of genealogical records, J. Hutchison and J. Vogel (1933:104) argued that the dynasty the ruling Katoch Rajputs established was among the oldest in India.

The Katoch rajas ruled Kangra as independent sovereigns for at least 600 years prior to the Muslim conquests of the eleventh century. In 1008 C.E. the rulers of Kangra and the neighboring hill state Chamba joined forces with Raja Anand Pal Shahi of Kabul against Mahmud of Ghazni in present-day Afghanistan (Charak 1978:138). Mahmud of Ghazni, the first of a series of Turko-Afghan Muslims to invade north India, defeated Anand Pal and went on to take the fort at Kangra in 1009.[8] This early military alliance between Kangra and Kabul suggests some of the political and economic interests that have linked Kangra with much wider regional political entities for centuries.[9] These linkages have served as important conduits for the diffusion of technologies such as irrigation from Central Asia to the western Himalaya, along with "technologies of power" such as the granting of entitlements in exchange for political legitimacy. They also indicate the long history of out-migration from Kangra for military service.

From 1009 to the dissolution of the Mughal empire in the mid-seventeenth century, the Katoch rajas negotiated with the Mughal regime for maximum political autonomy. At various times they ruled independently of Delhi, swore their allegiance to the Islamic dynasties that ruled from Delhi, and engaged in armed guerrilla resistance against them. The remoteness and inaccessibility of the hill states from the centers of Islamic rule in Delhi and Kabul helped ensure their relative autonomy during this period. George C. Barnes (1855:9) wrote that during this time, the hill rajas "enjoyed a considerable share of power, and ruled unmolested. . . . they built forts, made war upon each other, and wielded the functions of petty sovereigns." Some hill rajas raised their own Rajput armies and fought for the Mughal empire in far-flung provinces. In return for their services, the Muslim rulers appointed them to positions of authority within the Mughal regime and gave them rent-free estates (jagirs).

The garrison Mahmud of Ghazni left at Kangra Fort remained there only 34 years. Afterward, the Katoch rajas ruled as independent sovereigns for 300 years until 1365, when Sultan Firuz Tughluq, who occupied the throne in Delhi, laid siege to Kangra Fort. The siege ended with the surrender of Raja Rup Chand, after which the Kangra rajas paid a nominal tribute to Delhi. Preoccupation with competing claims to the throne following Firuz Tughluq's death in 1388 and subsequent internal conflicts meant that Kangra and the other hill states were only nominal tributaries until Akbar solidified Mughal control over them in the mid-sixteenth century. In the early sixteenth century Akbar annexed the whole of Kangra State and attempted, unsuccessfully, to secure control of Kangra Fort. His famous revenue minister, the Hindu raja Todar Mal, was deputed to oversee the annexation of the hill state. He left only a portion of Kangra Valley as a jagir to support the Katoch raja and annexed most of the rest of Kangra and portions of neighboring hill states. Upon returning to Delhi, Todar Mal reportedly told Akbar that he had "cut off the meat and left the bones," referring to the productivity of the land over which he had asserted Mughal control and that given to the Katoch raja as a jagir (Punjab District Gazetteer 1926:61).[10] The Mughals did not capture and establish a garrison at Kangra Fort until 1620, during the reign of Jehangir (Hutchison and Vogel 1933:146).

After 40 years of guerrilla resistance to the Mughal regime, waged from mountain redoubts in the protective heights of the Dhaula Dhar, whose ruins are still visible, the deposed Katoch rulers reconciled themselves to their status as subordinate tributaries and abandoned armed resistance. For the next 130 years the Katoch rajas paid tribute to the Mughal rulers. The reign of Raja Ghumand Chand (1751–74) marked the ascendancy of Katoch rule. In the mid-eighteenth century the Mughal empire was preoccupied with suppressing Maratha attacks from the south and Sikh revolts in the Punjab. Ghumand Chand took this opportunity to wrest control of many of the former territories of Kangra State from the Mughal governor, Saif Ali Khan, installed in the Kangra Fort. He also founded the town of Sujanpur, which became the seat of Katoch power, at the confluence of the Neugal and Beas Rivers. As an assertion of the growing ascendancy of Katoch political power, Ghumand Chand's *rani* (queen) sponsored the construction of a 12-mile-long kuhl known as Raniya Kuhl. Although it was subsequently destroyed by a flood, its repair was later sponsored by a rani of the Katoch raja Sansar Chand. She linked the kuhl's repair to a condition that a portion of the land revenue from the kuhl's command area be remitted to Sujanpur to support a state-sponsored temple complex there.

The Katoch dynasty reached its zenith under the rule of Raja Sansar Chand, who reigned from 1775 until his death in 1823. Sansar Chand consolidated Katoch control over the former territory of Kangra State, and in 1787 he gained control of Kangra Fort. He then launched a series of expansionist campaigns and subjugated many neighboring hill states.[11] Sansar Chand encouraged the arts, and his court, established on the banks of the Beas River, first at Nadoun and later at Sujanpur-Tira, attracted skilled artisans, storytellers, and performers. Under Sansar Chand's patronage the famous school of Kangra miniature painting flourished. He constructed many magnificent royal buildings and temples that still stand today. Sansar Chand also embarked on an impressive project of sponsoring the construction of some of the longest kuhls in Kangra Valley. His sponsorship of kuhls, like his support of temples, typified the "investment[s] in agrarian territoriality" that Ludden (1999:80) argued characterized precolonial Indian kingship. These investments, along with state patronage of the arts, served to simultaneously mark and strengthen the legitimacy of Katoch rule.

The political autonomy of Katoch rule lasted until Gurkhas from present-day Nepal invaded Kangra in 1805. The neighboring hill states that Sansar Chand had subjugated created a confederacy with the Gurkha commander, Amar Singh Thapa, promising to assist him against Sansar Chand in exchange for restoration of their independence. During the four-year Gurkha occupation of Kangra, anarchy reigned. A large portion of the local population fled to neighboring states.[12] Many of the kuhl irrigation systems were abandoned and fell into disrepair, though most were subsequently repaired. Barnes (n.d.:110) described the reconstruction in the early 1850s of one such kuhl, noting that "the people of their own free will . . . re-excavated the line at their own cost" and were able to bring irrigation water once again to villages 12 miles from the kuhl's danga.

Sansar Chand, from his refuge in besieged Kangra Fort, sought military assistance from the Sikh leader Ranjit Singh in order to oust the Gurkhas. Ranjit Singh, concerned that Gurkha aspirations to control the western Himalaya as far as Kashmir could threaten his sovereignty in Punjab, promised to assist Sansar Chand, but only on condition that Sansar Chand relinquish control of Kangra Fort to him (Hutchison and Vogel 1933:186). Sansar Chand agreed and with the help of Ranjit Singh defeated the Gurkhas in 1809 and forced them to retreat back across the Sutlej River. Ranjit Singh received possession of Kangra Fort and the revenue from the 66 villages that had been attached to it during the Mughal period. He appointed Desa Singh Majithia *subedar* (military commander) of the hill areas, and Pahar

Singh Man governor of Kangra (Singh 1977:233). Between 1811 and 1825, Ranjit Singh expanded the hill area under his control by reducing other, neighboring hill states—Haripur, Nurpur, Jaswan, Dutarpur, and Kutlehr— to the status of his tributaries (Barnes 1855:11–12). In most cases, he granted the ruling Rajput lineage of each state a jagir. Usually the jagir was large enough that the revenue it generated supported the ruling lineage but not large enough to enable the Katoch or other Rajput ruler to raise an army that might challenge Sikh supremacy. In this manner, "gifts" of revenue were used as subtle means to placate, gain the support of, and control potential political adversaries.

Sansar Chand, who retired to Alampur by the confluence of the Beas and Neugal Rivers after the Sikhs gained control of Kangra Fort, was compelled to go to Lahore annually to pay tribute to Maharajah Ranjit Singh.[13] Following Sansar Chand's death in 1823, his son Anrudh Chand also met with Ranjit Singh to pay an investiture fee and for confirmation of his ruling authority. In 1827, in order to avoid an unacceptable demand by Ranjit Singh that he give his two sisters in marriage to Hira Singh, son of the governor of Jammu—who was not a hereditary ruler and was therefore considered to be of lower social status than the Katoch rajas— Anrudh Chand and his immediate family secretly fled to neighboring Tehri Garhwal in Uttar Pradesh, which was under British control (Hutchison and Vogel 1933:194).

The departure of the Katoch raja provided Ranjit Singh the opportunity to assert Sikh control over Kangra State to an unprecedented degree. He granted a large jagir to Sansar Chand's younger brother, Fateh Chand, who had not left the country and is said to have set favorable terms for remitting the revenue from the rest of the state to the Sikh leader. Fateh Chand, however, died almost immediately, and when his son, Ludar Chand, failed to pay the amount demanded in the lease, the leased portion of the state was granted to two Sikh zamindars (noncultivating elite landlords), who tax-farmed Kangra for one and two years, respectively (Hutchison and Vogel 1933:194).[14] After this, Palam, a fertile *taluka* (district subdivision) in Kangra Valley, was given as a jagir to Nihal Singh. The town of Nadaun and its surrounding villages were given as a jagir to Jodhbir Chand, a younger son of Sansar Chand, who also received the title of raja. The rest of Kangra State was placed under the control of Lehna Singh Majithia, who, at his father's death, had assumed his father's position as subedar of all the hill states under Sikh control (Barnes 1855:12; Hutchison and Vogel 1933:194– 95; Singh 1977:269). In 1833, through the intercession of the British government, Ranjit Singh also gave a jagir worth 50,000 rupees to the two sons of Anrudh Chand, who then returned from Teri-Garhwal. Lehna Singh continued as governor of the hill states until the assumption of British control in the region in 1846.

Gift-Giving and Political Authority

As the frequent granting of jagirs in Kangra demonstrates, the control and exchange of land was one of the most important currencies used during the precolonial period to consolidate, strengthen, and maintain political power. For a ruler, whether a Katoch raja, a Sikh raja, a Mughal emperor, or an Afghan Durani, the importance and meaning of land derived from its use as a medium of exchange for negotiating sovereign claims to territory and for transforming potential adversaries into political allies.[15] British colonial rulers, well aware of the relationship between gift-giving and political authority, later sought to undermine the ability of native rulers to develop a following and enhance their authority, independently of colonial affirmation, by prohibiting them from giving jagirs—as Ajay Skaria (1999:236) has shown for the Bhil chiefs in western India.

As we have seen, rulers made gifts of land to persons who served the ruler in a military, administrative, or other capacity.[16] They also gave land to religious institutions such as temples and mosques and to religious leaders, theologians, and saints.[17] Land grants were given to potentially rival political groups as a way of securing their support for the ruling regime. The series of land grants made by Ranjit Singh to various members of the ruling Katoch lineage illustrates how land exchange could be used as a means to neutralize a former and potential future adversary.[18] In Kangra, at the assumption of British control of the district in 1846, approximately one-quarter of the district had been given as political jagirs, religious grants, and other miscellaneous grants to individuals (Barnes 1855:31–33).[19] This technology of power was common throughout the subcontinent. Ludden (1978:7) noted with regard to political authority in southern Tamil Nadu that "gifting became the constitutive ritual of kingship." Indeed, in Tamil Nadu by the eighteenth century, 60–80 percent of all cultivable land had been given away as *inam*, or tax-exempt land (Dirks 1992:179). In Kangra, gift-giving as a means of establishing and maintaining political legitimacy also included state sponsorship of kuhl construction and religious patronage.

When a ruler assigned a jagir to an individual or an inam to a temple or shrine, he transferred to that person or institution only the right to the revenue from the area encompassed within the jagir or inam. The existing array of rights to occupancy, cultivation, and other uses was left untouched.[20] This practice exemplifies precolonial notions of property relations that were based on overlapping sets of interests rather than on exclusive claims of ownership (Embree 1969:47). Irfan Habib (1963:118) suggested that in many areas, a "single owner cannot be located," and that instead one finds the allocation of "different rights over the land and its produce, and not one exclusive right of property."[21]

However, as Nicholas Dirks (1992:179) pointed out, land was only one of many mediums of exchange by which a ruler secured political legitimacy and maintained sovereignty. Dirks suggested that "the king ruled by making gifts, not by administering a land system in which land derived its chief value from the revenue he could systematically extract from it." In addition to gifts of land, rulers in Kangra distributed the hereditary right to cultivate a particular field, the rights held by transhumant Gaddis and Gujars to particular grazing runs, the rights to some inherited administrative posts, the right to operate a water mill or to erect a fish weir, and the right to set a net to ensnare game or hawks on a ridgetop. These rights were called *warisi*s and derived from the raja as separate, taxable tenancies (Baden-Powell 1892, 2:693–94; Barnes 1855:18–19; Lyall 1874:17). *Bartan*s, or customary use rights pertaining to untaxed, uncultivated areas used in common, included the right to graze livestock, cut grass and leaves for fodder, remove thorns for hedges, and collect dry wood for fuel. Cultivators, traders, artisans, and shopkeepers all had the right to use these commons in this manner.

The proof of entitlement to a particular warisi was the *pattah*, a deed that spelled out the rights and responsibilities the warisi entailed and the terms by which it could be renewed. Maintaining monopolistic control over the power to grant a pattah was central to the ruler's sovereignty. James B. Lyall (1874:21) mentioned that the rajas "jealously" guarded their monopoly to grant pattahs for warisis: "Under them [the rajas] no wazir or kardar [administrative officer] could give a pattah of his own authority." To do so would threaten the legitimacy of the ruler. In exchange for granting the entitlements specified in warisis and pattahs, the ruler received the political support of the grantee as well as a share of the benefits the entitlement produced. Thus, Lyall noted (1874:24), the rajas received "the best hawk caught in a net, the largest fish caught in a weir, a share of the honey in the bee-hives, and the fruit of the best fruit trees." [22]

Unlike tenure systems in the plains—where village boundaries invariably included uncultivated areas of common land used for grazing and where the locally regulated rights to those resources were a function of residency and landownership (Kessinger 1974)—tenure systems for uncultivated land in Kangra appear to have been less formal and at least nominally at the ruler's discretion. All individuals, whether or not they held rights to cultivated land or were even agriculturists, possessed usufructuary rights to uncultivated areas for subsistence purposes (Douie 1985 [1899]:69). These rights were generally subordinate to the ruler's right to grant a pattah to someone to bring a section of uncultivated land into cultivation.

In addition to giving grants of land, precolonial rulers in India sponsored the construction of irrigation systems and other public works projects and patronized temples in order to extend, solidify, and sanctify their domains of authority. Precolonial Katoch rulers were no exception; they or their family members sponsored the construction of 19 of the longest and largest kuhl irrigation systems in Kangra. Fourteen of these 19 state-sponsored kuhls are named after the raja or rani who built them. By naming kuhls after themselves, rajas and ranis ensured that their names would endure. Today, in contrast to the rulers who did not sponsor the construction or repair of kuhls, the names of those who did are common parlance for people who live in the areas through which the kuhls flow.

The construction dates of nine state-sponsored kuhls can be ascertained by using historical accounts to determine when the sponsor ruled or lived.[23] All of them were constructed between 1690 and 1805 (Table 4), and seven were constructed during the height of Katoch power, the last three decades of the eighteenth century.

The kuhls whose construction precolonial rulers sponsored are longer and more complex than those constructed by village landowners. Seven of the 19 state-sponsored kuhls were constructed in the Neugal watershed; the rest are scattered across other watersheds in Kangra Valley. The average length of these seven kuhls is 14 miles, and each conveys water to an average of 26 tikas. By contrast, in the Neugal watershed, kuhls constructed by landowners have an average length of 4 kilometers, and each irrigates an average of 4 tikas. The differences in scale between ruler- and landowner-sponsored kuhls are dramatic. They suggest that the importance of external support for kuhl regime persistence is directly related to the coordination requirements of kuhls and the scales at which they operate. Quite simply, the larger kuhls in the Neugal watershed might not have been constructed without state support; in most cases the labor mobilization required for their construction exceeded local capacities. This is especially true in cases

TABLE 4. Origin Dates of 9 of the 19 State-Sponsored Kuhls in Kangra and Palampur Tehsils, with Indicators of Scale for Kuhls in the Neugal Basin

Kuhl	Date Constructed	No. Tikas Irrigated	Command Area (ha)	Length (km)
Dewan Chand Kuhl	1690–1697	24	185	25
Kirpal Chand Kuhl	1690–1697	62	1,713	33
Raniya Kuhl	1759–1774	10	545	12
Rai Kuhl	1775	28	820	20
Giaruhl Kuhl	1760–1785	—	—	—
Dadhuhl Kuhl	1775–1805	—	—	—
Dai Kuhl	1775–1805	22	357	25
Dei Kuhl	1775–1805	—	—	—
Mian Fateh Chand Kuhl	1775–1805	23	256	20

SOURCES: Author's field notes; Charak 1978; Hutchison and Vogel 1933; *Riwaj-i-Abpashi* 1918.

where the downstream portions of ruler-sponsored kuhls convey water to the larh areas of hamlets, which are less productive than har areas. Because of the relatively low returns on labor investment in larh areas, it is unlikely that local landowners would have chosen to invest the resources necessary for bringing water long distances to irrigate relatively less productive fields, especially when rain-fed maize was a viable nonirrigated crop for larh regions.

What did ruler-sponsored kuhl construction entail? The *Riwaj-i-Abpashi* (Irrigation Customs, first prepared as part of the 1874 revised settlement of Kangra District) noted that the sponsors bore the expense of constructing the kuhl. What this actually meant probably varied from kuhl to kuhl. At the least, it would have entailed making the decision to sponsor a kuhl, arranging for its surveying and construction, and providing the materials and labor for these tasks. Raja Dewan Chand provided the funds for constructing Dewan Chand Kuhl, but he contracted the work out to someone else. Similarly, one of Sansar Chand's wazirs supervised the construction of Giaruhl Kuhl, with funds provided by Sansar Chand's mother.

The organization of labor for state-sponsored kuhl construction is difficult to determine. The *Riwaj-i-Abpashi* clearly refers to the monetary outlays required for constructing state-sponsored kuhls. The most significant, if not the only, expense must have been for paying laborers. Whether all workers were always compensated for their efforts is an open question whose answer probably depends partially on caste dynamics, the strength of state claims on corvée, and whether or not the workers were also those whose land the kuhl would irrigate. All workers were at least given the midday meal, one of the two main meals in Kangra.[24] Barnes, in his "Notes on the System of Irrigation Prevailing in the Upper Valleys of the Kangra District" (n.d.), referred to the construction of Kirpal Chand Kuhl in the 1690s and described the remuneration the laborers received. He noted that Kirpal Chand had sponsored the kuhl's construction because he was childless and desired to undertake a public works project that would perpetuate his name. He mentioned that Kirpal Chand was "munificent" in his "liberality to the people employed," because he gave them "six seers of rice, half a seer of dahl, and the usual condiments."[25] Additionally, every pregnant woman employed received "an additional half allowance in consideration of the offspring in her womb" (Barnes n.d.:111). This description, no doubt based on oral history accounts of events that occurred 150 years earlier, suggests that those pressed into service to construct state-sponsored kuhls did receive minimal in-kind compensation for their efforts.

Circumstantial evidence, based on oral tradition, indicates that corvée (*begar*) may also have been used to construct some state-sponsored kuhls. *Begar* is a Persian word that refers to the unpaid exploitation of labor. In the hill states of the western Himalaya it composed a system by which rulers exacted compulsory labor contributions from men for a wide variety of tasks, mostly related to transporting items such as timber for public works projects (e.g., bridges) and the baggage and loads of traveling government officers, the provision of wood and grass for encamped government representatives, and the conveying of messages and letters (Barnes 1855:67). Obligations to provide corvée were distributed according to principles of caste hierarchy and privilege. In general, Brahmans, some Rajput clans, state and village officials, and other wealthy or influential persons and their families were exempted from begar (Negi 1992:47).

The story "Brahmans Don't Do Begar" (see also Appendix 2) invokes divine sanction for the proscription against high-caste Brahmans doing begar. The story, part of the rich oral tradition of tales related to the kuhls, concerns the construction of the state-sponsored Kirpal Chand Kuhl (constructed between 1690 and 1697). Kirpal Chand's agent had asked two Brahman brothers, along with other local villagers, to contribute labor to help construct a particularly difficult section of the channel. Requesting Brahmans to participate in corvée violated the caste privilege that excused high castes from begar. The next day, after concluding their daily prayers, the brothers uprooted two large trees and, using them like brooms, began rolling two huge boulders, each the size of a two-story house, toward the difficult channel section. When the raja's agent came upon them, he recognized their spiritual abilities and asked their forgiveness for having asked them to contribute begar. To this day those two large boulders remain next to the kuhl, a testament to the ways in which social relations of privilege and hierarchy are inscribed onto the landscape and to the fact that corvée was employed to construct some state-sponsored kuhls.[26]

State sponsorship of kuhls was a means, much like land grants, by which a ruler could strengthen sovereign control over a region and legitimate his rule. For example, in 1752, after 130 years of Mughal rule, Raja Ghumand Chand regained control over much of the land the Katoch lineage had previously controlled. Soon thereafter, Ghumand Chand's rani sponsored the construction of Raniya Kuhl and through this demonstration of state capacity to mobilize resources reasserted the ruling authority of the Katoch dynasty.

Linkages between state-sponsored kuhls and religious patronage served to further consolidate the legitimacy of Katoch rule. Sometime between 1759 and 1805, for example, a flood destroyed Raniya Kuhl. A rani of Raja Sansar Chand's household offered to sponsor its reconstruction, on the condition that the village Saloh, which the kuhl irrigated, agree to remit 1,400 rupees annually toward the support of the Narbadeshwar temple in Sujanpur-Tira (fig. 26). Sujanpur, founded by Ghumand Chand, was the seat of Sansar Chand's political power and the center from which he ruled. This condition was agreed to, the kuhl was reconstructed, and to this day the village remits 1,400 rupees to the temple every year, despite complaints by the current *pujari* (priest) that the amount should have increased over time. Linking state sponsorship of a kuhl with religious institutions in this manner strengthened the basis of Katoch political authority and symbolically underscored the importance of Sujanpur-Tira as the regional center of political power. State-sponsored kuhls also constituted physical manifestations of state political authority distributed broadly across the landscape.

In Kangra, political authority based on the exchange of entitlement for support and on patronage of religious institutions clearly resonates with broader regional models of agrarian social power and state political institutions throughout the subcontinent. These models were conveyed to Kangra and took root there through the ongoing political and economic interactions that linked the region with other state regimes. State investment in kuhl irrigation was a statemaking strategy that served a political function similar to that of the granting of land (jagirs) and temple patronage.

FIG. 26. The Narbadeshwar temple in Tira-Sujanpur,
which is supported by revenue from Saloh village.

Sponsoring the construction of a kuhl was an effective way to generate
political support because not only cultivators but also artisans, traders, and
others benefited from the kuhl. In addition to providing irrigation water,
kuhls once met all the water needs of the villages through which they flowed.
This was especially true during the hot, dry pre-monsoon season, when
local springs were low or dry. Kuhl water satisfied household water needs
as well as those for livestock and the small gardens found in almost all
domestic compounds. Basketmakers soaked split bamboo and reeds in small
pools filled with kuhl water before weaving them into baskets. Potters used
kuhl water to turn their pottery-making wheels. Most kuhls powered at
least one, and some as many as twenty, water mills (*graths*) used for grinding
grain. Interestingly, many of the proprietors of the graths were widowed
women who supported themselves and their children (if they lived with
them) on the in-kind earnings they received for grinding others' grain
(*Riwaj-i-Abpashi* 1918).

State sponsorship of kuhls provided material benefits in addition to
symbolic ones, because the tax assessed on irrigated land was significantly
higher than that assessed on unirrigated land. For unirrigated tracts, the
raja's share varied from one-half to one-fourth, depending on the productivity

of the land. Irrigated tracts were usually assessed a rate of one-half of the gross produce (Anderson 1897:11). Other "cesses" (taxes) complemented the land revenue demands of the precolonial state. These included an army tax, a war tax, the weighman's cess, the money tester's cess, the watchman's cess, a cess to cover the cost of transporting the grain payments to the state granary, and even a tax to cover the costs of writing receipts for the revenue (Lyall 1874:37).

State sponsorship of kuhls did not lead to state ownership or ongoing involvement in kuhl management. Management authority for kuhl maintenance and repair, including the labor mobilization necessary for those tasks, and for water distribution was the responsibility of the family that held the warisi to the position of kohli. The right to be kohli of a state-sponsored kuhl was awarded by the ruler to a family or clan that had played an important role in the construction of the kuhl, probably either by providing a significant amount of labor or by supervising its construction. Although this is consistent with E. Walter Coward's (1990:81–82) suggestion that for some kuhls, the raja (or his agent) appointed the kohli and therefore exercised some control over the kuhl's management, it is unclear how much direct management authority the ruler exercised beyond designating which family or clan held the warisi to be kohli. In general, the ruler's involvement in kuhl management did not extend beyond awarding the right to be kohli; it did not extend at all to kuhls whose construction the state had not sponsored. In this regard, Barnes (1855:23) noted that the kuhls in Kangra "are managed entirely by the people, without any assistance from the government."

Although the precolonial state played important roles in the kuhls whose construction it sponsored, it is important to remember that the scale of state involvement in irrigation system construction, repair, and maintenance was limited overall. The majority of kuhls in Kangra were constructed and continue to be maintained and managed through the collective efforts of village communities. In Kangra, the construction of 694 multivillage kuhls, out of a total of 713, and of all of the more than 2,000 single-village kuhls was sponsored by local groups of irrigators or by individuals, not by state entities. Furthermore, and unlike in other regions in the subcontinent, responsibility for the repair and maintenance of all the kuhls in Kangra has historically rested with the irrigators themselves, not with state entities or powerful, noncultivating, landed elites.

This situation contrasts sharply with the degree of state and elite involvement in other "community" forms of irrigation in India, such as the tank systems of Tamil Nadu and the gravity-flow irrigation systems of south Bihar. In his study of irrigation in Sivagangai and Ramnad Districts of southern Tamil Nadu, David Mosse (1997a:10) noted that villagers historically never made contributions for major tank repairs, which they viewed as "government work . . . the responsibility and action of political overlords." In southern Tamil Nadu, the undermining of the political authority and economic viability of these elite intermediaries during colonial rule resulted in the decline and, in some instances, collapse of local irrigation systems.

A somewhat similar dynamic is observable in south Bihar, where zamindars played essential roles in the construction and maintenance of local irrigation systems. There, transformations in the methods for collecting revenue in the early twentieth century removed economic incentives for zamindars to continue to invest in irrigation works. During most of the nineteenth century, the prevailing system for determining the revenue due to landlords and the government was the produce rent system. Under it, revenue due the government was calculated as a proportion of agricultural production and either paid in kind or converted to a cash equivalent. Throughout the nineteenth century, zamindars had devised a variety of mechanisms by which to extract increasing surpluses from tenants through the produce rent system. They also invested in local irrigation systems, even coercing peasants by force to help maintain the irrigation works, because of the high rate of return they received on such investments (Sengupta 1980:174).

To provide relief to tenants from rack renting (the practice of charging excessively high rents), in the early twentieth century the colonial Revenue Department allowed tenants in south Bihar to petition to have their produce rent commuted to a fixed cash rent. In some cases, tenants and zamindars themselves negotiated such commutations. The result, as some but not all colonial administrators had feared, was a precipitous decline in the irrigation systems that had depended on zamindar investments. Following commutation to fixed cash rents, zamindars withdrew their support for maintaining irrigation works, because now they "had nothing to lose by the decline in irrigation" (Sengupta 1980:179) and nothing to gain by continuing to invest in local irrigation works. This was because the cash rent system was, in effect, a tax only on land, whereas the produce rent system had been a tax on land and irrigation together. Under the fixed cash rent system, increased production resulting from irrigation benefited only the tenant. Furthermore, by allowing irrigation systems to collapse, zamindars forced tenants to abandon their holdings through rent default and then made agreements with other tenants at higher rates. This led to declining agricultural productivity and eventually to demands to abolish the zamindari system.

In clear contrast to this sequence of events, in Kangra, when revenue was commuted to cash and fixed for 20 years in the first regular land settlement (1855), kuhl construction and irrigated agriculture expanded. The crucial distinction that accounts for this outcome was the absence of an intermediary landlord class in Kangra. There, the same cultivators who stood to benefit from increased agricultural production also had the capacity to construct and maintain the irrigation systems necessary to generate it. The distribution of cultivated land was relatively egalitarian, in comparison with that in regions where zamindars were present, and responsibility for constructing, repairing, and maintaining the irrigation systems was correspondingly more evenly distributed among irrigators. Kuhl regimes, unlike the irrigation systems in south Bihar or the tank irrigation systems of Tamil Nadu, were not so dependent on extralocal political support. The absence of zamindari tenure in Kangra, coupled with relatively egalitarian landownership patterns, explains the quite different effects of commuting in-kind revenue payments to cash that obtained in Kangra and Bihar.

The relatively limited role of the state in Kangri irrigation is further illustrated by a comparison with patterns of state investment in irrigation in Hunza, in the Northern Areas District of present-day Pakistan (Sidky 1996). In the valley of Hunza, because of steep and rugged mountain topography, only the state was able to mobilize adequate resources to construct gravity-flow irrigation systems. This took place during the eighteenth century, when the *mir* (ruler) of Hunza embarked on an ambitious campaign of statemaking. Local communities in Hunza relinquished control over water rights to the mir. In exchange, he mobilized the labor and resources necessary for the construction of irrigation systems. The resulting expansion of irrigated area enabled the mir to further expand and consolidate his political authority by establishing settlements in the newly irrigated areas and, using a now familiar technology of power, by granting tax-free land to leading families as a way to gain their allegiance. Furthermore, the increased revenue resulting from irrigated agriculture provided the mir with resources he used to acquire adjacent territories.

Thus, in Hunza, state investment in irrigation clearly contributed to centralization of authority and state formation. The relationship between state formation and irrigation was particularly strong there because of the state's monopoly control over the labor and materials necessary for constructing irrigation networks. In Kangra, on the other hand, the state held no such monopoly; individuals and villages were able to mobilize sufficient resources to construct most of the kuhls. In Kangra, the precolonial state played a more circumscribed role in irrigation management than it did elsewhere in the subcontinent. The role of the subsequent colonial administration in kuhl management displayed both continuities and discontinuities with that of the precolonial state.[27]

COLONIAL RULE AND KUHLS:
CONTINUITIES AND DISJUNCTURES

In Kangra, Sikh rule continued until the First Sikh War in 1845, when Ranbir Chand, with an army of Rajputs, assisted the British in expelling the Sikhs. In return, the British granted Ranbir Chand a tract of land and reimbursed him for expenses incurred in the war. Kangra came under British rule with the treaty of March 9, 1846, in which the Sikhs ceded the hill tracts between the Sutlej and Beas Rivers to the British. In 1848, three hill rajas, including the Katoch raja of Kangra, rose in insurrection against the British during the Second Sikh War of 1848–49. Following the violent suppression of the Katoch rebellion by British troops, the rajas were imprisoned in Almora, Uttar Pradesh (Barnes 1855:15). This marked the beginning of a century of British rule in Kangra.

The early years of British rule in Kangra were marked by both strong continuities with and disjunctures from precolonial administration. The first summary land registration settlement in Kangra District was made in 1846, immediately after the forcible annexation of Kangra from the Sikhs. This summary settlement was only a slightly modified version of the Sikh government's prior system of revenue collection. In some respects, the first regular settlement, made by Barnes, was also modeled on the Sikh system. Symbolic continuities with prior ruling regimes also existed. For example, British officers chose Kangra Fort as the first district administrative headquarters. Although the fort had a garrison and was close to the town of Kangra, the main reason for choosing it was to draw on its symbolic importance, "the prestige attaching to the name. . . . the same spot which had ruled so long the destinies of the hills still continued to remain the seat of local power—the center whence order emanated, and where supplicants repaired for redress" (Barnes 1855:15). As if to underscore the orderliness of British rule, Barnes, at the conclusion of his account of the tumultuous history of Kangra State, wrote: "I turn with pleasure from the narrative of wars and insurrections to the quiet details of our administration and the general statistics of the district" (1855:15).

Despite drawing on local referents that emphasized continuity with previous state regimes, British rule in Kangra differed significantly from precolonial political authority in several respects. The political legitimacy of the colonial administration in Kangra depended less on strategic exchange and alliances with local elites and more on superior military strength and the modernizing narratives of colonialism, progress, and development— the latter constituting key Enlightenment-era tropes concerning the legitimacy and meaning of government. Resources were valued not for their political currency but for their utilitarian potential to yield revenue if they were "properly" developed. Fostering that development led to a wide variety of state policies and interventions that together contributed to the colonial statemaking project in Kangra—a project that also included various levels of state involvement in kuhl irrigation. Thus, whereas the precolonial state had sponsored the construction of some kuhls in order to gain legitimacy, the colonial administration, through a variety of statemaking efforts such as the codification of irrigation customs, the establishment of judicial arenas, and the implementation of land tax assessment and collection systems, supported kuhl regimes as part of its broader effort to bring progress and development to the agrarian economy of Kangra.

This perspective shaped the policy content of the Revenue Department's early settlement reports. For example, the first regular settlement of Kangra promoted agricultural expansion and intensification (at the expense of forests), including the construction of new kuhls, and commuted in-kind payments to cash payments that were fixed for 20 years. Early colonial policies and institutions in Kangra also facilitated the exchange of land by converting inheritable rights to cultivate land into the right to alienate land. Steady increases in grain prices and the development of improved transportation linkages accompanied these changes. These processes resulted in unprecedented changes in the control over and access to land, investments in agricultural development (including the construction of new kuhls and expansion of irrigated agriculture), flows of resources between social groups, and the rise of a noncultivating, mercantile elite. Barnes's reference to the "quiet details of administration" notwithstanding, British rule wrought rapid change in Kangra.

Most of these changes, and indeed many features of the first regular settlement of Kangra, clearly bear the imprint of important debates among colonial officials regarding the administration of India's agrarian economy. These debates formed part of the deliberations that took place during the latter half of the eighteenth century over the most effective way to govern the agrarian system of Bengal. They were heavily influenced by the tumultuous political events taking place in France and the United States, patterns of landownership in Great Britain, and Enlightenment-era utilitarian, physiocratic, and political economy schools of thought (Guha 1981 [1963]). Several key principles relating to the relationship between private property, trade, and the creation of wealth emerged out of these deliberations and were enshrined in the early land settlements in India.

A central supposition was that the primary source of wealth was agriculture and that secure rights in land were a necessary precondition for people's investing labor and capital in agriculture in order to create the value that in turn would satisfy the government's revenue demands. Consequently, establishing the security of private property became a paramount goal of early land settlements. Colonial administrators also transplanted the British notion of the gentleman farmer to India and sought to create the conditions under which the "improving landlord" would act like one. In addition to securing rights in private property, this involved developing a market for land and generally encouraging the free trade that would, presumably, enable generation of the capital necessary for increasing agricultural productivity.

In Bengal, as elsewhere in north India, colonial administrators concealed the European roots of the principles the land settlements embodied by claiming (and in some cases no doubt believing) that settlements represented a return to an imagined native precedent. By the middle of the nineteenth century, when the British defeated the Sikhs and took control of the Punjab, the emphasis on native precedent had developed into an explicit commitment to establishing agrarian land rights on the basis of local custom. However, British colonial land policy in Kangra demonstrates the extent to which such a commitment could mask the dramatic changes that occurred through the settlement process.

The Influence of Settlement on Land Tenure and Agriculture

After four years as district commissioner of Kangra, George C. Barnes conducted its first regular settlement. In determining rates of assessment, Barnes was guided by the rent rolls from the prior Sikh government and the summary British settlement of 1846. In fact, as Lyall pointed out 20 years later, Barnes's settlement was "nothing more than the old native assessment very slightly modified" (quoted in Anderson 1897:12). The primary changes consisted of a reduction in assessment rates on unirrigated areas and the removal of the host of extra taxes that had accompanied the land tax.

Although rates of taxation remained remarkably consistent between the precolonial and colonial regimes, the methods of tax payment and the nature of rights in property were significantly altered. The colonial state, rather than legitimating preexisting property rights systems (its stated intention), wrought dramatic changes in the nature of rights in private cultivated land and collectively used commons areas. The case of collective rights in the commons is one example. Prior to the first settlements in the Punjab, cultivating households held allotments of land (shares) that consisted of strips of land of equivalent productivity.[28] Appurtenant to these shares were proportional rights in the commons—the uncultivated areas. Shares in the commons included usufructuary rights in grazing and wood collection as well as the right to break up and cultivate a household's "share" of the commons. On the basis of the size of their shares, allotment holders jointly contributed labor for collective investments in agriculture such as masonry wall building for irrigation, and they paid, generally in kind, the revenue assessments of the precolonial state.

The first regular settlements of the Punjab divided this agricultural community into two groups, cultivators and tenants, according to principles of ancestry that had previously held no bearing on the work of agriculture, the allotment of rights in the commons, or the corporateness of the community of cultivators. Cultivators who were descendants of the founders of the village were newly classified as landowners—that is, proprietary rights holders—whereas cultivators who were not members of the founding lineage were classified as either hereditary or at-will tenants, depending on the number of years they had been cultivating their allotment—a minimum of 12 to be considered hereditary tenants. Furthermore, because tenants were now no longer classified as shareholders, their shares (rights) in the village commons "passed into oblivion" (Smith 1996:32). Thus, the colonial administration redefined the village community on the basis of nineteenth-century evolutionist anthropological theories of genealogy and patrilineal descent rather than according to the actual pattern of land use based on allotments. This process disenfranchised "nonlandowning" families from the legitimate use of uncultivated areas.[29]

The reification of an imagined community based on membership in the dominant lineage undermined the rights of other social classes. As Neeladri

Battacharya noted (1996:46), "the colonial regime of customary law thus sharpened the opposition between outsiders and insiders, the 'agriculturalists' and the 'non-agriculturalists', the proprietary body and the lower castes." Although the effects of these transformations in property rights were most evident with regard to forest resources and the ability to expand agricultural production, they also affected irrigation management in the Punjab by undermining collective interest in maintaining irrigation works.

Other effects accompanied the settlement process. In Kangra, as in other districts of greater Punjab, the "ancient and time-honored custom" of paying rent in kind was reversed by commuting in-kind to cash payments (Barnes 1855:52). The switch was part of the then prevailing utilitarian philosophy of agricultural development in Europe. That Barnes embraced this philosophy is strongly suggested by his comments on the effects on farmers of substituting cash for in-kind payments: "It has taught them habits of self-management and economy, and has converted them from ignorant serfs of the soil into an intelligent and thrifty peasantry" (1855:52).

That the first revenue settlement of Kangra District was seen as an appropriate vehicle for teaching farmers "habits of economy" and converting them into an "intelligent and thrifty peasantry" speaks volumes about nineteenth-century conceptions of the liberal state, the art of government, and the rationale for withholding the (ostensibly universal) right to consensual government from the empire's colonies. Under the view formulated by the Physiocrats and utilitarians during the eighteenth and nineteenth centuries, habits of thriftiness and economy were necessary prerequisites for securing the conditions necessary for laissez-faire government. Laissez-faire government, which "works through and with interests, both those of individuals and, increasingly, those attributed to the population itself" (Burchell 1991:127), required the existence of the very interests that were the objects of its regulation. In Western societies, these interests were presumed to be a natural expression of a self-regulating population oriented toward the creation of wealth. During this period the economy evolved into a primary field of government intervention, and the individual, recast as "'economic man," became "the correlate and instrument of a new art of government" (Burchell 1991:127). Regulation of the population in order to promote the rational efforts of its members to express and realize their self-interests, particularly with respect to the economy, became a central element of this new art (Foucault 1991).

Influential nineteenth-century utilitarians such as James Mill and John Stuart Mill argued, however, that colonized populations had not reached the stage of progress, of historical maturation, necessary for the realization and application of liberal principles of government (Mehta 1999). The "universal" liberal principles of freedom and equality applied only to populations that had reached the appropriate level of civilization (Mehta 1999). Colonized populations lacked the habits and interests that constituted the objects of regulation in the liberal laissez-faire state. Thus, the art of government in the colonial state involved the simultaneous creation and regulation of such habits and interests. The powerful commitment to a teleology of progress among liberal thinkers, which rendered such populations "backward," simultaneously justified withholding from them government by consent and generated the reformist zeal of utilitarians in India as they sought to realign and advance colonized societies along the path of progress Western societies had already taken.

This is why the first settlement of Kangra involved, as Barnes informs us, teaching the habits of economy, thriftiness, and self-management— already presumed to exist in Western societies—that were the essential precursors to the establishment of government by consent. The challenge of the project and the associated "indefinite temporizing" of the narrative of progress ensured that this would be a long process (Mehta 1999:111); fulfilling the white man's burden was going to take time. In the meantime, in Kangra, the arts and techniques of government entailed transforming "ignorant serfs" into an "intelligent peasantry" and, through the laissez-faire regulation of the population and the field of economic activity, creating the conditions that would allow "economic man" to thrive.

One of the central conditions necessary for the development of economic interests was, in liberal thought, the presence or, where they had not yet developed, the establishment of secure private property rights. This hallmark physiocratic idea was thought to be central to agricultural production and more general efforts to create wealth. In this respect, too, Barnes's settlement did not disappoint. Although he did not explicitly acknowledge this effect, by conveying the same rights in land that had been granted to landowners in the North-Western Provinces (present-day Uttar Pradesh), Barnes conferred full proprietary rights in cultivated land to people who had previously held inheritable rights to use the land but not the right to sell or transfer it. Although this was certainly consistent with prevailing utilitarian and physiocratic schools of thought, subsequent Revenue Department officers tried to sidestep the momentous transformation that had been wrought and that far exceeded their formal authority. For example, Alexander Anderson (1897:9), trying to downplay the significance of this move, argued that the introduction of the right to alienate land was an unintended consequence, a "mere incident of the [first] settlement."

Whether intended or not, this new right had far-reaching consequences once rights holders realized they had been granted the power of alienation. Between 1850 and the second settlement in 1870, in Kangra and Palampur Tehsils only 4.6 and 2.5 percent of the total cultivated area had been mortgaged, respectively. By 1890, in Kangra Tehsil, 14 percent of the total cultivated area was under mortgage, and an additional 5 percent had been sold (Anderson 1897:9). Land alienations were greatest among Rajputs, a pattern consistent with what Bernard Cohn reported for districts in the United Provinces near Benaras during 1795–1850 (Cohn 1987:369; Connolly 1911:6).

Settlement officers unanimously attributed the increase in alienated land to the need to raise capital for bride-price payments among high-caste Rajputs as well as upwardly mobile Rathis and Thakurs seeking to legitimate their claims to Rajput status (the dowry system gradually supplanted the practice of bride price during the late nineteenth century) (Anderson 1897; Connolly 1911; Middleton 1919). During this period the price of a bride increased tenfold, from 20–40 rupees to 200–400 rupees (O'Brien 1891a:9; Parry 1979:243). Some Rathi, Rajput, and Brahman clans sought to enhance their status by providing a dowry when giving a daughter away in marriage rather than accepting bride price, yet often they were still obligated to pay a bride price in order to get a daughter-in-law. This practice had severe consequences on the household economy, as E. O'Brien noted (1891a:6): "When [land] owners are in the habit of giving daughters gratis and buying brides for themselves, they are always poor and in debt and their land is certain to be mortgaged."

Other reasons for people's desire to raise capital by alienating land included the purchase of cattle and bullocks, expenditures on marriages and death ceremonies, and debts incurred in order to undertake the long pilgrimages that expanding transportation networks had made easier (Lala Moti Ram, cited in O'Brien 1890:6). The expanding market economy and increasing opportunities for wage labor also fueled land alienation (Parry 1979:25). The increasing monetized sector of the economy facilitated payment of land taxes, which had been converted from grain payments "at easy rates" into money (Barnes 1855:52).[30]

In Kangra, land transactions increased dramatically during the latter part of the nineteenth century. Recent changes in property rights and the introduction of a bureaucratic set of procedures and laws (e.g., district courts, land laws, and codified statements of rights regarding landownership) that provided the means for transferring property from one owner to another made these land transactions possible.[31] Urban-based moneylenders and other urban groups began to accumulate land under these laws. Between 1870 and 1890, approximately 25 percent of total agricultural land sales and 24 percent of total agricultural land mortgages in Kangra Valley were made to persons who had not owned agricultural land before 1870 (O'Brien 1889, 1890, 1891a, 1891b), primarily urban-based moneylenders. The transfer of agricultural land to moneylenders was actually more extensive than these figures suggest; many of the remaining sales and mortgages were made to people who, although classified as "old" agriculturalists, were "money-lenders pure and simple" (Anderson 1897:9).

The Punjab Land Alienation Act of 1900 was an attempt to slow these forms of land transfers, which the colonial administration feared would lead to reduced agricultural production and revenue, by prohibiting "non-agricultural" castes from purchasing agricultural land.[32] Of course the category "non-agricultural caste" was in part an artifact of the settlement process, which had sharply defined the boundaries of the proprietary community on the basis of genealogy and had, in the process, demarcated other groups as "non-agricultural." Nevertheless, the act did slow the transfer of land. In Dehra and Hamirpur Tehsils of Kangra District, for the nine years preceding and following passage of the land act, the percentages of total cultivated land mortgaged declined from 13.8 to 3.8 and from 9.5 to 3.5 percent, respectively (Connolly 1911:6).

Following the first settlement, the cultivated area in Kangra also increased. By 1890 it had increased 8–10 percent. Hill slopes that previously had been cultivated infrequently were now terraced and cultivated annually, and forested areas were converted to agriculture. This agricultural expansion, consistent with that described by Minoti Chakravarty-Kaul (1996) for the greater Punjab but on a much smaller scale, was facilitated by a provision of the first regular settlement that shifted authority over the expansion of agriculture into uncultivated areas such as forests from the ruler to the landholders of a hamlet. This "revolution in the old state of property" (Lyall 1874:19) converted the landholders of each hamlet into a co-proprietary class and created and transferred to them ownership rights in the commons (in which they previously had only usufructuary rights).[33] By converting use rights into ownership rights, treating landowners as coparcenary groups that were now jointly responsible for paying the land tax, and granting them the collective right to collect certain miscellaneous rents from the commons, the settlement process in effect created a type of community that hitherto had not existed.[34]

The transfer to landholders of rights in these areas may have been an unintended consequence of the application of land-use categories from the plains in the hill states, or it may have been an intentional, if implicit, policy to promote agricultural expansion and intensification by simplifying the process of bringing new areas under cultivation and more intensively cultivating already cultivated areas. Evidence suggests that it more likely was the former. In the Punjab, early village settlements were conducted by itinerant field surveyors (*amins*) from the North-West Provinces (NWP), who went from settlement to settlement, working on a pro-rata basis (Smith 1996:159). Because the village-level record of rights (known as the *iqrar-nama* and later as the *wajib-ul-arz*) in Kangra was probably drawn up by itinerant amins from the NWP, it is highly likely that land-use categories were imported from the plains to the hills. Barnes's admonition to a subdistrict *tehsildar* "to write down the actual practices as observed . . . and not to fill up details [of the iqrar-nama] after his own imagination" (1855:67) suggests that this was a real threat. This possibility is made the more plausible by Barnes's having noted that in the preparation of the record of rights for each hamlet, he himself gave the subject headings and elicited information with questions and even suggestions. The resulting confusion is easy to imagine. As Neeladri Battacharya (1996:34) noted regarding the general difficulty of codifying custom in the Punjab, "baffled villagers produced answers which interrogators helped to mould."

Even if trained local patwaris, and not itinerant amins, compiled the record of rights in Kangra, the possibility for importing nonlocal categories of property rights was high because the patwari training manual, "Educational Course for Village Accountants," was based on the author's experiences in the North-West Provinces. Furthermore, the author, Ram Saran Das, was transferred from the NWP to oversee settlement operations in the Cis- and Trans-Sutlej territories following their acquisition by the British after the 1846 Sikh War. Therefore, whether the Kangra settlement was conducted by amins from the NWP or by patwaris whose training was based on Ram Das's manual, land-use categories from the NWP could easily have been transferred to Kangra despite the lack of local referents for those categories.

The history of the term *shamilat*, referring to village common property, in Kangra exemplifies this process. It was introduced in Kangra as a land-use category during the first regular settlement. A term imported from the plains, *shamilat* had no pre-British referents in Kangra.[35] Twenty years after the first settlement, Lyall argued that landholders had not manufactured their own title to the commons by putting "shamilat" in the village record of rights but rather that "the real inventors of the definition [of shamilat] were the native officials and clerks who worked under Mr. Barnes" (1874:31), who had inserted "shamilat" as the heading in the village records. The creation of shamilat as a land-use category encouraged the expansion of agriculture by granting landholders the right to break up and cultivate the commons, free of extra taxes, for the duration of the settlement. This was consistent with colonial policy encouraging agricultural expansion and conversion of forests to agricultural lands in other regions, such as the plains areas between the Ganga and Jamuna Rivers, during the preceding decades (Mann 1995:211–12).

Following the transfer of rights in uncultivated areas from the state to the newly created community of co-proprietary landholders and the designation of those areas as "shamilat," Revenue Department officials attempted to privatize as much of them as they could. Barnes (1855:67) described how he approached areas described as shamilat:

> Whenever . . . I saw an opportunity, I insisted on a partition of the estate according to the number of shares. Every inch of profitable ground was divided and allotted to one or another of the co-partners. I ignored as far as my means would allow the very name of "Shamilat," for experience has assured me that the smallest portion left in common will act as a firebrand in the village. It is sure to lead to dissension, and forms, as it were, a rallying point for the discontented and litigious to gather round.

Quite possibly the "discontented and litigious" people Barnes referred to were those whose usufructuary rights had been nullified through the vesting of common land in the community of landowners, thus disenfranchising nonlandowning groups.

The incentives to expand agriculture provided by the introduction in Kangra of new forms of property rights were further strengthened by a 20-year fixed assessment and increasing grain prices. One outcome of these processes was the construction of new kuhls by collectivities of agriculturalists and by influential individuals. In Palam Subdistrict, between 1851 and 1890, 146 acres of uncultivated area were converted to agriculture and irrigated by newly constructed kuhls or extensions of preexisting kuhls (O'Brien 1890:14). Between 1850 and 1916, 41 new kuhls were constructed in Kangra Valley (*Riwaj-i-Abpashi* 1918). In 1855 Barnes observed that after the first settlement, single-cropped fields were double-cropped and new kuhls were "projected and executed" (1855:63). In 1897 Anderson remarked on the "new watercourses" that had been constructed since Lyall's first revision of the settlement in 1874 (1897:60). And L. Middleton, in the introduction to the second edition of the *Riwaj-i-Abpashi*, noted that the records pertaining to kuhl irrigation drawn up during Lyall's revised settlement were no longer accurate, because of new kuhl construction (*Riwaj-i-Abpashi* 1918).

The primary landowning castes during this period were (and continue to be) Rajputs, Brahmans, Rathis, Thakurs, and Girths. Table 5 gives the ownership of cultivated land by caste for Kangra District in 1919, and Table 6 gives landownership statistics by caste for Kangra Valley in 1897. Table 5 shows that together, the two highest castes, Brahmans and Rajputs, owned just over 50 percent of the total cultivated land. In 1931 they composed 44.2 percent of the district's population. Table 6 demonstrates a similar

TABLE 5. Percentages of Cultivated Land in Kangra District by Caste, 1919

Tehsil (Subdistrict)	Brahman	Rajput	Rathi	Girth	Other
Palampur	21.0	20.6	17.5	9.1	31.8
Kangra	11.5	21.3	5.8	33.1	28.3
Nurpur	12.6	55.1	10.0	2.5	19.8
Total	14.9	35.6	11.3	12.4	25.8

SOURCE: Middleton 1919:3.

TABLE 6. Land Ownership by Caste, Kangra Valley, 1890

Caste	No. Holdings	Cultivated Area (ha)	Average Holding (ha)	% of Total Holdings
Girth	5,466	9,676	1.8	14.4
Brahman	5,869	16,723	2.9	25.0
Mahajan	1,282	4,194	3.3	6.3
Rajput	5,557	15,259	2.8	22.8
Rathi	4,061	11,827	2.9	17.6
Other	6,332	9,344	1.5	13.9

SOURCES: O'Brien 1889, 1890, 1891a, 1891b.

trend in Kangra Valley and also illustrates the relatively small differences in average landholding size between castes.[36] The Mahajan caste, composed primarily of traders, had the largest average landholding. During the British period, many Mahajan families accumulated land and wealth as traders and moneylenders. These two tables clearly show the absence of wealthy, landed elites in Kangra.

The Influence of Settlement on Property in Kuhls

Consistent with the colonial government's interest in progress—in this case through agricultural expansion and revenue generation—the Revenue Department facilitated, subsidized, and generally supported the expansion of irrigation networks. This process involved a variety of statemaking practices through which the colonial government could shape and encourage private investment and growth in Kangra's agrarian economy while simultaneously fashioning itself in the image of the liberal vision of government (though shorn of principles of freedom and equality). These practices included regulating the construction of new kuhls, codifying irrigation customs and rights, mapping kuhl networks, and shifting dispute resolution from the village level to the district courts. The codification of irrigation customs reflected the mid-nineteenth-century emphasis on using custom as the basis for determining land rights. Settlement officers asserted that state claims to the natural waterways of the district represented a continuity rather than a change from previous customs. Lyall (1874:56) wrote:

> In order to retain in its hands the power of making new irrigation channels where needed, the Government directed all Settlement Officers to assert its title to all natural streams and rivers. In Kangra the title of Government, by old custom of the country, was particularly clear, and I accordingly asserted it subject, however, to existing rights of use possessed by shareholders of canals, owners of water-mills, or persons entitled by custom to erect "chip" or fish-weirs in certain places. . . . The actual beds of streams and the water in them belong to the Government.

Permission to construct a new kuhl could not be granted unless the government had a record of the existing network of kuhls. This was prepared as part of the 1874 revised settlement of Kangra. Cognizant that a village-level record of irrigation rights would reveal only a partial picture of multivillage kuhls, the settlement officer responsible for the revised settlement directed that a watershed-scale record of irrigation rights for the two tehsils with the greatest density of irrigation networks—Palampur and Kangra—be prepared. The resulting compendiums described the origins, histories, locations, command areas, and methods of construction of the more than 715 multivillage kuhls in Palampur and Kangra Tehsils, as well as the intervillage rights and responsibilities associated with them. It also included summary descriptions of the more than 2,000 single-village kuhls in the two tehsils. The document included a glossary of specialized irrigation terms, a section on the customary rules governing the construction of new kuhls, and maps of every stream showing the position of each kuhl and its headworks, main channels, and the villages it flowed through. These statements of irrigation rights were bound and copies kept at the Palampur and Kangra Tehsil offices. They constituted the first edition of the *Riwaj-i-Abpashi.*

The *Riwaj-i-Abpashi* represented the first time that complex irrigation customs guiding the measurement and distribution of a single kuhl's water to as many as 60 different hamlets were reduced to writing. Settlement officers determined the customs and practices relating to a specific kuhl by calling a public meeting and asking those present to describe their customs and practices. After being written down, they were read aloud, suggested changes were incorporated, and prominent village leaders then attested to the veracity of the statement with their thumbprints or signatures.

Lyall himself acknowledged the difficulty of creating accurate statements of irrigation rights in this manner: "Probably these statements are sometimes incorrect. . . . the custom is often vague and difficult to define" (1874:243). The alien frames of reference of such settings, the challenges of verification, questions concerning who had standing to speak, and lingering uncertainties about the purpose of the inquiry no doubt bedeviled these attempts to codify irrigation customs in Kangra, as they did the creation of other village records of custom in the Punjab (Battacharya 1996). Though irrigation customs might have appeared vague to a settlement officer, one wonders whether they appeared equally vague to the shareholders whose irrigation water depended on them. Furthermore, dominant factions well represented at the general meeting might have presented the settlement officer with a picture of rights in a kuhl that favored their own interests over those of subordinate claimants. It is not surprising that the process of codifying custom would be used by dominant social groups to solidify claims. This was certainly the case with respect to the codification of rights of inheritance and succession in greater Punjab, a process through which customs related to women's succession and inheritance were systematically undermined, especially because women could not participate in public forums to claim their rights.

Indeed, the *Riwaj-i-Abpashi* occasionally acknowledges such conflicts explicitly. In some cases, after describing intervillage rights and responsibilities with regard to a specific kuhl, it notes that members of a hamlet contested the version of rights that were recorded and refused attestation. It also refers sometimes to ongoing litigation over contested water rights. Social groups appear to have taken full advantage of the new arena to assert competing claims to kuhl irrigation water and to negotiate favorable rulings regarding the intervillage distribution of responsibility for kuhl maintenance and repair.

The expansion of irrigated agriculture, construction of new kuhls, and court decisions regarding irrigation soon outdated the statements of irrigation rights compiled as part of the 1874 settlement. The tension created by disjunctures between the static, inflexible, and no doubt partial record of irrigation rights and the dynamic social system that undergirded it led to the revision of the original *Riwaj-i-Abpashi* during the third revised settlement, from 1913 to 1919.[37] As noted in the preface to the revised edition, it was necessary to update the *Riwaj-i-Abpashi* because the original was incomplete, judicial decisions regarding water rights were at variance with it, and new kuhls had been constructed.

The reference to new judicial decisions is interesting. With local conflict resolution forums having been supplanted by the colonial judicial system, it became common practice in late-nineteenth-century north India to use the court system as an "arena in the competition for social status, and for political and economic dominance" through ongoing litigation, rather than using it actually to settle disputes (Cohn 1987:610). Similarly, threatening recourse to the colonial administration for resolving conflict was a strategy deployed against rivals (Skaria 1999:245). Lyall acknowledged this dynamic in Kangra. With respect to the use of courts to resolve struggles over scarce water, he noted that disputants used the courts "to frighten the opposite party" instead of "getting a useful decision"; as a result, the courts rendered "many unintelligible and impractical judgements" (1874:243). Thus it seems that, as elsewhere in north India, the colonial judicial system in Kangra was used as an arena for iteratively advancing claims and counterclaims to kuhl water rather than for settling claims permanently.

Despite the strategic use of courts as arenas for competing over social status and material wealth, the *Riwaj-i-Abpashi* eventually was viewed as a legal record of right that could be used as the basis for judicial decisions regarding water disputes. Initially, it was not intended to be a binding contractual document between villages and the Revenue Department. Instead, it was part of a much wider effort during the latter half of the nineteenth century to codify customary law in settlement reports, statistical reports, and, later, district gazetteers (period reports that provide comprehensive information on social, economic, agricultural, geographic, and other conditions within a district). Information contained in the formal compilations of customary law "had the legal value of evidence of custom, not the presumption of truth which was accorded an entry in a record of rights" (Smith 1996:156). The *Riwaj-i-Abpashi* explicitly stated that the codification of custom did not constitute legally binding rights and obligations. Part 9 of the 1918 edition included the following entry from the 1868 edition: "These conditions does [sic] not form an agreement between government and farmers. Rather this is a system in practice of defined customs and agreement between farmers of different villages."

Regardless of the extent to which the *Riwaj-i-Abpashi* constituted a legally defensible record of water rights and customs, it did have numerous ramifications for statemaking and governmentality that warrant review here. These concern the creation of new, state-centered arenas for claiming rights related to agricultural expansion and the construction of new kuhls, the supplanting of village-level conflict resolution forums by colonial courts of law for resolving disputes related to water, and the institutionalization of new forms of knowledge regarding kuhls. These elements are related to statemaking because of the ways in which they solidified the role and legitimacy of state involvement in water management in Kangra. Having codified irrigation customs in the *Riwaj-i-Abpashi,* the colonial government effectively transferred to itself the power to regulate kuhl systems. In doing so, the government enhanced its own legitimacy as well as the likelihood that people would concede it authority over themselves in this domain. The link between knowledge—in this case irrigation knowledge—and governmentality was explicit, as is demonstrated in the following statement by Charles Tupper, one of the architects of the effort to codify customary law in the Punjab: "The better the people are understood, the better they will be governed" (Tupper 1854:98, quoted in Battacharya 1996:37). Here we see the link made between codification of custom and ability to govern. Some specific examples illustrate these points.

The process of codifying irrigation rights created new, state-centered arenas for negotiating water rights among water users and between water users and the government. Groups that were in conflict over water allocation probably saw the creation of the *Riwaj-i-Abpashi* as an opportunity to solidify their water claims or at least to express their discontent with the existing manner of water distribution. In one case, that of Kanduhl Kuhl, the *Riwaj-i-Abpashi* described the distribution of water among 12 villages in terms of the numbers of days and nights each village could claim the kuhl's water and in what order. It also mentioned that a measured portion of the kuhl's flow was always to be reserved for Kandwari village, whose landowners in the late eighteenth century had mobilized labor to repair the previously defunct kuhl and then named it after their village. The text noted that the residents of Kandwari contested the water rights the other villages claimed and argued that these villages were claiming new rights that had not existed in the past. It also stated that farmers from three villages alleged that the residents of a cluster of four villages were claiming water earlier in the season than was their right. The entry for this kuhl concludes by noting that the claims of the cluster of four villages were rejected and that all present except the residents of Kandwari agreed to the final statement of rights. A reference to an 1889 civil court case concerning Kandwari's rights to the kuhl's flow indicates that the conflict between Kandwari and neighboring villages had been ongoing.

The negotiations that took place during the preparation of the record of rights were important, as no doubt the participants recognized, because the written record became the template against which future disputes over water were to be resolved, as it still is today. In many cases it reinforced existing power relations, strengthening the position of local elites and weakening the basis for future counterclaims. One example is the case of Sapruhl Kuhl, named after the Girth (agricultural caste) clan that constructed it in the late eighteenth or early nineteenth century. The constraints of elevation and gravity dictated that the kuhl, before bringing water to the Girth village, flow through an upstream, high-caste, Rana village. The *Riwaj-i-Abpashi* notes that sometime between the completion of the kuhl and the assumption of British control over the region, the Ranas forcibly appropriated all the kuhl's water and killed some of the Girths. Since then, the water rights of the downstream Girth village have been reduced to only eight days of dol rights, and to this day conflicts between these two groups continue. The act of writing did not concretize previously fluid relations but did further marginalize already marginal groups and strengthen the dominant position of others.[38]

The recording of irrigation rights also eroded the kohli's authority by creating an alternative repository of knowledge about water rights, the *Riwaj-i-Abpashi*, which constituted legitimate evidence in an alternative dispute resolution arena—the district courts. The courts, as alternative, state-sanctioned sources of expertise and conflict resolution, tended to undermine the specialized knowledge of the kohli and his ability to resolve conflicts. Thus, the long-term decline of the kohli's authority, more recently exacerbated by regional economic changes—especially the increasing importance of nonfarm employment and remittance income—extends back to the codification of irrigation custom.

The emergence of the district court during colonial rule as an alternative to local dispute resolution arenas has several implications. First, it suggests that the codification of irrigation customs did not necessarily ossify fluid social relations, as has sometimes been argued regarding the effects of colonialist knowledge, but rather helped to create a new arena within which to negotiate contested social claims to water. This new arena operated according to a different legal logic and jurisprudence tradition from that which had existed previously in the region. To operate effectively in this arena required a different set of skills, organizational structures, and forms of expertise. Once these skills were developed, local groups used this arena to effectively advance claims against rival claimants, including sometimes state entities.

For example, in the late 1980s a proposed government-sponsored expansion of an upstream kuhl in the Neugal watershed (funded in part by an international development organization) threatened the water supply of the next downstream kuhl. Farmers from the downstream kuhl formed a kuhl committee for the express purpose of representing their interests in court. They successfully sued the Irrigation and Public Health Department of the state of Himachal Pradesh. The lawsuit hinged on the *Riwaj-i-Abpashi*, which described the nature of the farmers' water rights, including injunctions against upstream diversions that might threaten the kuhl's water supply. In this case, farmers used the colonial codification of their "customary" water rights and a "modern" dispute resolution forum to successfully defend their "traditional" water rights against the state's attempts to expand irrigated agriculture and promote development.

In addition to codifying irrigation rights and customs, the colonial administration provided resources for the reconstruction of kuhls following natural disasters and adjudicated water conflicts during periods of water scarcity. In the introduction, we saw how the colonial administration mobilized military labor and resources for the reconstruction of kuhls destroyed in the 1905 earthquake. The administration also played third-party roles in resolving water disputes. Although I did not examine historical court records for specific decisions in water disputes, every settlement report from the first revised settlement of 1874 through the third revised settlement of 1916 refers to the role of the Revenue Department and the district court system in resolving disputes over kuhl water, especially during periods of water scarcity. For example, Revenue Department notifications 37 and 38 of March 20, 1907, authorized the district collector to "regulate the flow of the natural channels" of Kangra Valley. Notification 117 of October 1, 1907, restricted the exercise of that authority to "seasons of drought and with the object of supplying water to canals or to the cultivation of lands which are likely to be injuriously affected by the obstruction of natural channels"—that is, the diversion structures of upstream kuhls. This power was exercised in 1914. The *Riwaj-i-Abpashi* notes that because of a drought that year, the downstream kuhls of Baner Khad were receiving inadequate water. The district deputy commissioner appointed an official to distribute the water more equitably between upstream and downstream kuhls. He was instructed to ensure that the lower 16 of the 32 kuhls in the watershed each receive one *nala* of water.[39]

By the time of the third revised settlement of Kangra District (1913–19), the colonial administration was indirectly promoting the construction of new kuhls through a provision known as a "protective lease" (Middleton 1919:xii). It postponed the application of higher rates of tax assessment on newly irrigated land until the foregone revenue payments were equivalent to the total cost of the kuhl's construction, at which time the assessment rates associated with irrigated land would apply. Thus, the protective lease protected agriculturalists from tax increases until they had recouped, through lower tax remittances, the costs incurred in constructing the kuhl, at which time the usual higher assessment rates for irrigated land would be applied. These costs were equivalent to the monetary value of the labor and materials the landowners provided to construct the kuhl. This was a clear attempt to encourage investment in agricultural productivity by providing a subsidy for kuhl construction in the form of a reduced rate of land tax assessment.

The British government also sponsored the construction of two new kuhls. One was built to supply water to the growing market town of Palampur, whose growth the British encouraged as a trading center with Afghanistan and eastern Turkistan, where they sought a market for Kangra green tea. After constructing the kuhl, the government handed it over to the association of traders and businesspeople to manage and maintain. The second kuhl the government constructed diverts water from Gaj Khad in Kangra Tehsil. Although it currently irrigates agricultural land, its initial purpose probably was to provide water to the adjacent town of Dharmsala, which the British had established as a hill station and the headquarters for the district administration.

STATEMAKING AND COMMUNITY-MAKING

We have seen how kuhl regimes constituted sites for precolonial and colonial statemaking in Kangra. Consistent with precolonial models of territorial sovereignty, political authority, and statemaking based on the exchange of resources for political support and legitimacy, the precolonial state sponsored the construction of some of the longest and most complex kuhls in Kangra Valley and then handed their management over to the villages they irrigated. In return, precolonial rulers were able to strengthen the legitimacy of their rule, especially when they linked the construction of a new kuhl or the reconstruction of a destroyed one with temple patronage, as in the case of Raniya Kuhl.

The colonial state, too, was involved with kuhl regimes in a manner that demonstrates the intertwining of statemaking with the governance of agrarian systems and the permeability of state-society boundaries (Mitchell 1999). A strong economic and utilitarian rationale, consistent with the prevailing nineteenth-century liberal theory of government, conditioned the colonial state's involvement with kuhl regimes. This perspective has direct links with the eighteenth-century physiocratic notion that land is the primary source of wealth and secure private property rights are a necessary precondition for securing the investments needed to release land's inherent value. According to this rationale, the role of government is to create the conditions necessary to allow the "natural" expression of economy and, where necessary, to reform and develop social institutions to enable "economic man" to express his inherent interests.

The liberal theory of government, imbued with reformist zeal in the colonial context, informed both the statemaking enterprises in which kuhl regimes figured and the social transformations the colonial administration wrought. Indeed, when we review the various forms of colonial engagement with resources and people in Kangra and the governance structures developed to guide that engagement with an eye to their social effects, we see that statemaking processes simultaneously involved community-making, both as process and as outcome. Community-making refers to the specific ways in which state-society interactions modify and contribute to the creation of particular types of communities and social relations. Community-making, as a corollary of statemaking, draws attention to the ways in which the arts and rationalities of governance not only legitimate government but are also implicated in the process of crafting particular types of communities and distributions of social power and privilege. In specific, identifiable ways, the state-society dialectic creates particular state structures and communities.

The urge to guide and promote the expansion of the agrarian economy in Kangra led to the variety of statemaking processes I have reviewed: land settlements, codification of irrigation rights, establishment of judicial arenas for conflict resolution, imposition of state authority to distribute water during periods of drought, and mobilization of state resources to help repair kuhls destroyed by floods or earthquakes. These actions not only established and strengthened the legitimacy and necessity of colonial government but also contributed to community-making by modifying relations among social groups and between them and state entities. Many of these community-making modifications related to property rights, colonial concepts of community, the devolution of authority to the local community, the codification of custom, and the classification of social groups.

For example, the transformations the colonial state wrought in the nature of private and common property, in combination with the use of a definition of community based on anthropological principles of agnatic relationship, generated a powerful set of processes that strengthened the social position and authority of landowning groups. Assigning responsibility for paying the government's land tax to the collectivity of landowners in a hamlet and devolving to them the authority to expand cultivation into uncultivated common land further strengthened the power of the emerging village community thus specified. The codification of irrigation customs and rights and the establishment of courts provided important arenas through which social groups could challenge the rights and claims of others and advance their own. In some cases, statemaking introduced new categories of social difference, such as the binary agriculturalist-nonagriculturalist distinction, which, when used as the basis for state interventions such as the Punjab Land Alienation Act, became reified and imbued with social meaning. All of these processes contributed to the creation of specific types of communities with particular constellations of social power in Kangra. The social effects of these processes varied by social group and were inflected by the ways in which they interacted with attributes of regionality.

Colonial statemaking and community-making interacted with regional social and economic processes with which the state was involved but over which it exerted little absolute control. These included shifts in the control of land among social groups fueled by rising bride prices and the gradual adoption of the practice of dowry, increased investment in agriculture, increasing grain prices, improved transportation infrastructure, and the increase in absentee landownership. One outcome of these changes was agricultural expansion and a concomitant flurry of locally sponsored kuhl construction. These regional processes of economic and social change continued, and in many respects accelerated, during the post-independence period, to which I now turn.

4

PATTERNS OF CHANGE

DURING THE LAST 30 YEARS OR SO, THE INCREASING PERVASIVENESS OF the market economy has wrought deep-seated and far-reaching changes in Kangra. In Palampur, Kangra, Dharmsala, Baijnath, and other market towns in Kangra Valley, once-scarce consumer durables such as electronics, household appliances, scooters, and motorcycles are displayed prominently in the storefronts that line the busy thoroughfares. The tremendous rise in nonfarm employment that has coincided with the expansion of the market economy provides the cash needed to purchase these goods. Concomitantly, attitudes among the younger generation about work and livelihood have undergone sea changes. Partly as a result of the increased availability of public education throughout the region, many, if not most, youths today seek wage work. They generally prefer government employment, with its security and pension plan, when they can get it, but they are willing to take almost any job over full-time agricultural work. This is partly because of the small sizes of agricultural holdings (as discussed in chapter 2); few households today own enough land to be self-sufficient. The Kangri phrase *cuch gainda cuch bainda* refers to the common practice of cobbling together a living though part-time wage work and agricultural work or through full-time employment and weekend farming (women, who generally do not work outside of the house, shoulder a heavier share of the agricultural work).

Powerful discourses of development and modernity are also heightening the divide between "old Kangra" and new values and patterns of work, consumerism, and livelihood. In some respects, kuhls and their customs, practices, and stories are part of old Kangra. They are associated with an earlier period in which almost all households shared great dependence on agricultural production and kuhl water. With the rapid expansion of the market economy, few people now would not prefer working a government desk job, with paid vacation, over slogging in knee-deep mud behind a pair of bullocks pulling a wooden plowshare under the hot May sun.

Not all households, however, have access to nonfarm employment. The differential distribution of access to nonfarm employment has changed the pattern of dependence on kuhl water. Households with access to new economic opportunities such as secure nonfarm employment are less willing to contribute the labor and other resources necessary for the maintenance and repair of kuhls, especially when the opportunity costs of their labor are foregone cash wages. The resulting tensions are not unique to kuhl regimes. In many situations, increasing market-based economic opportunities weaken people's bonds of common dependence on the benefits common property resources provide (Jodha 1985; Polanyi 1944). The resulting erosion of common property resource regimes is not due simply to the increased opportunity costs of labor for those with nonfarm employment. It is also related to the diminishing salience of village-based authority structures and to challenges to caste-based inequality, as well as to other, broader social changes in the region. In Kangra, as regional economic opportunities expand and the electoral politics of democracy flourish, conflicts arising from caste-based inequalities increase, and people's willingness to accept those inequalities decreases. With regard to kuhl regimes, these processes have resulted in increasing absenteeism for khana, the declining ability of the kohli to enforce rules, increasing conflicts between head-end and tail-end farmers and communities, and contractions in command areas.

These effects are not distributed evenly across all kuhl regimes. Rather, significant spatial and temporal heterogeneity shapes their distribution. The potential for caste-, class-, or locationally derived conflict among the irrigators of a kuhl and the degree of reliance on the irrigation water a kuhl provides shape the tensions arising from increasing nonfarm employment as well as the means people employ to resolve those tensions. Currently, kuhl regimes vary in their degree of role specialization and organizational formalization from having no specialized roles, formal rules, or written records to having multiple watermasters, a formal committee with elected officers, extensive written records, and sophisticated methods for measuring water flow. They also vary in the extent of state involvement in their water management, from operating independently of the state to being managed entirely by the Himachal Pradesh Irrigation and Public Health Department.

This tremendous variation in the organizational characteristics of kuhl regimes reflects their differential responses to the stresses arising from increasing nonfarm employment. The varied roles the state of Himachal Pradesh plays in the management of kuhls can best be accounted for as a process of negotiation between various state agents and the persons involved in kuhl management. Local social and ecological influences shape the content of this negotiation and its outcomes in terms of state involvement in water management. This view contrasts sharply with the more common notion of the undifferentiated application of a homogenous state irrigation "policy" across a socially and ecologically differentiated landscape.

THE EFFECTS ON KUHLS OF
INCREASING NONFARM EMPLOYMENT

Increased nonfarm employment has affected kuhl regimes in four primary ways, both social and economic. It has decreased participation in collective kuhl maintenance work activities, increased inequality between head-end and tail-end farmers in terms of water consumption and contributions for system repair and maintenance, led to a decline in the authority of the kohli and his ability to enforce customary rules, and resulted in changing cropping patterns. When a household's (primarily male) labor supply is incorporated into the nonfarm economic sector, the supply of labor and incentive to contribute to the maintenance and management of common resources is concomitantly reduced. This is particularly true for activities such as the repair and maintenance of a kuhl's physical structure, from which gender-based norms exclude women.[1] When participation in nonfarm, income-generating opportunities reduces dependence on local resource systems, forms of authority that evolved in a context of mutual dependence on local natural resource endowments are likely to be weakened and become more easily contested. The resulting differentiation among people in terms of their dependence on local resources, although moderated by ideologically compelling norms of reciprocity, hierarchical relations, and the strong local bias against buying food grains, nevertheless weakens the legitimacy of rules and the ability of village-based authorities to enforce them.

Declining Participation

Increasing nonfarm employment has reduced the incentive for some households to participate in communal kuhl maintenance and repair activities. Consequently, rates of participation have declined in some kuhl regimes. Without exception, kohlis told me their most difficult problem was mobilizing farmers for kuhl maintenance. In order to bolster participation and provide a basis for sanctioning absent farmers, many kuhl regimes now maintain attendance registers.[2] Though all attendance registers record who contributes labor and who does not, the dynamics of declining participation vary from kuhl to kuhl. Participation in khana may decline for political or economic reasons among big or small landowners. In some kuhls, participation may have been low previously, whereas in others, low participation may be a recent phenomenon.

Evidence from three kuhls—Kathul, Pathan, and Raniya—shows how participation in khana has declined over time, but for different reasons in different regimes. Kathul Kuhl, whose construction two traders from the nearby town of Nagrota Bhagwan paid for during the colonial period, carries water approximately 5 miles to the villages of Paror and Kharot. It irrigates about 70 hectares. Laxman Das, the kohli for Kathul Kuhl, often decried farmers' declining interest in kuhl maintenance. He described the increasing difficulty with which he and the kuhl committee, created in part to back up the kohli's decisions, mobilized labor for khana. In 1991, for example, the few farmers who turned out for khana were unable to complete the channel maintenance all the way to the danga. As a result, no water from the Neugal River flowed into the kuhl's main channel that year; only ephemeral streams provided irrigation water, and that only after the monsoon started. Because of the lack of water for field preparation and the insecurity of water supply, most farmers were forced to sow paddy using the lower-yielding but less water-intensive battar method.

The following year, after much browbeating by the kohli and members of the kuhl committee, more than 90 farmers participated in khana and danga construction for Kathul Kuhl. Once they had completed their work and the kohli had performed puja, water from the Neugal River flowed through the kuhl's main channel. With a relatively certain water supply secured, farmers utilized the mach method of paddy sowing that year. Nevertheless, the ongoing difficulty of mobilizing enough labor for adequate kuhl maintenance threatens the ability of the current kuhl regime to maintain the physical integrity of the kuhl without either reconstituting its own operating rules or changing the nature of its relationship with the state.

Regional increases in nonfarm employment restrict the pool of labor available for khana. Spatially heterogeneous social and ecological factors, however, mediate this regional dynamic and shed light on the kohli's difficulties. These factors include Kathul Kuhl's irrigation primarily of larh areas. As labor scarcity due to rising nonfarm employment increases, communal labor supplies are scarcest for tasks such as irrigating larh areas that yield the lowest returns. Overall dependence on Kathul Kuhl water is also relatively low because once the monsoon begins, water from ephemeral streams can be diverted and used for irrigation. Furthermore, residents of the village of Paror, through which the kuhl flows, no longer rely on Kathul Kuhl to provide hydropower for grinding grain or to meet other domestic water needs. Dependence on the water from this kuhl would have been much greater prior to the availability of public faucets for domestic use and before electricity-powered mills supplanted kuhl-powered mills (graths). These site-specific factors have weakened the web of dependence on the water this kuhl provides. Together, they account for Laxman Das's difficulty in mobilizing labor to maintain the kuhl's infrastructure. Other indicators of system stress in this kuhl regime include an increasing ratio of battar- to mach-sown paddy fields and shifts from paddy to maize production in some larh fields.[3]

Attendance registers for nearby Pathan Kuhl indicate that the number of farmers participating in its khana has declined in recent years, too. An influential member of the Pathan caste constructed Pathan Kuhl during the precolonial period when Kangra was under Mughal rule. It carries water approximately three miles from the Neugal Khad to the villages of Paror and Kharot, where it irrigates about 45 hectares. Table 7 shows the number of days called for khana on Pathan Kuhl every year from 1978 through 1991 in terms of the number of farmers who turned out on each of those days. The maximum number of farmers participating in khana on a given day fell from 90–100 to 30–40. The total number of workdays farmers contributed for khana per year also declined. Some of the variation may be attributed to yearly fluctuations in the labor requirements for kuhl maintenance, but the declining maximum number of farmers who participated on any given day, the declining number of workdays contributed per year, and—as observed by the kohli, Dhyan Singh—the fact that fewer farmers now participated than had earlier all suggest that participation in khana for Pathan Kuhl was indeed declining.

TABLE 7. Number of Days Called for *Khana,* by Number of Farmers
Who Came Each Day, Pathan Kuhl, 1978–1991

Year	Number of Farmers Each Day									Total Days Called	Total Person Workdays
	10–20	21–30	31–40	41–50	51–60	61–70	71–80	81–90	91–100		
1978	4	2	3	2	—	—	—	1	1	13	485
1979	9	3	2	1	—	—	1	—	—	16	389
1980	1	3	1	1	1	—	1	—	—	8	315
1983	4	1	1	1	—	1	—	—	—	8	226
1985	—	1	2	—	2	—	—	—	—	5	215
1986	5	2	1	—	—	2	—	—	—	10	274
1987	5	2	2	1	—	—	—	—	1	11	328
1988	4	1	2	—	1	1	—	—	—	9	258
1989	6	2	1	1	—	—	—	—	—	10	213
1990	6	3	1	—	1	—	—	—	—	11	247
1991	2	2	3	—	—	—	—	—	—	7	189

SOURCE: Kohli's records (records for 1981–82 and 1984 missing).

What accounts for declining participation in Pathan Kuhl? A review of
the kuhl committee's meeting minutes from 1978 through 1990 reveals a
series of common conflicts that, when considered in conjunction with the
effects of increasing nonfarm employment, shed light on the dynamics of
declining participation. One recurring theme is the complaint by the kohli,
as well as by farmers residing in Kharot, that farmers in the adjacent,
upstream village of Paror used water from Pathan Kuhl but did not
contribute to its maintenance. Furthermore, they argued, Paror farmers
took more than their entitlement of water as specified in the *Riwaj-i-
Abpashi.* To attempt to address this issue, the kuhl committee passed
resolutions directing the farmers of Paror to heed the kohli's call to come
forward and contribute labor on the announced day. The resolutions noted
that the kuhl committee considered excuses such as "I didn't hear the kohli's
call" to be inadequate.

Other conflicts noted in the minutes are concerns by small landholders
(those holding 2–3 kanals, or 0.3–0.5 ha) that their holdings were too small
to warrant full participation in communal work projects and a long litany
of complaints that Kharot farmers lodged against the kohli in 1982. These
included allegations that he had received payment in exchange for nighttime
water deliveries to farmers not entitled to the kuhl's water, that he favored

his own fields during periods of water scarcity, and that farmers had been forced to seek temporary water delivery from the kohli of an adjacent kuhl *bhai bundi se* ("through brotherhood") because Dhyan Singh had organized khana too late and an early monsoon cloudburst and flood had destroyed the kuhl's diversion structure. The farmers of Kharot also stated that during times of water scarcity, Dhyan Singh was reluctant to install bamboo measuring devices (thellu) at each outlet, because doing so would reveal the extent of water scarcity (and, by implication, the inadequacy of his management).

The committee minutes noted other problems with the kuhl's management—for example, erosion-causing livestock grazing on the kuhl banks, damage to the kuhl's danga by local fisherfolk, illicit removal of sand from the kuhl for cement-making, and the refusal of recalcitrant farmers to allow the kuhl to flow through their land. In response to these problems the kuhl committee had at times recommended that the state government be approached to take over management of the kuhl, offered cash rewards for information leading to the apprehension of persons harming the kuhl's channel, and set the rather large fine of 500 rupees to be levied against persons who did not follow the rules that the committee promulgated.

Given the litany of conflicts that the minutes describe, it is not surprising that attendance registers record declining rates of participation in khana. It is perhaps more surprising that the kuhl continues to function at all. Several factors suggest why it does. Pathan Kuhl irrigates only the highly productive, rice-growing har areas of both Paror and Kharot, alternative water supplies are unavailable, and the water-intensive mach method is used for sowing paddy throughout the kuhl's command area. Judging from household landownership information contained in the committee records, socioeconomic inequality is not great in Paror, nor does it appear to be in Kharot. The records Dhyan Singh and the kuhl committee keep are among the most complete and best maintained that I saw. Formed in the early 1950s, the kuhl committee is among the older committees in the watershed. It facilitates the acquisition of government funds for kuhl maintenance and repair and, as suggested by its detailed meeting minutes, provides a forum for evaluating and resolving conflicts that arise among farmers or between the kohli and a farmer. Dhyan Singh has been kohli since 1971, when he retired from the army. His father served as kohli from 1940 to 1971. The kuhl appears to be organized with a degree of efficiency and organization that reflects Dhyan Singh's years in the military, where he served as an officer responsible for training new recruits. The high degree of dependence on kuhl water and the tight organization of the regime seem to provide adequate incentive for farmers to work through conflicts as they arise.

Examining the dynamics of khana in a third kuhl, Raniya Kuhl, sheds further light on the diverse causes of declining participation. As discussed in the previous chapter, the precolonial ruling Katoch lineage sponsored the construction of this kuhl, which brings water approximately seven miles from the Neugal River to the village of Saloh. The reasons for the decline in participation in Raniya Kuhl differ from those for Kathul and Pathan Kuhls. Kishori Lal, the lower-caste kohli for Raniya Kuhl, remembered that only 10 years earlier, 80 to 100 men would show up for the four days required to complete khana. In 1988, so few farmers turned out for khana that Kishori Lal called it off and instead collected money from the village to pay migrant laborers from Rajasthan to do the work. In 1993, only 21 individuals, many of them boys under 15 or men over 55, turned out for khana.[4] Kishori Lal repeatedly expressed frustration at his inability to force the larger landowners to either contribute labor or pay for laborers in their stead, and at the overall decline in farmer turnout.

Several factors seem to account for declining participation in Raniya Kuhl. Although the kuhl irrigates all the har areas of Saloh, alternative water supplies are available from a nearby ephemeral creek following the onset of the monsoon. The dominant reason, however, seems to be the existence of caste- and land-based inequalities between cultivators and tenants in Saloh. There, caste intersects with landownership—the three or four largest landowning families are Brahmans. Although I did not attempt to determine household landownership, participant observation and informal interviews indicated that these families owned most of the har land in the village. Their holdings almost certainly exceeded the current ceiling on landholding size. They were leased informally to tenants who gave the owner half the production in rent. This share arrangement exceeded the legal share that owners might demand. Lower-caste small landowners resented the discrepancy between landholding size, contributions for kuhl maintenance and repair, and water use. In their view, the large landowners contributed less labor for khana than did the small landowners yet used more kuhl water.

In contrast to the tightly organized committee for Pathan Kuhl, the committee for Raniya Kuhl, which was also formed in the 1950s, maintained no records. It did not support Kishori Lal, and it appeared to represent the interests of the large landowners. The president of the committee was one of the oldest men in Saloh, a Brahman, and the largest landowner. When asked what the committee did, he said (paraphrasing) that "we formed the committee years ago and we made rules, but because the rules were not obeyed or followed, what is the point of having a committee at all?"—at which point he threw his arms up in (feigned?) frustration and resignation.

Because of the difficulty of managing the kuhl, Kishori Lal and other village representatives traveled at their own expense to Simla, the state capital, to request the Irrigation and Public Health Department to assume responsibility for managing it. The request was denied, partly because the large landowners of Saloh opposed the proposal out of concern that the government might impose an area-based water tax.

Participation for khana in Raniya, Pathan, and Kathul Kuhls has declined, but the reasons vary from kuhl to kuhl. Declining dependence on kuhl water accounts for declining participation in Kathul Kuhl. The "pull" of nonfarm employment accounts for it in Pathan Kuhl, whereas the "push" of inequality explains it for Raniya Kuhl as low-caste small landholders exit a regime characterized by relatively high caste- and land-based inequality.[5] Declining participation, though a common phenomenon, has different causes and effects.

Increased Inequality among Users

The burden of kuhl maintenance has probably always tended to fall more heavily on downstream users than on upstream users. The *Riwaj-i-Abpashi* acknowledges this inequality when it states that tail-enders are responsible for maintaining and repairing the kuhl. It is often the case, though not always, that when a kuhl irrigates multiple hamlets, the upstream hamlets are predominantly high caste and the downstream hamlets low caste. In these instances, the rules codified in the *Riwaj-i-Abpashi* tend to reinforce the positions of dominant social groups. This tendency conforms to Bourdieu's analysis of the relationship between rules, practice, and action, in which he suggests that rules tend to reflect the interests of powerful individuals or groups. He notes that "the rule's last trick is to cause it to be forgotten that agents have an interest in obeying the rule" (1977 [1972]:22).

Numerous de facto rules that attempt to shift responsibility back upstream considerably soften this stark statement as it applies to the privileges upstream, high-caste hamlets enjoy in Kangra. Rules such as the tup-to-tup rule for khana and the common responsibility of all irrigators for danga construction and khana above the most upstream tup soften locationally derived inequalities. Nevertheless, declining dependence on agriculture and the consequent weakening of the bonds of interdependence among households have reduced the leverage these rules previously provided downstream users to influence the contributions of head-enders for system maintenance. The weakened ability of downstream water users to influence head-enders' actions strengthens the strategic advantages of head-end location and leads to more frequent free riding. In this case, the intersection of caste and locational differences amplifies inequalities between head- and tail-enders.

Buhli Kuhl exemplifies these processes. Farmers from the 17 hamlets irrigated by this kuhl constructed it sometime during the precolonial period. Its main channel is approximately six miles long, and its command area, at 300 hectares, is relatively large. High-caste Rajput families live near the head of the kuhl, and low-caste households are concentrated around the tail. The kohli of Buhli Kuhl, Vichitra Singh, is a Rajput from one of the head-end hamlets. Prior to the increased availability of alternative economic opportunities, common dependence on kuhl irrigation water muted inequalities deriving from caste and position and gave the kohli the leverage to enforce customary rules allocating responsibility for kuhl maintenance and repair between head- and tail-enders. However, as Vichitra Singh explained, "cooperation has disappeared because now people have money." Nonfarm employment opportunities have reduced upstream Rajput households' dependence on agriculture and, by extension, on kuhl water for irrigation. Downstream, lower-caste households have been less successful at obtaining nonfarm jobs, and the jobs they do obtain are relatively low wage. The resulting fragmentation of common dependence on kuhl irrigation water, combined with caste antagonisms, has reduced the leverage that rules and sanctions gave the kohli and downstream users to compel upstream farmers to contribute labor to repair and maintain the kuhl. Consequently, despite the kohli's attempts to coerce upstream hamlets to contribute, free riding has increased and Rajput contributions for kuhl maintenance and repair have declined.

The resulting inequalities grew to the extent that nearly the full burden of maintaining and repairing the kuhl fell on downstream households, while upstream households through whose land the kuhl flowed continued to divert water for irrigation. In protest, the downstream households withdrew from the kuhl. They now divert water for irrigation from nearby small, ephemeral streams that flow only after the onset of the monsoon. With no pre-monsoon water supply for irrigation, residents of the downstream hamlets now sow paddy using the less productive battar method. Although downstream households no longer bear the burden of maintaining and repairing Buhli Kuhl, they must contend with reduced rice and wheat harvests and with increased risk of crop loss from drought or hail. The kohli who preceded Vichitra Singh correctly foresaw the consequences of increasing conflict and diminishment of the kohli's authority—he had predicted that when he was no longer kohli, Buhli Kuhl would become defunct.

The contraction of the command area of Buhli Kuhl does not signal a general decline in social capacity for collective action. Rather, downstream low-caste households and hamlets refused to continue to participate in an increasingly unequal regime. Although Buhli Kuhl is the only kuhl regime in the Neugal watershed from which downstream hamlets withdrew their participation to protest increasing inequality, exercising one's exit strategy as a form of protest is not uncommon. For example, David Mosse (1997a) suggested that low-caste groups withdrew their labor contributions for tank maintenance and management in Tamil Nadu to protest and challenge their subordinate status. He noted that "the abandonment of water management systems here is not the result of a passive process of decay or decline, but the result of active strategies to redefine social and service identities" (1997a:31).

To varying degrees, tensions strain relations between upstream and downstream water users in almost all kuhls in the Neugal watershed, especially in the larger, multivillage ones. This holds true even if the head-end and tail-end villages are of the same caste. For example, the committee meeting minutes for Pathan Kuhl, which irrigates the adjacent Rajput villages of Paror (upstream) and Kharot (downstream), contain numerous references to the fact that farmers from Paror do not participate in khana yet freely use the kuhl's water for irrigation.

In some cases the tension can escalate into violent confrontations. One historical example of this, with contemporary ramifications, is the case of Sapruhl Kuhl. Members of the Girth caste initially constructed this kuhl to convey irrigation water to Kharot and Paror. Oral history recounts that a Gaddi (nomadic herder) who lived in the Gaddi village of Kandi at the foot of the Dhaula Dhar surveyed the kuhl's path. While grazing his flocks in the Dhaula Dhar above the valley, he determined from his vantage point the optimal route for the kuhl. He scattered pulse seeds in a line to mark the route. Later, they germinated, and the Girths excavated the kuhl's channel using the sprouted grain to guide their work. The sponsors

FIG. 27. The shrine at which the sacrificed
daughter-in-law is worshiped, Sapruhl Kuhl.

reportedly paid the excavators rice in volume equivalent to the stones, sand,
and dirt they removed. The kuhl, approximately nine miles long, transports
water from the Baner River watershed (adjacent to the Neugal watershed)
to Kharot and Paror in the Neugal watershed.

Initially, the kuhl would not convey water. Only after sacrificing the
daughter-in-law of one of the Girths by walling her into the kuhl's masonry
did the kuhl flow. To commemorate the event, farmers from Sapruhl Kuhl
worship the daughter-in-law every year at a small temple erected near the
kuhl's danga (fig. 27).[6]

Both oral history and the *Riwaj-i-Abpashi* recount that residents of
upstream Rajput hamlets through whose land the kuhl flowed coveted its
water. In order to gain rights to the kuhl, the Rajputs of the village Lahla
attacked the Girths from Kharot and renamed the kuhl. To help establish
their ownership, they also destroyed a rock inscription near the head of
the kuhl that declared it to be for the Girths of Kharot (fig. 28). The
upstream hamlets were able to restrict the water rights of Kharot and Paror

FIG. 28. The place where the rights of Paror and Kharot residents
in Sapruhl Kuhl are said once to have been engraved in stone.

villages to 16 days and nights of dol. Later, during the colonial period, their
rights were further reduced to only 8 days and nights. The *Riwaj-i-Abpashi*
notes that at the time of its compilation, one of the upstream villages was
contesting the dol rights of Kharot and Paror and the case was pending
with the district commissioner. Residents of Kharot and Paror still refer to
the kuhl by its original name, Sapruhl Kuhl, after the Girth clan that initially
constructed it.

Both downstream Girths and upstream Rajputs employed strategies to
naturalize their claims to the water from this kuhl. These strategies involved
inscribing markers of their water claims onto the landscape—literally, in
stone. Such markers constitute distillations of history and social relations
mapped onto space, part of the contested process of making places by
stretching out social relations over space (Massey 1994:2). Place, constituted
in this way, can also become a site for contesting and renegotiating social
relations. By renaming the kuhl and destroying the rock inscription near
its head, upstream Rajputs attempted to erase the history of Girth claims

to the kuhl. Girth farmers from Paror and Kharot, on the other hand, maintain the social memory of their original rights to the kuhl by recounting the sacrifice of the daughter-in-law and by annually commemorating the event at the temple erected in her honor. The phrase "our blood is in that kuhl," which the kohli used to describe the Girth water claims, invokes the woman's sacrifice and serves as a device to legitimate the rights of Paror and Kharot to the kuhl's water.

Other stories establish the "naturalness" of the downstream villages' rights to the kuhl. One story recounts an incident in which farmers from Paror and Kharot, contesting the rights of the upstream Rajput water users, worshipped at the sacrificed woman's temple. They prayed that if the kuhl belonged to the downstream villages, then the upstream villages should not receive its water. Immediately afterward, a landslide blocked the kuhl's main channel. The upstream farmers were unable to clear the debris until the downstream farmers (the proven rights holders) from Paror and Kharot offered to help. The story ends by stating that this was the manner in which the farmers of Paror and Kharot were able to gain back at least eight days and nights of dol rights in the kuhl.

A more secular piece of evidence that downstream farmers marshal in support of their water claims is the fact that the villages of Paror and Kharot pay the tax for a small patch of land at the kuhl's diversion structure, even though the diversion structure is approximately 10 miles from the boundary of either village. They argue that the original sponsor of the kuhl purchased the plot when the kuhl was built; in their view this further legitimates their claims to the kuhl's water.

Conflicts between the downstream villages of Paror and Kharot and the upstream Rajput village of Lahla continue to this day. I walked the length of Sapruhl Kuhl with its kohli, Laxman Das (also the kohli for Kathul Kuhl), during the period of downstream dol rights. As we passed by the fields of upstream landowners (those whose ancestors had wrested control of the kuhl from the downstream Girths), the kohli noticed that several were illicitly using the kuhl's water for field preparation and mach. Rather than angrily confronting the farmers and shouting insults (a frequent occurrence under such circumstances), Laxman Das continued to walk alongside the kuhl and, without pausing, called out a reference to their illicit water use loudly enough that the farmers were sure to hear. Laxman Das explained later that it was not worth his risking bad relations and recriminations with the farmers of the upstream villages, especially when the downstream villagers' rights to the water lasted for only eight days and nights. This reflected a general sentiment that neither the kohli nor the 12 pairs of farmers from Paror and Kharot who guarded the kuhl around the clock during the time of their dol rights could entirely stop illicit water use by upstream Rajput villages.

Declining Kohli Authority

Earlier I described the inability of the kohli of Buhli Kuhl to enforce rules for pushing the burden of khana upstream and up the social hierarchy. This inability reflects the general erosion of the kohli's authority. The topic was a common theme in many of my conversations with kohlis. The declining authority of the kohli is tightly linked to increasing nonfarm employment and the declining salience of caste- or ritual-service-based authority systems.[7] The salience of village rules and norms declines as households shift their economies from subsistence agriculture to nonfarm, market-based activities. Participation in wider economic systems, when it reduces dependence on local systems, weakens forms of authority that evolved in a context of mutual dependence on local natural resources. Previously, common dependence on local resource systems constituted the basis for regulating communal activities and the source of legitimacy for rules governing those activities. The fragmentation of this dependence has weakened the legitimacy of rules and the ability of caste- or service-based authorities to enforce them.

The declining authority of the kohli reflects these processes. Previously, kohlis were respected; some were feared and associated with supernatural powers. Many farmers recounted how, when the demand for kuhl water peaked for field preparation and paddy sowing and water supply was at its annual minimum, the kohli used to walk the kuhl, overseeing water distribution and resolving water conflicts on the spot. His long turban and cane were adequate reminders of his authority and helped ensure that his word held. In some cases, his knowledge about the control, transport, and distribution of water extended to supernatural realms. The kohli's role as officiant in the puja to the kuhl's *devi* (goddess) and to Quaja Pir reinforced his authority. Local stories tell how kohlis provided water for their kuhls during droughts by supplicating the kuhl's devi. The story "Never Argue with the Kohli" (Appendix 2) illustrates the negative consequences of questioning a kohli's decision and the appeal he can make to supernatural forces to enforce it. Often, the right to be kohli was a valued warisi, an inheritable right similar to that pertaining to property in land or a family's claim to hold a village office, which often stemmed from having played an important role in the initial construction of the kuhl.[8]

In recent years the authority and respect accorded the kohli have declined. The hereditary right to be kohli is in some cases now a liability rather than a privilege. Fifteen years ago, the Brahman clan that held the hereditary right to the position of upstream kohli for Raniya Kuhl relinquished its claim to that position. The last kohli from the clan said that he quit because he could no longer resolve conflicts between farmers or mobilize them for khana. In his words, farmers "no longer minded" him. Many current kohlis say they would prefer that their sons get nonfarm jobs and not assume the responsibilities associated with what they consider to be the relatively thankless, difficult, and poorly remunerated responsibilities of the kohli.

Many kohlis also face increased difficulty in collecting their in-kind payments at harvest time. The minutes of committee meetings are replete with admonitions stating the rates at which the kohli was to be compensated and the sanctions that would be applied to those who did not pay him. Mosse (1997a) described farmers' resistance to compensating water tenders in the tank systems of Tamil Nadu as a challenge to the social relations that governed water management and to the water tenders themselves. Reluctance to pay the kohli his agreed-upon share of the harvest similarly constitutes a challenge to the institution of kohli. Those most reluctant to contribute to him are most likely those who benefit least from kuhl irrigation water and who depend on agriculture only minimally.

One of kohlis' most often repeated complaints was about the frustrations associated with trying to accomplish khana with fewer men than previously. In some cases the work had been left undone. In 1988, Kishori Lal, kohli of Raniya Kuhl, hired migrant laborers for the spring khana, and in 1991 the khana for Kathul Kuhl was left unfinished. Kishori Lal also described the difficulty he faced in collecting the monetary payment a household was expected to contribute in lieu of providing labor for canal cleaning. He said he would go to the same house only three times. If by the third visit payment was not forthcoming, he would not return. To continue asking for payment would be an affront to his honor and self-respect. This appears to be a general phenomenon—kohlis and farmers alike mentioned the increasing difficulty with which kohlis were able to resolve water conflicts and ensure compliance with their decisions.

Changing Cropping Patterns

The fourth way in which increased nonfarm employment has affected kuhl regimes is by causing changes in cropping patterns. Labor shortages for kuhl maintenance and repair, resulting from increased nonfarm employment, have led to increasingly uncertain water supplies, especially in the downstream portions of some kuhls. Shifts in the method of paddy seed sowing and location-specific changes in cropping patterns reflect farmers' responses to these conditions. Most changes in cropping patterns are related to declining water availability; they include shifts from sprouted to dry seed paddy sowing, from sugarcane to wheat, and from paddy to maize. Farmers in Kangra Valley prefer to sow mach over battar because of its greater yield, but in the downstream portions of four kuhls, the area sown using the dry seed method has increased while sprouted seed sowing has decreased. The increasing risks of water scarcity, especially in larh and tail-end areas, offset the productivity advantage of sowing sprouted seeds.

In response to location-specific declines in water availability, farmers have begun to substitute maize for paddy in the downstream portions of the command areas of larger kuhls. Maize requires much less water than paddy. Usually, only one irrigation is necessary, just prior to field preparation. During the winter months, households use maize flour to make a nourishing unleavened bread enjoyed with spinach or mustard greens topped with *desi ghee* (homemade clarified butter). The shift from paddy to maize has occurred almost exclusively in the larh regions of the command areas of some kuhls. This shift is a response to reduced flows in the kuhl's main channel and consequent reductions in water delivery to larh areas, which have lower priority for irrigation than har areas.

A third cropping pattern change concerns the cultivation of sugarcane. The spatial distribution of sugarcane, given its heavy water requirements, is a good indicator of changing patterns of water availability. Sugarcane has virtually disappeared from the tail-end sections of kuhls and the larh areas of most villages; invariably, wheat has replaced it. However, its cultivation has also declined substantially throughout Kangra Valley. The general decline of the area planted to sugarcane is perhaps more strongly related to the availability of relatively inexpensive processed sugar and other sugarcane products grown in the plains states of neighboring Punjab and Haryana than to changes in kuhl water availability.

A final change in cropping patterns concerns what Yashwant Negi (1993) called "social fallow." That is, some farmers in Himachal Pradesh have simply stopped cultivating some irrigated paddy fields, but they have done so because of severe household labor shortages rather than for the more common purpose of restoring a field's productivity before resuming cultivation.[9] The uncultivated fields now produce valuable fodder that is harvested for livestock feed. The decision to cease cultivating fields results from a combination of factors, including increasing household labor shortages and water scarcity as well as regional fodder shortages, especially during the winter. In Kangra, fodder supplies during winter months are so inadequate that farmers from Punjab find it lucrative to truck crop residues to Kangra, where they are sold as fodder.

KUHL REGIME RESPONSES TO THE STRESSES ASSOCIATED WITH INCREASING NONFARM EMPLOYMENT

The tensions arising from increasing nonfarm employment have differentially affected the 39 kuhls in the Neugal watershed. The diverse responses among kuhl regimes to these tensions reflect each regime's particular social and ecological characteristics. Ten regimes persist relatively unchanged; these kuhls are informally managed without a kohli. Twenty kuhl regimes modified their organizational structure at both the operating and the institutional levels (Ciriacy-Wantrup 1969). Responses at the operating level included changing the remuneration rates for the kohli, reorganizing the mobilization of resources for kuhl maintenance and repair, and formalizing kuhl management activities. Their day-to-day management is the responsibility of generally one, but in a few cases two or more, hereditary or elected kohlis. Responses at the institutional level included the formation of kuhl committees, with their varied structures, functions, mechanisms of accountability, and degrees of effectiveness, and the renegotiation of relations between individual kuhl regimes and the state government. It is these institutional-level responses that I deal with in the following subsections.

The remaining nine kuhls, since the late 1960s and early 1970s, have been managed by the Himachal Pradesh Irrigation and Public Health Department (IPHD). The panchayats (elected village councils) of the areas these kuhls used to irrigate negotiated with the IPHD for it to assume responsibility for kuhl management under the Himachal Pradesh Minor Canals Act.[10] The state government's management of these nine kuhls constitutes a direct and total subsidy because it has yet to assess or collect any water tax from the farmers whose land the kuhls irrigate.

The IPHD's direct involvement in managing these nine kuhls, and the indirect involvement of other state agencies and departments through occasional grants for the repair of committee-managed kuhls, has been instrumental in preserving the overall viability of the kuhl networks in the Neugal watershed. The reasons for the willingness of these state agencies to participate in irrigation management, although varied, are grounded in the ideology of the developmentalist, socialist welfare state. More instrumentalist motivations within the IPHD include increasing the department's power relative to other departments and justifying an expanding budget. The expectation of political support in return for financial subsidies for kuhl repair is a less direct but nevertheless significant motivation that informs the giving of subsidies by the civil administration and, on occasion, of grants brokered by locally elected political leaders.

Kuhl Committees: Structure and Function

In the Neugal watershed, 14 kuhl regimes have formed committees, all since 1950. Local officers of the Punjab state government organized the two earliest kuhl committees (for Pangwan and Pathan Kuhls) in the early 1950s as part of a more general effort to form agricultural cooperative societies to disseminate green revolution technology, subsidize agricultural inputs, and improve access to rural credit. When these two committees were created and registered under the 1860 Cooperative Societies Registration Act, they were given a set of bylaws specifying the purpose of the committee, membership criteria, the committee's officers and their duties, the records it should maintain, and its general functions. Because the committees are registered, an officer of the Department of Cooperative Societies audits their account books annually. Of the 14 kuhl committees in the Neugal watershed, only these two are registered under the 1860 act.[11]

These two initial "cooperative irrigation societies," as they were originally called, constituted the organizational blueprint on which irrigators modeled subsequent kuhl committees. All kuhl committees share a remarkably similar corporate structure. Each consists of a governing head of elected officers that includes a president, sometimes a vice-president, and a secretary and treasurer. Elections are usually held once a year. The voting members of the committee sometimes include landowners and cultivators within the kuhl's command area.

Kuhl committees were formed for three reasons: to increase the legitimacy of the kohli, to facilitate acquisition of government funds for

TABLE 8. Reasons for the Establishment of Kuhl Committees
in the Neugal Watershed

Kuhl	Year Started	Reason Started
Bhradi	1970	D
Bhagotla	1986	L
Kathul	1970	L, G, D
Sapruhl	1965	L, G
Pathan	1952	L, G
Makruhl	1974	L, G
Samruhl	1950s	L
Raniya	1952	L, G
Taruhl	1989	L, G
Chamruhl	1989	L, G
Masanol	1974	L
Pangwan	1954	L, G
Sonia	1950s	L, G
Gagruhl	1977–78	L

SOURCE: Author's field notes.

KEY: L = to increase legitimacy of kohli; G = to facilitate acquisition of government funds for kuhl repair; D = to defend against external threats to a kuhl's water supply.

kuhl repair, and to defend against external threats to a kuhl's water supply (Table 8). The relative importance of each of the three varied from kuhl to kuhl. The most common reason was to strengthen the declining authority of the hereditary kohli by providing more formal, rule-governed institutional support for the position and creating additional accountability mechanisms. In this regard, committees fulfill three functions: they provide an arena above the kohli for resolving conflicts between farmers and for backing up the kohli's decisions, they create rules governing kuhl maintenance and repair, and they provide the means to monitor and enforce rules and to sanction rule violators.

Kuhl committees constitute a level of decision-making authority one step removed from and above that of the kohli. They neither compete with him for authority nor supplant his authority. The importance of a hierarchy of arenas for resolving conflicts was articulated by nearly every farmer I interviewed. Almost without exception, farmers explained that a conflict between two people regarding water would travel up to higher arenas of conflict resolution until it reached the one that had the authority and enforcement capacity to match the strength of the conflict. Ranked in terms of enforcement capacity from lesser to greater, these arenas were the kohli, the kuhl committee, the panchayat, and the subdistrict magistrate (SDM), the police, or both.[12]

The minutes of committee meetings contain numerous references to the ways in which kuhl committees reinforce the kohli's authority. Resolutions commonly reinforce his authority to block unauthorized water diversions and withhold water from those who steal it or use it out of turn, especially during times of water scarcity. Sonia Kuhl serves as an example. This kuhl irrigates 25 hectares in the Rajput village of Panapar, in the downstream portion of the Neugal watershed. On July 20, 1987, its committee decided that because of water scarcity, the kohli, with the help of a carpenter, would install bamboo flow regulating devices (thellu) at every diversion point beginning the next day. In anticipation of upcoming water conflicts, the committee emphasized that water would be withheld from the fields of farmers who stole or misused it and that the committee would hold those farmers responsible for any resulting damage to other farmers' crops. The committee also stated that those who fought with the kohli would be referred to the subdistrict magistrate in Palampur. Meeting minutes also sometimes reflect a committee's self-conscious recognition of the limits of its own and the kohli's power. For example, on July 10, 1980, the committee for Gagruhl Kuhl, a small kuhl adjacent to Sonia Kuhl, declared that it would not be responsible for resolving nighttime quarrels over water.

Frequently, committees also uphold the kohli's right to a specified share of the harvest of the kharif crop and, often in response to complaints by the kohli, intervene to help him collect his share from reluctant farmers. Committees commonly pass resolutions stating that farmers who do not pay the agreed-upon fines for not participating in khana or for water stealing will be referred to the village panchayat *pradhan* (elected head). The committee for Gagruhl Kuhl asked the panchayat pradhan to collect the overdue fees from farmers who had not paid their share of the stonecutter's fee for repairing a collapsed section of the kuhl.

A kuhl committee can also provide an arena for discussing and resolving conflicts between the kohli and farmers dissatisfied with his work. In 1982 a group of farmers from Kharot, during a kuhl committee meeting, lodged an extensive set of written complaints against Dhyan Singh, the kohli of Pathan Kuhl. They accused him of water mismanagement and inadequate organization for kuhl maintenance and repair and expressed their dissatisfaction with his attitude. They stated that Dhyan Singh did not understand his role, considered himself an important person, and did not understand how to "take work from farmers," referring to the mobilization of labor for khana, kuhl repair, and danga construction. They alleged that he quarreled with and "abused"—shouted and yelled at—farmers. The minutes noted that at this point the kohli interjected that he had no need of their grain payment. The committee responded to some of these complaints by ruling that requests for water from those without formal water rights had first to be approved by the committee before the kohli could actually arrange for the water delivery. Although it is unclear whether and how the committee resolved the issues the farmers raised, it is probable that they reflected an ongoing set of dynamics. Several years later the committee noted that Dhyan Singh had pledged to work "honestly and sincerely." Among other things, the meeting minutes noted that the kohli was not a dictator and that neither flattery nor threats were acceptable ways of obtaining water from him.

Committees also attempt to resolve conflicts between farmers. For example, in April 1988 the committee for Pangwan Kuhl considered an ongoing conflict in which a farmer in the upper portion of the kuhl's command area had blocked the water channel, depriving 26 downstream farmers of water during the rabi season (when irrigation water is used for wheat and potato production). The downstream farmers submitted a written application to the committee, asking its members to resolve the issue. Despite multiple attempts, after a 15-day period the committee determined that it could not prevail upon the upstream farmer to allow water to flow through the channel. It referred the issue to the panchayat and asked the subdistrict magistrate also to investigate the case. The issue resurfaced in July of that year when water scarcity prior to the monsoon was at its peak. The committee visited the area where the kuhl had been blocked and noted that the channel, which the patwari (village revenue officer) had reopened, had again been blocked. While the committee members were unblocking the channel, family members of the upstream farmer came and threatened the committee by saying they would kill anyone who opened it. The committee members were able to convince the family to allow water to flow for 24 hours to save the paddy crop of the 80 to 90 affected downstream kanals. The committee noted in its minutes, however, that if the channel was blocked again, it would take no more action, because of the danger of possible bloodshed.

In addition to resolving particular conflicts or forwarding them to a decision-making arena with greater authority, committees make decisions regarding general kuhl management. Such decisions are usually made when all the irrigation society members meet just before or during the hot season before the monsoon begins. At these meetings, members discuss current issues and conflicts (particularly those related to the upcoming irrigation season), review prior rules, and sometimes develop new rules, and committee officers make their reports. A common management decision made during the late spring meeting is to set the date for khana, or else to instruct the kohli to set the date and notify irrigators, often by beating a drum and calling out the announcement.

Additional meetings are called as necessary throughout the kharif season. Meetings are often held in June to determine the order and conditions under which the kuhl's water will be rotationally distributed to farmers for field preparation. The committee generally sets the order (including date and time period) in which secondary and tertiary channels will receive water. Accompanying this decision are statements reiterating that only the kohli is authorized to guide the kuhl's water from channel to channel and that farmers who did not participate in that season's khana will not receive water unless they pay the determined fines. At these meetings, committee members emphasize that it is the farmers' responsibility to finish their field preparation during the time they are allotted water and that neither the committee nor the kohli is obligated to provide more water if field preparation is not completed within the specified time. These meetings also are forums for discussing issues related to kuhl maintenance and repair, including problems with the quality of khana and suggested rule changes.

After the period of rotational water distribution, kuhls with low water flows, because of less-than-average snowfall the previous winter, declining kuhl maintenance, water theft, or upstream diversions, often shift to a regulated, continuous-flow water distribution system. Near the end of the period of rotational water deliveries, a meeting is held to discuss the installation of thellu at every tup in the kuhl. The committee or the kohli may recommend installation of thellu to help ensure equitable water distribution and to reduce the inevitable conflicts between farmers that arise under these conditions. The kuhl committee meets, generally approves the kohli's recommendation, and authorizes the construction and installation of thellu for each tup. The kohli supervises this process. If water scarcity worsens to the point that even with thellu installed, portions of the kuhl's command area are not receiving their share of the rationed water, then the kohli suggests that rotational water delivery be substituted for continuous-flow irrigation. If the committee agrees, then in consultation with him it determines the timing and order of the rotations. The irrigation schedule is written in the proceedings book, and at the specified time and date the thellu are removed and rotational water delivery begins. This practice is common to all the kuhl committees on the right bank of the Neugal River from Pathan Kuhl through Gagruhl Kuhl.

Perhaps one of the most important written records committees and kohlis maintain is the attendance register. Kohlis note in attendance registers which families provided labor for khana and which did not. Some registers, such as those for Pathan Kuhl (discussed earlier), illustrate declining rates of participation, but others do not. Table 9, which summarizes information contained in khana attendance records for four kuhls—Masanol, Bhagotla, Gagruhl, and Pangwan—shows that participation in these four kuhls generally did not decline between 1974 and 1993. Each of them irrigates only har areas for which no alternative water sources are available. Each kuhl has a committee. The irrigator groups of all but one kuhl (Bhagotla) are multicaste, but in none of them does land appear to be as unequally distributed as it is in Saloh village (Raniya Kuhl).

Table 9 does show that rates of participation were generally low, that they varied from year to year, and that except for Bhagotla Kuhl, they were not declining. The declining participation rate for Bhagotla Kuhl may have been related to the creation of a kuhl committee and the election of a new kohli in 1986, the year attendance records were started. I suspect that prior to 1986, attendance had already declined, probably because of nonfarm employment. In response, the irrigators created a kuhl committee and chose a new kohli. The increasing rate of nonfarm employment, the assumption that attendance records would not have been instituted without a need for them, and statements by the kohlis of all these kuhls that participation had declined suggests that without attendance records, participation would have been lower or that if attendance records had not improved participation rates, they at least had given the kohli and kuhl committee leverage for assessing fines against farmers with high absenteeism.

Does low participation imply free riding? Are the same people absent each time khana is called, or are most people absent part of the time? Table 9 shows that participation rates for Pangwan Kuhl—that is, the percentage of those requested to participate who were actually present—varied from 23 to 29 percent between 1990 and 1993. Analysis of the names in the attendance registers for Pangwan Kuhl reveals that out of a total of 66 irrigators, other than three individuals, no farmer except the kohli was present for more than half the announced workdays. Thirty-five irrigators

TABLE 9. Average Rates of Participation in *Khana* for Masanol, Gagruhl, Bhagotla, and Pangwan Kuhls, 1974–1993

	Masanol			Gagruhl			Bhagotla			Pangwan		
Year	D	W	P	D	W	P	D	W	P	D	W	P
1974	2	51	58	—	—	—	—	—	—	—	—	—
1975	4	60	41	—	—	—	—	—	—	—	—	—
1976	4	93	52	—	—	—	—	—	—	—	—	—
1977	4	90	47	—	—	—	—	—	—	—	—	—
1978	11	205	40	—	—	—	—	—	—	—	—	—
1979	6	159	59	5	97	30	—	—	—	—	—	—
1980	6	126	37	13	243	29	—	—	—	—	—	—
1981	9	278	51	13	164	20	—	—	—	—	—	—
1982	—	—	—	16	211	21	—	—	—	—	—	—
1983	—	—	—	13	276	33	—	—	—	—	—	—
1984	—	—	—	7	149	33	—	—	—	—	—	—
1985	—	—	—	7	124	28	—	—	—	—	—	—
1986	—	—	—	2	63	49	1	30	65	—	—	—
1987	—	—	—	3	49	38	1	30	65	—	—	—
1988	—	—	—	7	185	41	4	69	60	—	—	—
1989	—	—	—	8	134	26	1	15	34	—	—	—
1990	—	—	—	1	27	42	1	17	37	13	240	25
1991	3	81	46	19	325	27	1	15	34	16	275	23
1992	2	91	70	18	365	32	1	20	43	7	138	25
1993	—	—	—	33	355	17	1	15	34	16	381	29

NOTE: Between 1982 and 1987, Masanol Kuhl had collapsed. Prior to 1986, khana attendance records were not maintained for Bhagotla Kuhl. Attendance records for remaining data gaps were lost, misplaced, or otherwise unavailable.

KEY: D = number of days called for khana; W = total number of person workdays contributed; P = percentage of those requested to participate who were actually present.

came for 20 to 50 percent of the announced workdays, 12 came between 10 and 20 percent of the time, 11 came between 5 and 10 percent, and 4 never came. Of the four who never came, two were women from woman-headed households. There are strong proscriptions against women's participating in khana, so unless there is a son in the family who can be sent, these households are excused. These attendance records show that low participation rates do not necessarily imply that a minority of farmers contributes the majority of the labor for khana. In Pangwan Kuhl, most farmers participate in khana fewer than half the days for which khana is called. The committee fines those who rarely or never come.

The specific configuration of social relations among the irrigators of a kuhl shapes the differential meaning and effectiveness of structurally similar committees. Every kuhl regime that maintains attendance records has also developed some system for collecting fees from or imposing fines on households that do not contribute labor for kuhl maintenance. The money collected is used to purchase materials and supplies, such as shovels and cement, for kuhl repair and maintenance. The issue of fines for absenteeism during khana is a recurring theme during committee meetings. A common de jure rule is that for every day a household does not contribute labor, it must give the equivalent of a laborer's daily wage (25–30 rupees in the early 1990s). But because participation in khana averages only 25 to 50 percent of the people expected to contribute labor, implementing and enforcing this rule is extremely difficult and time consuming, if not impossible. The de facto solution is to fine only households that are very absent—that in a particular year never contribute labor or perhaps provide labor only once or twice. The Pangwan Kuhl committee has created a rule that is feasible to implement. Rather than assessing the daily wage rate for every day of absence, a fine of 30 rupees is levied for every six days of absence. The effect of this rule is to encourage farmers to turn out for khana two or three times a year, which is what most do anyway. This solution to the problem of rule-breaking behavior conforms closely to game theory modeling in which "measured reactions" rather than the "grim trigger strategy" counter small deviations from the rule (Ostrom, Gardner, and Walker 1994).

In contrast to the kohli of Pangwan Kuhl, the kohli for Raniya Kuhl, Kishori Lal, neither maintains accurate attendance records nor even attempts to collect fines. This is because of the high level of conflict among the kuhl's irrigators, who are riven by caste and wealth inequalities and whose committee a few large landowning families control. In Samruhl Kuhl, a fine system initiated in the early 1980s caused women from de facto woman-headed households (a result of male out-migration) to have to participate in communal work parties. In response, in 1983 the kuhl committee, which included two women members, and irrigators resolved the issue by substituting a monetary fee based on the area a household cultivated (1.0 rupee per kanal) in lieu of labor contributions (the fee was increased to 1.5 rupees per kanal in 1989 and to 2.0 rupees per kanal in 1990).

These three examples illustrate the quite different functions played by structurally identical kuhl committees. The Pangwan Kuhl committee's fine system effectively mitigated against the pull of nonfarm employment; the committee for Raniya Kuhl was a means (albeit unsuccessful) for local elites to maintain their threatened hierarchical authority; and the committee for Samruhl Kuhl was an effective vehicle for shifting from labor to monetary contributions for kuhl maintenance and repair. The innovation of substituting monetary for labor contributions for khana, first instituted by the committee for Samruhl Kuhl in the early 1980s under the leadership of a female committee president, had been adopted by several other kuhl regimes in the Neugal watershed by the early 1990s.

Apart from setting fines for failing to participate in khana, committees levy fines and fees for other reasons. They may charge membership fees for the irrigation society (membership is open to both owner-cultivators and tenant-cultivators) and fees to cover expenses for kuhl repair (e.g., stonecutter fees and materials). Fees are sometimes based on a sliding scale, calibrated to landownership. The committee for Gagruhl Kuhl decided in 1979 to charge large landowners twice as much as it did small landholders to cover the costs of repairing the danga. In Pathan Kuhl, farmers with four kanals of land or less were exempted from charges for khana altogether. Some committees levy fines for water stealing, and the committee for Pathan Kuhl even established a reward system: if the danga was damaged by fishers (or downstream water users), then a 50-rupee reward was given to the person who identified the responsible parties. A reward of 10 rupees went to anyone who reported on farmers who made illegal holes to allow water to flow into their fields.

As I mentioned earlier, the second of the three reasons (and the second most common one) for the formation of kuhl committees was to facilitate the acquisition of government funds for kuhl repair and maintenance. Committees represent the common interests of the irrigation society to various branches and departments of the state government in order to gain such monetary support. A kuhl regime that has a committee can more easily request government money than can one without a committee. The ability of a committee to acquire government funds derives from its accountability to government agencies and the ability of its officers to approach government officials. A block development officer or subdistrict magistrate is more likely to authorize funds for kuhl repair if they are channeled through an organized committee that can be held accountable for the money than through an individual kohli. A kohli may not have received higher secondary education nor be skilled in the bargaining and negotiation that inevitably accompany local-level government funding. In most cases the officers of a kuhl committee have those skills and can be more successful than the kohli at acquiring government grants.

There are numerous examples of committees interacting with branches of the state government. The committee for Samruhl Kuhl successfully petitioned the block development officer several times for funds to help rebuild portions of its main kuhl channel. The committee for Sonia Kuhl requested the Public Works Department to repair a bridge over a kuhl that had collapsed and flooded adjacent fields. The Pangwan Kuhl committee also successfully requested funds from the block development officer to repair sections of its main kuhl channel that had been destroyed by floods.

Interactions with the state government are not limited to requests for funds and support. The two cooperative irrigation societies, which are registered under the Cooperative Societies Registration Act, are also audited annually by officers of the Department of Cooperative Societies. The audit focuses primarily on the societies' financial management. Although financial accountability is important even for kuhl committees, it is less a high-stakes issue for them than for agricultural cooperative societies, which provide loans and agricultural inputs at subsidized prices to their members.

The third primary reason for forming kuhl committees is that they can defend irrigators against external threats to the kuhl's water supply. Two kuhl committees were formed primarily for this purpose. Threats to a kuhl's water source usually derive from an upstream claimant, which might be a village through whose land the kuhl flows or a state-managed kuhl whose diversions threaten the water flows of its downstream neighbors. In the case of Bhradi Kuhl, its shareholders organized a kuhl committee to protect their water interests, which were threatened by the state-sponsored construction of an adjacent upstream kuhl. The committee mobilized financial resources from its members and challenged the Irrigation and Public Health Department in court. In 1988, the district court decided the case in favor of Bhradi Kuhl, against the state of Himachal Pradesh. Creating a kuhl committee enabled the irrigators of Bhradi Kuhl to mobilize more resources, to be held more accountable for managing those resources, to have greater standing in the district court, and to more effectively represent their interests in the courtroom than they would have been able to do without a committee.

Kuhl Committees and the State

The rational, bureaucratic organization of kuhl committees, as well as their formal rules of operation, reflect the imperatives of conforming to an organizational mold recognized and legitimated by the state. The form of the committees certainly did not spring from local idioms of social organization. Instead, it reflects the hegemonic imprint of the modern, bureaucratic nation-state on local resource management organizations. Recall that the first two kuhl committees, termed cooperative irrigation societies, were formed at the instigation of local officers of the Punjab state government involved in forming agricultural cooperatives and that the officers gave the organizational template for the committee structure. The institutionalization of this organizational form within the modern Indian state accounts for the striking similarity in the corporate organization of all kuhl committees.

The number of village-level societies, cooperatives, and committees has mushroomed since the community development initiatives of the 1950s. Government agencies organized many of these. If registered with the Department of Cooperative Societies, the block development officer, or any other government agency, a committee must conform to the specified organizational structure. This explains the structural similarity between, for example, women's village organizations in the nearby Changar region and kuhl committees in Kangra Valley. The organizational structure of these local societies, cooperatives, and committees, which arose autonomously, without government involvement, conforms to the dominant organizational template.

The structural similarity of formalized local organizations is consistent with theories in political science and sociology associated with new institutionalism. Pamela Tolbert and Lynne Zucker (1983) argued that the institutional environment affects organizational structure primarily by legitimating a "new procedure, position, or element of structure," especially when hierarchically higher elements of the environment—that is, regulatory agencies or institutions with the power to provide financial or technical support—establish implicit or explicit requirements that the organization must satisfy before support will be given. Tolbert and Zucker's analysis explains the relatively rapid diffusion of kuhl committees as a key organizational response to a hierarchical institutional environment—the rational bureaucratic nation-state, which legitimates certain organizational forms. In order to successfully negotiate and interact with the civil administration, irrigators are subtly compelled to organize themselves in a manner consistent with the organizational norms of the institutional environment in which they find themselves.

The creation of kuhl committees also sheds light on the transnational workings of modernity and statemaking. This issue comes into focus when we notice the striking resemblance between the organizational template irrigators adopted for kuhl committees in Kangra and the organizational form Hispano irrigators utilized in the American Southwest when they incorporated their community-based, gravity-flow irrigation systems (*acequias*) in the 1960s. Gregory Hicks and Devon Peña (2003) described how irrigators of one acequia in the Culebra watershed of southern Colorado bowed to pressure from the state engineer's office to incorporate their irrigation system in order to qualify for government grants to subsidize the cost of "modernizing" the main irrigation channel—that is, lining it with concrete to reduce leakage. The state engineer's office perceived such leakage as inefficient and, ignoring the important ecosystem services associated with "leakage," had pressured the irrigators to incorporate, apply for government support, and line the main channel (Hicks and Peña 2003:143). The "boilerplate" organizational model that the San Luis People's Ditch consequently adopted included bylaws and an organizational structure in all respects similar to that of the first two "cooperative irrigation societies" in the Neugal watershed.[13]

The remarkable similarity between the template in the Neugal watershed and the boilerplate in the Culebra watershed is not coincidental; on the contrary, the two share the same statemaking roots. We can trace these shared roots back to the emergence of "modern," "scientific" models of agricultural development during the first half of the twentieth century in the United States (Berry 2003).[14] Kim Berry shows how, during the early 1950s, international development agencies exported to newly independent India the same model of "progressive" agricultural development and gender relations that the U.S. Agricultural Extension Service had promulgated in North America. In India this model was interpolated with discourses of nation-building and the creation of an Indian modernity. It became the basis for much of the agricultural development and extension work in India during the years immediately following Independence, including the work of officers of the Punjab Cooperatives Department in Kangra. Berry notes that the model incorporated key elements of North American modernity, including state support for efficient resource use and an absolute faith in science and technology. Thus the template for kuhl committees and the boilerplate for acequia incorporation were poured from the same rational, bureaucratic mold. The former is a product of the politics of nation-building and transnational development aid in India, and the latter, a product of the faith in science and technology that is one of the hallmarks of North American modernity and governmentality.

What have been the effects of the bureaucratization of kuhls on the forms of authority that are salient for their management? In short, the creation of kuhl committees and increased interaction with the state has enlarged the basis of authority for kuhl management from charisma, personality, and local knowledge to include also literacy, wealth, and demonstrated ability to negotiate with government bureaucracies. Under some conditions, especially where interaction with the state is a vital concern of the kuhl regime, this may have shifted authority for water management away from the hereditary position of watermaster toward the elected members of the committee. In most cases, committees function to back up or support the authority of the kohli to manage the kuhl, mobilize labor, and resolve conflicts. In such cases the authority roles embodied in committees and based on literacy, wealth, and the ability to successfully negotiate with the state complement those of the kohli, based on local knowledge and force of character.

Committees, structured in the image of rational bureaucracy, legitimate forms of authority that differ significantly from those of the watermaster. Committees validate forms of authority based on social and economic status and the ability to interact with and skillfully negotiate grants from civil administrative officers and local political representatives. The people who possess these characteristics are generally the more politically and economically influential members of the community, the local elites. These are the people who are most frequently elected to be committee officers. In some kuhl regimes, committee officers make decisions regarding water management, water distribution, and conflict resolution that the kohli previously made. In these instances the kohli, rather than being the autonomous authority regarding water management that he previously was, now implements the committee's decisions. Whereas previously kohli was a hereditary position, now, in some kuhl regimes with committees, the committee and members of the irrigation society nominate and elect a person to be watermaster for a specified term. These "temporary" kohlis have significantly lower social status than the permanent, hereditary kohlis in the watershed, such as Kehar Singh of Menjha Kuhl and Dyan Singh of Pathan Kuhl. They are viewed more as semiskilled laborers for whom this is a way to increase their household's meager income.

Does the bureaucratization of kuhl management consolidate elite authority? The answer seems to depend on the degree of inequality and latent conflict among a kuhl's irrigators. Where inequality in terms of landholding size and wealth is relatively high, bureaucratization further consolidates the authority of the local elite, as occurred in Raniya Kuhl. The committee for Raniya Kuhl, dominated by large landowning and high-caste farmers, opposes rules governing labor contributions based on landownership and has blocked moves by the watermaster and other farmers to petition the Irrigation and Public Health Department to take over management of the kuhl for fear that a tax based on landholding size would be assessed. Consequently, large landowners in this kuhl regime now receive a disproportionate share of water relative to their labor contributions. Also, the kohli for Raniya Kuhl, a low-caste stonemason, does not receive the committee's support for collecting fines from households that do not contribute labor for kuhl maintenance and repair. Consequently, free riding has increased. In situations of relatively unequal wealth distribution and manifest or latent conflict among irrigators, kuhl committees' consolidation of authority can exacerbate preexisting fault lines. In such cases the committee may undermine the kohli's authority and strengthen the power of local elites.

On the other hand, the committees of kuhls whose irrigators are more homogeneous in caste and wealth can be effective vehicles for formalizing water management rules and negotiating with the district civil administration for small grants for kuhl repair and maintenance. Even under these conditions, however, bureaucratization tends to shift authority away from the kohli to the committee, because of the different forms of authority that circulate in the realms in which committee members operate. In the shift from relations based on status to those based on social contracts, the role of kohli, when transformed from a permanent hereditary role to a temporary appointment, loses prestige.

FACTORS SHAPING INSTITUTIONAL CHANGE IN KUHL REGIMES

How can we explain the various trajectories of institutional change among kuhl regimes and their differential abilities to persist? The framework offered in this section accounts for the effects on kuhl regimes of the rising opportunity costs of labor associated with increasing nonfarm employment as well as the responses of kuhl regimes to those effects. In particular, it accounts for the differences among kuhl regimes with regard to these effects and associated responses. The framework incorporates three of the four strands described in chapter 1—the social and ecological characteristics of individual kuhl regimes, negotiated relationships with the state, and the effects of regionality on the organization of irrigation institutions.

The first strand involves the ways in which farmers balance the risks and benefits associated with kuhl irrigation water against the costs of the collective action necessary to provide that water. The second strand encompasses the potential role of the state in kuhl management. The state, for the purposes of this analysis, is the totality of different agencies and bureaucracies—in short, "officialdom"—with which irrigators may negotiate for benefits regarding kuhl management, in which they may seek recourse for conflict resolution, or which they may challenge in court when state claims to resources threaten local access and control of water. This strand involves analysis of the nature and effects of the interface between state institutions, local government (including village panchayats), and kuhl regimes. The last strand, regionality, concerns the influence of the social, historical, and institutional landscape of kuhl irrigation on the pattern and nature of kuhl regime responses to the changing context of irrigation.

The first strand—social and ecological variables—informs the analysis of the different effects of nonfarm employment on kuhl regimes. Two multidimensional factors designated "reliance" and "differentiation" describe, respectively, the degree of irrigators' reliance on kuhl water and their socioeconomic differentiation. These factors have both social and ecological components. Together, they provide the basis for discriminating among kuhl regimes in terms of the effects of increasing nonfarm employment. "Reliance" is high when alternative water supplies are unavailable and the kuhl irrigates the fertile and productive har fields adjacent to the Neugal River; it is low when the reverse conditions obtain. "Differentiation" is high when a kuhl irrigates more than one village, the irrigators of the kuhl comprise multiple castes, and land distribution is relatively unequal; it is low when the reverse conditions obtain.

Reliance and differentiation mediate the effects of nonfarm employment. Together, these two summary concepts describe the dependence of irrigators on kuhl water and the potential for conflict among them. Figure 29 summarizes the expected effects of increasing nonfarm employment on kuhl regimes and their probable responses according to degrees of reliance and differentiation. As nonfarm employment increases, the relative reliance and differentiation of a kuhl regime will influence the willingness of irrigators to continue to contribute labor, money, or both for kuhl maintenance and repair. These factors also influence the degree of conflict among irrigators stemming from the fragmentation of common dependence on kuhl water. When reliance is high and differentiation is low, increasing nonfarm employment will minimally affect the kuhl regime.

Differentiation

	Low	High
High Reliance	Effect Minimal Response No formalization No state intervention	Effect Moderate Response High formalization State involvement No signs of collapse
Low	Effect Indeterminate Response Indeterminate	Effect High Response State control of kuhl or signs of potential collapse

FIG. 29. Predicted degree of effect of
nonfarm employment on kuhl regimes and
response, by nature of "reliance" and
"differentiation."

Under these conditions the low coordination requirements of the regime, the relatively equal distribution of incentive to contribute to maintaining and repairing the kuhl, the high productivity of the land the kuhl irrigates, and the lack of alternative water sources minimize potential conflict among resource users.

When reliance and differentiation are both high, increasing nonfarm employment will lead to conflicts within the kuhl regime even though the kuhl irrigates productive har areas and post-monsoon alternative water sources are unavailable. Socioeconomic differentiation among the regime members diversifies the opportunity costs of labor and time across households; those with greater access to nonfarm employment opportunities will be less willing to contribute to the provision of the collective good. Asymmetrical relations governing inputs as well as access to the benefits of the commons may be tolerated to the extent that resource users consider such asymmetry legitimate (O'Neil 1987:172–74). However, when access to nonfarm employment constitutes an increasingly available and attractive exit option (Hirschman 1970), people's willingness to tolerate inequality may decline (Bardhan 1993a:91), as it did in Raniya Kuhl. The conflicts that result from differential opportunity costs for labor and decreasing tolerance for unequal distributions of entitlements and responsibilities, when combined with the high coordination and resource mobilization requirements associated with large-scale systems, challenges the ability of kuhl regimes with high differentiation to maintain their integrity. At the same time, the fact that these are also high reliance kuhl regimes suggests that people have a strong incentive to resolve the conflicts generated by social differentiation, rather than allow the kuhl to collapse.

When reliance is low and differentiation is high, the difficulties associated with mobilizing adequate labor for maintaining and repairing the kuhl and managing conflict will be greatest, because the benefits are fewest. The benefits of maintaining the kuhl are few because of the low productivity of the land the kuhl irrigates, the availability of alternative post-monsoon water sources, or both. The difficulties of maintaining the regime's integrity derive from the user group's being socially and economically differentiated, which leads to greater conflict, and from the high coordination costs of managing a regime that involves multiple villages and irrigates relatively large command areas. For these kuhl regimes, internal stress will be highest and incentives to remain in the regime lowest.[15]

The processes that influence the tensions, conflicts, and stresses in kuhl regimes also shape the responses regime members make to those conditions. The degree of regime formalization, the extent of negotiated state intervention in regime management, and the likelihood of regime collapse depend on the nature of reliance on the benefits the regime provides and the degree of social and economic differentiation within the regime. The high dependence on kuhl water, low coordination requirements, and low conflict potential of high reliance–low differentiation kuhl regimes suggest that these kuhls will be informally organized, with no kohli, and managed independently of state involvement. Irrigators using kuhls that deliver water mostly to high-value crops and who are themselves characterized by social and economic differences (high reliance–high differentiation kuhl regimes) will likely formalize their regime's management structure by creating a committee and formal management rules, and they will negotiate with state authorities for grants for kuhl repair and maintenance. Exigencies emanating from the imperative to interact and negotiate effectively with "officialdom" will influence the organizational character of regime formalization. Kuhls that convey water to low-value crops and whose irrigators are divided by class or caste inequalities (low reliance–high differentiation) will likely show signs of potential collapse or be managed by the Irrigation and Public Health Department. Indicators of potential collapse include shifts in methods of paddy sowing from the water-intensive but higher-yielding sprouted seed method to the less water-intensive and lower-yielding dry seed sowing method, shifts from paddy to maize in larh areas, and contractions in the command areas of kuhls.

Observed Patterns of Kuhl Regime Response to Increasing Nonfarm Employment

We can explore the explanatory capacity of the framework just presented by classifying kuhl regimes according to their expected responses to increasing nonfarm employment, based on their degree of reliance and differentiation. The extent to which expected responses correspond with actual responses reflects the degree to which the framework incorporates the key factors influencing kuhl regimes. A comparison of expected and observed responses, by kuhl, shows that the observed extent of formalization and state intervention in kuhl management and of indications of potential collapse matches the expected extent for 32 of the 39 kuhl regimes in the Neugal watershed.

All 11 low reliance–high differentiation kuhl regimes are either managed by the Irrigation and Public Health Department or show signs of possible system collapse. Three kuhl regimes (Ghran, Patnuhl, and Ghughrul Kuhls) are under IPHD management that were not expected to be, and one kuhl (Menjha Kuhl) shows unexpected signs of potential collapse. The hamlets within the command area of both Ghran and Ghughrul Kuhls are undergoing rapid urbanization associated with the growth of the nearby town of Palampur as a district commercial center. Agricultural areas are being converted to residential and commercial uses. Rates of nonfarm employment are extremely high in the hamlets these kuhls irrigate (88 percent and 85 percent, respectively, as derived from hamlet-level census information). Given these unusual economic circumstances, there was little opposition to the IPHD's proposal to take over management of Ghran Kuhl when its diversion structure and main channel were subsumed by the large cement structure the department constructed for an adjacent cluster of department-managed kuhls. Similarly, Ghughrul Kuhl came under IPHD management because the intensification and diversification of competing urban and agricultural claims for water exceeded private conflict resolution capacities.

Patnuhl Kuhl, too, was not expected to be under department management, given its high reliance and high differentiation. But because less productive larh areas make up approximately one-third of the kuhl's command area and ephemeral streams provide alternative post-monsoon water sources for portions of its har fields, it probably would have been more accurate to classify the regime as having intermediate rather than high reliance. The combination of unusually high indicators of differentiation (the kuhl has four kohlis and a relatively large command area—525 hectares—and irrigates portions of 25 different hamlets) and characteristics that suggest intermediate rather than high levels of reliance suggests that the incentives to maintain the regime's integrity were inadequate to overcome the substantial challenges to collective action required to maintain the kuhl.

Menjha Kuhl was not expected to show signs of potential collapse, yet it did. The ratio of paddy sown with sprouted to dry seed has decreased in its har areas, while in its larh fields maize has begun to replace paddy. The command area of the kuhl has contracted toward the head end. This is probably due to a combination of factors including the proximity of Menjha village to the town of Palampur, which may exacerbate the effects of increasing nonfarm employment, the fact that it has no substantial larh areas within its command area, and its relatively large command area (140 ha).

The observed outcomes confirm the expectation that high reliance–high differentiation kuhl regimes will formalize their organization and continue to function without signs of potential collapse. Ten of the 13 high reliance–high differentiation kuhls formalized their management structures. The three exceptions were Ghughrul, Menjha, and Patnuhl Kuhls, which I have discussed. In addition, three kuhls—Masanol, Bhradi, and Bhagotla Kuhls, all of which were classified as high reliance–low differentiation—that were not expected to form committees did so.

Prior to the early 1970s, Masanol Kuhl had neither a kohli nor a kuhl committee. The irrigators themselves managed the kuhl informally. In the early 1970s, Shri Phulli Ram returned from Rajasthan, where he had been a heavy equipment operator on a large government irrigation project. The kuhl's irrigators asked him to be kohli for Masanol Kuhl, which a flood had destroyed several years earlier and which had since lain dormant. Phulli Ram agreed to be the first kohli for this kuhl. At the same time, a committee was formed to help him mobilize adequate labor to reconstruct the kuhl. The committee was able to secure a grant from its elected representative in the Legislative Assembly to purchase materials for the repairs.

Bhradi and Bhagotla Kuhls also have committees, despite their low differentiation. As described previously, the irrigators of Bhradi Kuhl had organized a committee to facilitate their court case against the IPHD. The kuhl committee for Bhagotla Kuhl was formed in 1986, at the same time the present kohli was chosen. The previous kohli was from a small (fewer than 10 households) upstream hamlet. Although caste and wealth were not divisive issues, the kuhl committee was formed to bolster the new kohli's authority in anticipation of water conflicts based on the locational asymmetries of the two hamlets.

The last class of kuhls, those with high reliance and low differentiation, were expected to remain informally organized with minimal state intervention. Eleven of these 15 kuhl regimes matched the expectation, whereas four kuhls already discussed—Masanol, Bhradi, Bhagotla, and Ghran Kuhls—did not.

Three Classes of Kuhls

The composite factors "reliance" and "differentiation" explain much of the variation among kuhl regime responses to the stresses resulting from expanding nonfarm employment opportunities under conditions of access to state assistance and subsidies and state willingness to assume management of defunct kuhl systems. The seven kuhl regimes that did not respond as anticipated indicate a slight trend among kuhls to be more formalized and have greater degrees of state intervention than expected.

Three broad classes of kuhl regimes emerge from the analysis. Those in the high reliance–low differentiation category are informally organized, with few if any rules, sanctions, or enforcement mechanisms. None has a kohli or a kuhl committee. The stresses resulting from increased nonfarm employment have negligibly affected these kuhl regimes, because of their low potential for conflict among irrigators, their relatively low organizational complexity, and the fact that they irrigate predominantly fertile paddy and wheat-growing fields for which alternative water sources are unavailable.

The farmers of high reliance–high differentiation kuhls have formalized their management structures. All of them have kohlis and, except for Mahang and Loharal Kuhls, have created committees. None of these kuhls exhibits signs of potential collapse. Each kuhl regime has received at least 10,000 rupees (approximately US$250) from the block development officer, the district commissioner, or the Forest Department for kuhl repair work. The high reliance characteristics of these kuhls buffer the tensions generated by increasing nonfarm employment—they are the only sources of irrigation water for highly productive and highly valued paddy and wheat fields.

Regime formalization (the creation of committees and fine systems and formalization of monitoring and sanctioning rules) enables irrigators of these regimes to manage internal stress as well as to broker government grants.

All low reliance–high differentiation kuhl regimes have either been taken over by the Irrigation and Public Health Department or exhibit signs of potential collapse. The high differentiation of these regimes made them particularly vulnerable to increasing levels of conflict resulting from increased nonfarm employment because these irrigators were already riven by preexisting fault lines. Additionally, their low degree of reliance reduced the risks associated with withdrawing from the kuhl because of the availability of alternative post-monsoon water sources, the relatively low productivity of the kuhl's command area, or both. The combination of low reliance and high differentiation in these regimes generated high levels of internal stress and few incentives for investing the resources necessary for their management.

At the watershed level, increasing nonfarm employment opportunities initiated a sequence of responses that produced new patterns of authority and organization for water management. Some kuhl regimes persisted unchanged, some transformed their management structures and negotiated with state authorities for monetary grants, and others came to be managed by the Irrigation and Public Health Department. These differential patterns of change have created a web of multijurisdictional, interconnected kuhls that appear highly resilient at the watershed level, especially with regard to the stresses associated with increasing nonfarm employment. In the next chapter, I address kuhl regime responses to the stresses associated with destructive floods and earthquakes.

5

NETWORKS OF INTERDEPENDENCE

THE FOURTH STRAND OF THE EXPLANATORY TAPESTRY HAS TO DO WITH the role of networks of physical and social linkages between kuhl regimes in enabling their persistence by buffering individual regimes against the effects of recurring environmental shocks such as floods and droughts. Networks can provide kuhl regimes with crucial pulses of resources—generally water but sometimes also labor—following destructive floods. The vignette at the beginning of the introduction described the water-sharing agreement the kohlis of Menjha and Patnuhl Kuhls negotiated in 1952 following the flood unleashed when a temporary landslide dam burst in the headwaters of the Neugal River. After farmers from both kuhls had repaired Patnuhl Kuhl, water from it was diverted for three years into Menjha Kuhl until it, too, was again operational.

Networked kuhl regimes also seem better able to cope with drought than non-networked regimes. In 1989, the monsoon rains were late, creating water shortages for some kuhl regimes in the lower reaches of the Neugal watershed. On June 26, the president of the committee for Sonia Kuhl, Jagat Ram Ohri, lodged a formal request with the committee of Pangwan Kuhl, the next upstream kuhl. He noted that the farmers of Sonia Kuhl were unable to continue with field preparation and paddy sowing because there was little or no water in the kuhl. He asked the committee of Pangwan Kuhl to give the Sonia Kuhl farmers water from Pangwan Kuhl for 48 hours, to allow them to complete their field preparations and paddy sowing. The committee agreed and directed its kohli to notify Mr. Ohri that the full water flow of Pangwan Kuhl would be diverted to Sonia Kuhl for 48 hours.

Without an interkuhl water transfer, farmers from Sonia Kuhl would have had to revert to sowing dry paddy seed (battar).

To what extent does coordination among kuhls reduce the vulnerability of individual kuhl regimes to the risks and stresses associated with environmental shocks such as floods and droughts? Does interkuhl coordination contribute to the resilience—defined as the capacity to absorb disturbances (Holling and Gunderson 2002)—of individual kuhl regimes by buffering them from such shocks? Do interkuhl networks that provide pulses of additional water and labor during periods of intense, short-duration disturbance represent important sources of redundancy that contribute to the persistence of individual kuhl regimes and the overall integrity of the multikuhl irrigation network?

To explore the issues these questions raise, I focus on interkuhl irrigation networks. Networks can be thought of as "vehicles of action" (Hanf and O'Toole 1992:171) through which coordination is organized and problems solved. In the Neugal watershed, the pattern of overlapping kuhl systems creates a network of interconnected regimes. The degree of overlap influences the extent of interconnectedness; within a single watershed there may be clusters of overlapping kuhls as well as kuhls that do not overlap with others. Employing the perspective of a "net thrower"—Todd LaPorte's (1995) term for someone whose vantage point overlooks an entire network—enables description of the overall pattern and linkages that constitute the watershed-level kuhl irrigation network. The network itself is composed of individual "nodes" such as Mr. Ohri, who has the perspective of what LaPorte calls a "net rider."[1] In the rest of this chapter I explore the interconnectedness of individual kuhl regimes, the extent to which it is related to coordination between regimes, and the effects of coordination on regime persistence. I assess the ways in which networks provide redundant sources of needed resources, buffer kuhls from environmental disturbances or stress, and potentially contribute to their resilience.[2]

A "NET THROWER" PERSPECTIVE ON KUHL NETWORKS

Tables 10 and 11 show the pattern of overlapping kuhl networks on the right and left banks, respectively, of the Neugal River. The tables, in which both kuhls and "revenue villages" (mauzas) are arranged from upstream to downstream, provide a basis for differentiating between sets of kuhls that are more or less tightly interconnected. From the village perspective (reading the rows left to right, by village), the tables indicate that most villages are engaged with upstream kuhls that irrigate their larh areas and with downstream kuhls that irrigate their har areas. For example, on the right bank, Sapruhl Kuhl (no. 5) irrigates the larh fields of Kharot village, and Pathan, Rai, and Makruhl Kuhls (nos. 6–8), which lie downstream from Sapruhl Kuhl, irrigate the village's har fields. The same pattern may be observed from the kuhl perspective (reading columns from top to bottom, by kuhl). Generally, kuhls irrigate har and then larh areas of different villages as they flow downstream. For example, on the left bank, Diwan Chand Kuhl (no. 2) irrigates the har fields of three upstream villages and the larh fields of two downstream villages.[3]

The number of kuhls per village can be used as a proxy indicator of the degree of interconnectedness among kuhl regimes. This indicator is based on the assumption that a kuhl that irrigates a village that no other kuhls irrigate is less interconnected than a kuhl that irrigates a village irrigated by several other kuhls. For example, on the right bank, Bhagotla Kuhl (no. 3) is the least interconnected. It irrigates only one village, and it is the only kuhl that irrigates that village. In contrast, Sapruhl Kuhl (no. 5), also on the right bank, is more interconnected because from one to three other kuhls irrigate each of the three villages it irrigates.

Interconnectedness refers to the density of irrigation networks with which a particular kuhl is engaged. The elevational distribution of a village's arable land influences the degree of interconnectedness—a kuhl that irrigates a village whose arable land is dispersed across several elevational niches tends to be more interconnected than one that irrigates a village whose arable land is concentrated at a single elevation.[4] Interconnectedness, measured as the extent of interkuhl linkage, provides opportunities for coordinating water management between kuhl regimes. Interconnected regimes are better able to coordinate among themselves for joint water management than are regimes that are not interconnected. Interconnectedness among overlapping kuhl regimes may increase the resiliency of the watershed-level irrigation network by providing alternative (redundant) sources of water, labor, and other resources during periods of disturbance and shock. If coordination between kuhl regimes buffers individual regimes and reduces their vulnerability to environmental shocks, then it is likely that interconnected regimes are better able to persist than regimes that are not part of an interkuhl network.

Interconnectedness can also lead to conflict between kuhl regimes, because of competition for scarce water supplies. However, intervillage caste affinities, kin and marital ties, and the value of maintaining positive social

TABLE 10. Har (H) and Larh (L) Areas Watered by Kuhls (Numbered) for Villages on the Right Bank of the Neugal River

Village	1	2	3	4	5	6	7	8	9	10	11	12	13	14	15
Kandi	H	H	—	—	—	—	—	—	—	—	—	—	—	—	—
Bhagotla	—	—	H	—	—	—	—	—	—	—	—	—	—	—	—
Lalla	—	—	—	L	H	—	—	—	—	—	—	—	—	—	—
Paror	—	—	—	L	L	H	—	—	—	—	—	—	—	—	—
Kharot	—	—	—	—	L	H	H	H	H	H	H	—	—	—	—
Panapar	—	—	—	—	—	—	H	H	—	—	—	H	—	—	—
Gaggal	—	—	—	—	—	—	H	—	—	—	—	H	H*	—	—
Dhera	—	—	—	—	—	—	L	—	—	—	—	H	—	H	H*
Nora	—	—	—	—	—	—	L	—	—	—	—	—	—	—	—
Purba	—	—	—	—	—	—	LH	—	—	—	—	—	—	—	—

NOTE: Kuhls are arranged from upstream to downstream as follows: (1) Bhradi, (2) Chanogi, (3) Bhagotla, (4) Kathul, (5) Sapruhl, (6) Pathan, (7) Rai, (8) Makruhl, (9) Samruhl, (10) Pangwan, (11) Sonia, (12) Gagruhl, (13) Majettli, (14) Bal, (15) Natyrya. An asterisk (*) indicates that the kuhl is independent of others in the same village.

TABLE 11. Har (H) and Larh (L) Areas Watered by Kuhls (Numbered) for Villages on the Left Bank of the Neugal River

Village	1	2	3	4	5	6	7	8	9	10	11	12	13	14	15	16	17	18	19	20	21	22	23	24
Bandla	H*	H	H	H	H	H	—	—	—	—	—	—	—	—	—	—	—	—	—	—	—	—	—	—
Ghugar	—	H	H	—	H	H	H	—	—	—	—	—	—	—	—	—	—	—	—	—	—	—	—	—
Sidhpur Rani	—	—	—	—	—	L	L	H	H	H	H	H	H	—	—	—	—	—	—	—	—	—	—	—
Sidhpur Sarkari	—	—	—	—	—	—	—	L	H	H	H	H	—	—	—	—	—	—	—	—	—	—	—	—
Khlet	—	H	H	H	—	H	—	—	—	—	—	—	—	—	—	—	—	—	—	—	—	—	—	—
Menjha	—	—	—	—	—	—	—	H	—	—	—	H	L	H	—	—	—	—	—	—	—	—	—	—
Battu Palam	—	—	L	—	—	—	—	—	—	H	H	—	—	—	—	—	—	—	—	—	—	—	—	—
Jasun Samola	—	—	H	—	—	—	—	H	—	—	—	—	—	—	—	—	—	—	—	—	—	—	—	—
Raipur	—	—	H	—	—	H	H	—	—	—	—	H	—	H	—	—	—	—	—	—	—	—	—	—
Henja	—	—	—	H	—	—	H	—	—	—	—	—	—	H	—	—	—	—	—	—	—	—	—	—
Arla	—	—	—	—	—	—	—	—	—	—	—	—	—	—	—	—	—	—	—	—	—	—	—	—
Saloh	—	—	L	—	—	—	H	—	—	—	—	L	—	—	—	—	—	—	—	—	—	—	—	—
Sulah	—	—	—	—	—	—	—	—	—	—	—	—	—	—	H	H*	H*	H*	H*	H*	H*	—	—	—
Paror	—	—	—	—	—	—	—	—	—	—	—	—	—	—	H	—	—	—	—	—	—	—	—	—
Garla Sarkari	—	—	L	—	—	—	—	—	—	—	—	L	—	H	—	—	—	—	—	—	—	—	—	—
Garla Dei	—	—	L	—	—	L	—	—	—	—	—	—	—	H	—	—	—	—	—	—	—	—	—	—
Bhawarna	—	—	—	—	—	L	—	—	—	—	—	—	—	—	—	—	—	—	—	—	—	—	—	—
Ninaon	—	—	—	—	—	—	—	—	—	—	—	—	—	L	—	—	—	—	—	—	—	—	H	—
Daroh	—	L	—	L	—	—	—	—	—	—	—	—	—	—	—	—	—	—	—	—	—	—	H	H
Ghar Jamula	—	—	—	—	—	L	—	—	—	—	—	—	—	—	—	—	—	—	—	—	—	—	—	—
Mundi	—	L	—	—	—	L	—	—	—	—	—	—	—	—	—	—	—	—	—	—	—	—	—	H
Bandahu	—	—	—	—	—	L	—	—	—	—	—	—	—	—	—	—	—	—	—	—	—	—	—	—

NOTE: Kuhls are arranged from upstream to downstream as follows: (1) Ghran, (2) Diwan Chand, (3) Mia Fateh Chand, (4) Dai, (5) Ghughrul, (6) Kirpal Chand, (7) Raniya, (8) Mahang, (9) Loharal, (10) Taruhl, (11) Chamruhl, (12) Patnul, (13) Menjha, (14) Sangar Chand, (15) Masanol, (16) Spein, (17) Sulah da Cho, (18) Saldian, (19) Macchlena, (20) Karni, (21) Rein da Cho, (22) Bouru da Cho, (23) Upperli, (24) Buhli. An asterisk (*) indicates that the kuhl is independent of others in the same village.

relations based on generalized norms of reciprocity mitigate against interkuhl conflict. In his study of tank irrigation in Tamil Nadu, David Mosse (1997a:17–18) also noted that interconnectedness tended to promote coordination more than competition.

A "NET RIDER" PERSPECTIVE ON KUHL NETWORKS

Table 12 shows the various kinds of interkuhl coordination I observed and the kuhls that engaged in them. There were five types of interkuhl coordination: water sharing under conditions of drought or damage to kuhls; sharing of the same diversion structure; having a joint watermaster for both kuhls; joint water guarding during periods of water scarcity; and water sales. Water-sharing arrangements between kuhls were the most common form of coordination. During the period of field research, four clusters of from two to seven kuhls shared water. Water-sharing arrangements typically involved temporary water transfers from an upstream kuhl to a flood-damaged downstream kuhl for the duration of the repair work. For example, during the 1993 monsoon the Neugal River flooded and washed out the shared diversion structure and cliffside section of the main channel for Mahang and Loharal Kuhls. The kohli for the two kuhls arranged a water-sharing agreement with the kohli of the next upstream kuhl, Raniya Kuhl. Throughout the 1993 summer agricultural season, water from Raniya Kuhl was diverted into the main channels of Mahang and Loharal Kuhls. By the end of the year the repairs were still incomplete, and the water-sharing arrangement with Raniya Kuhl continued.

TABLE 12. Kuhls Engaged in Each of Five Types of Coordination
on the Right and Left Banks of the Neugal River

| | Type of Interkuhl Coordination | | | | | |
Kuhl	Water Sharing	Shared Diversion Structure	Joint Water-master	Joint Water Guarding	Water Sales	Interlinkage Measure
Right bank						
Bhradi	—	—	—	—	—	2.0 (H)
Chanogi	—	—	—	—	—	2.0 (H)
Bhagotla	—	—	—	—	—	— (L)
Kathul	—	—	—	X_1	—	1.5 (M)
Sapruhl	—	—	—	X_1	—	2.0 (H)

Pathan	X_1	—	—	—	—	2.5 (H)
Rai*	X_1	—	—	—	X_1	1.7 (M)
Makruhl	X_1	—	—	—	—	4.0 (H)
Samruhl	X_1	—	—	—	X_1	5.0 (H)
Pangwan	X_1	—	—	—	—	5.0 (H)
Sonia	X_1	—	—	—	—	5.0 (H)
Gagruhl	X_1	—	—	—	—	3.0 (H)
Majettli	—	—	—	—	—	1.0 (L)
Bal	—	—	—	—	—	1.0 (L)
Natyrya	—	—	—	—	—	1.0 (L)
Left bank						
Ghran*	—	X_1	—	—	—	1.0 (L)
Dewan C.*	X_2	X_1	—	—	—	3.2 (H)
Mia Fateh*	—	—	—	—	—	2.7 (H)
Dai*	—	—	—	—	—	3.0 (H)
Ghughrul*	—	—	—	—	—	4.0 (H)
Kirpal C.*	—	—	—	—	—	2.6 (H)
Raniya	X_3	—	—	—	—	4.3 (H)
Mahang	X_3	X_2	X_1	—	—	4.2 (H)
Loharal	X_3	X_2	X_1	—	—	6.0 (H)
Taruhl	—	X_3	X_2	—	—	5.0 (H)
Chamruhl	—	X_3	X_2	—	—	5.0 (H)
Patnuhl*	X_4	—	—	—	—	3.7 (H)
Menjha	X_4	—	—	—	—	5.0 (H)
Sangar C.*	—	—	—	—	—	2.5 (H)
Masanol	—	—	—	—	—	0.5 (L)
Spein	—	—	—	—	—	1.0 (L)
Sulah	—	—	—	—	—	1.0 (L)
Saldian	—	—	—	—	—	1.0 (L)
Macchlena	—	—	—	—	—	1.0 (L)
Karni	—	—	—	—	—	1.0 (L)
Rein	—	—	—	—	—	1.0 (L)
Bouru	—	—	—	—	—	1.0 (L)
Upperli*	—	—	—	—	—	1.5 (M)
Buhli	X_2	—	—	—	—	2.5 (H)

KEY: An asterisk (*) indicates a kuhl currently managed by the Irrigation and Public Health Department. X_n identifies which kuhls were engaged in a particular interdependent relation. The interlinkage measure for a kuhl is the ratio of the number of other kuhls that irrigate each of the villages it irrigates to the number of villages the kuhl itself irrigates. When the ratio (y) is less than or equal to 1, interlinkage is low (L); when $1 < y < 2$, interlinkage is medium (M); and when $y \geq 2$, interlinkage is high (H).

Interkuhl water-sharing arrangements also occasionally emerged during the hot, dry, pre-monsoon season. Ranvir Singh, a former kohli of Pangwan Kuhl who was then president of its kuhl committee, described how, during his tenure as kohli, a severe water shortage, combined with upstream diversions, left no water in the Neugal River. In order to receive the minimum water necessary for pre-monsoon field preparation, Ranvir Singh negotiated with the kohlis of the next five upstream kuhls not to divert water for a 24-hour period. On the designated day, all five kuhls were shut down; water flowed downstream in the Neugal riverbed to Pangwan Kuhl, where the readied diversion structure diverted it to the fields for a single flood irrigation that provided adequate water to prepare the fields for dry seed paddy sowing (battar).

Coordination implies interdependence. Todd LaPorte's definition of interdependence as "an exchange relationship of at least one resource between at least two persons" (1975:7) is useful for teasing out the nature of interdependence.[5] He distinguished between two types of interdependent exchange relations that may obtain between two individuals or groups. First, group A may be dominant over group B—in other words, B depends on A for a necessary resource. Second, groups A and B may be mutually dependent on each other for a resource both need.

At first glance, interkuhl water-sharing arrangements appear to conform to the first type of interdependent relationship (A dominant over B). An upstream kuhl (A) is dominant over a downstream kuhl (B) because until kuhl B is repaired, it depends on A for water. For example, Pangwan Kuhl was dependent on the actions of upstream kuhl regimes in order to receive even a minimal supply of water. However, when a longer time frame is used to analyze interkuhl relations, the structural positions of dominant and subordinate regimes can shift. Because floods and their damage to kuhls are random and unpredictable, there is no assurance that a kuhl regime that at one time is asked to provide water temporarily to farmers whose downstream kuhl is damaged will not at a later time be itself damaged by a flood and forced to request a water transfer from the next upstream kuhl regime. In order to preserve its future option to request water from an upstream kuhl, it will likely agree to a request from a downstream kuhl regime in the present. In this manner the structural positions of dominant and subordinate shift over time unpredictably. This shifting dependence encourages cooperative responses from regimes that occupy temporarily dominant positions.[6]

Introducing time into the analysis of interkuhl water transfers helps to explain why an upstream kuhl regime would share water with a temporarily damaged downstream regime with no possibility of direct reciprocation. Fritz Scharpf (1978:353) acknowledged the importance of time and the broader structure of interorganizational relations when examining a specific interorganizational interaction: "Many interactions (interorganizational), however, are not of a one-shot nature. They occur in the context of more stable relationships with their past histories and their expectations of future transactions. Within this broader context, individual interactions which, taken by themselves, would be disadvantageous to one party might still be acceptable."

Although the structural relationship between two kuhl regimes may conform to unilateral dependence (*A* dominant over *B*), their observed behavior more closely approximates that expected from organizations engaged in a mutually dependent interorganizational relationship. Over time, within a context of shared environmental vulnerability, unilateral dependence begins to look more and more like mutual dependence. This is because the ability to access resources such as water and labor through an interkuhl sharing arrangement functions as an insurance policy that enables individual kuhl regimes to reduce their common vulnerability to extreme emergencies.[7]

By examining instances of interkuhl coordination over time, we see that the overall level of cooperation within the interkuhl network is greater than that which exists between any two kuhls at a particular time. Barry Wellman (1988) reported an analogous dynamic in his analysis of community networks in Toronto, Canada. Using the concept of "network balance" (1988:170), he showed that general reciprocity at the network level always exceeded that between any two network ties (nodes). He attributed network balance to the structural embeddedness of ties and to the tendency for reciprocal relations between individuals to reach an equilibrium. In his analysis, network balance emerged by expanding the spatial scale of analysis. For kuhls, network balance emerges by expanding the temporal scale of analysis. In either case, the result is the same: "Do unto others as you would have your network do unto you" (Wellman 1988:171).

To a certain extent, interkuhl water transfers defy the predictions of rational choice theory. Because of the imperative of gravity, kuhl regimes that share water with other, downstream regimes will most likely never be able to ask the beneficiary regime to return the favor—in Kangra water doesn't run uphill (yet). So why should a self-interested regime be willing to share water with an adjacent downstream kuhl? Rational choice theory says it would not be willing to do so, yet we have seen that interkuhl water sharing is the most common form of coordination among kuhl regimes. Part of the answer lies in the observation that a kuhl regime preserves its option of asking an adjacent upstream kuhl for a water transfer in the future by complying with a current request from a downstream kuhl for water.

In addition to this long-term, pragmatic instrumentalism, Gregory Hicks and Devon Peña (2003) draw our attention to the importance of what they call the "civic commons" in structuring relations among common property resource managers and users. As they illustrate for the acequia irrigation systems of the American Southwest, equity and necessity—the hallmarks of the civic commons—rather than efficiency and formal allocation principles are the basis for determining water allocation among acequias in a common watershed (Hicks and Peña 2003:107). In Kangra, the force of the civic commons extends to the most upstream kuhl regime in the watershed, which will never be able to benefit from a water transfer in the event of an emergency and thus would be expected to be least willing to share water with an adjacent downstream kuhl. Rather than the system of interkuhl water transfers unraveling from the top down, as rational choice theory would lead us to expect, irrigators develop a commitment to maintaining the networks of social relations within the watershed.[8] This commitment, often expressed as *bhai bundi se* ("through brotherhood"), which is used to describe interkuhl sharing arrangements, constitutes the basis for the willingness of even the most upstream kuhl regime to supply water to adjacent kuhl regimes during emergencies.

This is not a unique or unusual feature of networks, although it is somewhat inconsistent with rational choice explanations of cooperative behavior. Brian Uzzi (1997), for example, noted that a central principle of game theory is that players will abandon cooperative strategies and revert to self-interested behavior when they know the end of the game is near, because self-interested strategies can yield higher short-term payoffs. In contrast to this expectation, he observed that when the end of the game was in sight, networked players, like the most upstream kuhl regime, continued to engage in cooperative behavior (1997:55). Uzzi noted that in this manner, embedded networks of social relations can reallocate a resource in a manner that produces Pareto improvements, that is, improvements for one person that do not make another worse off. Uzzi accounted for the pervasiveness of cooperative behavior, even within an end game, by describing the emergence of commitments to relationships within a network that transcend their short-term economic character—just as in a collective commitment to the social relations that compose the "civic commons."[9] This is partly due to the multiplex relationships that bind people together and the value people place on maintaining them. Other examples of interkuhl relations, though less inconsistent with game theoretic predictions, further demonstrate the importance of interkuhl relations to the persistence of kuhl regimes.

Sharing a diversion structure is another form of coordination between two or more kuhl regimes. When a flood or earthquake destroys the diversion structure and cliffside channel section of a kuhl, the channel of an adjacent kuhl (if one exists) may sometimes be used to convey water for both kuhls. The redundancy provided by the adjacency of water channels represents insurance against vulnerability to destructive flooding. The main channel and diversion structure of the adjacent kuhl can take over the function of the destroyed structure and channel and thus maintain continuity of water flow. If farmers reconstruct the destroyed diversion structure and cliffside channel section, as was the case for Menjha Kuhl in 1952, then the prior resiliency of the adjacent cluster of kuhl regimes is restored. If the sharing arrangement becomes permanent and the destroyed structure and channel are not reconstructed, then the vulnerability of the irrigators who use the joint infrastructure is greater than before.

In some cases, adjacent kuhls in the Neugal watershed share diversion structures. For example, Taruhl and Chamruhl Kuhls, located in the upper portion of the watershed, use a joint diversion structure and cliffside channel section. The *Riwaj-i-Abpashi* notes that although they originally had separate diversion structures, they were combined following a flood or earthquake. Approximately half a mile below the headworks, the single common channel splits into the two original channels, at which point the water is divided into two equal parts. Each member of this pair of kuhl regimes also engages in other forms of joint water management. For example, a single committee and one committee-appointed kohli manage this pair of kuhls.

Another example of a shared diversion structure and main channel section is that of adjacent Mahang and Loharal Kuhls. The construction of Mahang Kuhl was sponsored by a Rajput, and it was named after his clan. A Brahman clan sponsored the construction of Loharal Kuhl, just downstream of Mahang. Sometime in the late nineteenth century, the Brahman clan requested permission from the Rajput clan to relocate Loharal Kuhl's diversion structure upstream of Mahang Kuhl so that sufficient water would flow into the kuhl's channel. Although the Rajputs refused the request, they did agree to share their diversion structure and cliffside channel section (*Riwaj-i-Abpashi* 1918). The farmers of the two kuhls jointly repair and maintain the kuhl upstream of the point where the main channel bifurcates. In this case and the preceding one, sharing the diversion structure was a response to inadequate water flow and a destructive flood, respectively. Although the sharing ensures the availability of irrigation water for the short run, the resulting overall decline in the density of the kuhl network reduces the system's redundancy and its ability to maintain its integrity in the face of further environmental perturbations.

Joint water guarding is the fourth type of interkuhl coordination for water management. A good example is the coordination between the villages of Paror and Kharot to guard, maintain, and repair the seven miles of main channel shared by Kathul and Sapruhl Kuhls during the eight days when Paror and Kharot had dol rights to the water in Sapruhl Kuhl. The period of dol was from 16 to 24 Jeth, or late June, a time characterized by relatively high water scarcity and high water demand. During this time, 24 farmers divided into 12 pairs, 8 from Paror and 4 from Kharot, to patrol the kuhl's channels for eight 24-hour shifts. Each pair of farmers carried staves, food, and bedding. They guarded the kuhl's water against diversions by upstream farmers, watched for breaches in the channel, and repaired small breaks. To repair large breaches they called for reinforcements from Paror and Kharot. In 1992, more than 90 men from the two villages assembled to repair a large nighttime breach. A similar number helped repair a large breach the following year. Laxman Das, the kohli for both kuhls, remarked that previously the water guards had sheltered at night in the more than two dozen graths (watermills) that Sapruhl Kuhl powered. Because the graths no longer operated, the men now had to sleep along the bank of the kuhl. He also noted that aside from their physical presence at strategic spots susceptible to water stealing, guards were relatively limited in the sorts of sanctions they could apply against illicit water users. Physical violence was not worth it, he said, especially because the dol rights were only for eight days whereas the negative effects on relationships would be long-lasting.

A fifth form of interkuhl coordination is the sale of water rights. I found only one example of this among the kuhl regimes of the Neugal watershed. If the exception proves the rule, then this lone example of a historic water sale underscores the extent to which water rights are appurtenant to landownership in Kangra. The *Riwaj-i-Abpashi* describes the transfer of water rights in Samruhl Kuhl from the village of Panapar to the farmers of downstream Naura. A member of the Rathi caste had sponsored the construction of Samruhl Kuhl during the period of Sikh rule in Kangra (1809–45). The first edition of the *Riwaj-i-Abpashi* (1868) noted that the farmers of Naura purchased water rights in Samruhl Kuhl by paying 92 rupees and 9 *topa* of paddy.[10] To this day, prior to 24 Jeth (mid-June), the kohli for Samruhl Kuhl diverts its total flow into Rai Kuhl, which conveys the water to Naura, approximately 10 miles downstream. After 24 Jeth, the farmers of Panapar can use as much of the kuhl's water as they need. Although not mentioned in the *Riwaj-i-Abpashi*, the farmers of Naura apparently purchased water rights in the kuhl only for the period prior to 24 Jeth (or else that water transfer condition was negotiated at a later date). Because Panapar and Naura are both predominantly Rajput villages, it is likely that caste-based affinities (marital, kin, etc.) linked them and facilitated the sale of rights to the kuhl. The sale of a permanent yet seasonal water right, rather than a one-time sale of a quantity of water, presents an interesting contrast with practices in other regions of India, such as water sales between operators of indigenous tank irrigation systems in Tamil Nadu (Mosse 1997a:19) and farmer-to-farmer water sales in Bihar (Shah and Ballabh 1997).

To what extent is interconnectedness related to interkuhl coordination? Table 12 gives a quantitative indicator of the density of the interkuhl network within which each kuhl is embedded. The indicator, which expresses the degree of interlinkage among kuhl regimes, is the ratio of the number of other kuhls that irrigate each of the villages a kuhl irrigates to the number of villages the kuhl itself irrigates. The ratios are grouped into three categories representing different network densities. Ratios of less than 1.0 indicate low density, ratios greater than or equal to 1.0 but less than 2.0 indicate medium density, and ratios greater than or equal to 2.0 suggest that the kuhl regime is embedded in a relatively dense network.

Not surprisingly, all but three examples of interkuhl coordination are between kuhl regimes embedded in relatively high-density irrigation networks. Of the 19 kuhl regimes engaged in one or more forms of interkuhl coordination, 16 are highly interconnected, 2 are moderately interconnected, and 1 is minimally interconnected. All five of the kuhls that are involved in two or three kinds of interdependent relations are highly interconnected. The one minimally interconnected kuhl (Ghran Kuhl, left bank no. 1) shared a diversion structure with the next downstream kuhl (Diwan Chand, no. 2). This was a short-lived arrangement, however. After a relatively brief period during which the diversion structure was shared, separate structures were again constructed. Many, if not most, forms of interkuhl coordination are ephemeral. The examples listed in Table 12 are undoubtedly a small sample of all the incidents of interkuhl coordination that have taken place in the Neugal watershed. However, they do illustrate the point that dense, interdependent kuhl networks enable interkuhl coordination.

EXPLAINING THE COHERENCE OF NETWORK STRUCTURE

Understanding how and why networks of interkuhl relations cohere over time requires not only examining interkuhl networks as "emergent phenomena" (Benson 1975) but also exploring their cultural and historical components (Scott 1983), their social embeddedness (Granovetter 1985), and the extent to which the technical characteristics (LaPorte 1995) of gravity-flow irrigation systems constitute the basis for interkuhl exchange and coordination.

The technical constraints of gravity-flow systems, in conjunction with the topographic variation found in most villages, produce the dendritic pattern of main kuhl channels in the Neugal watershed (fig. 30). The network of kuhl channels constitutes an ecologically and technologically conditioned template of interconnectedness that offers the possibility for interdependent, interkuhl exchange relations to emerge. Figure 31 shows how the dendritic patterns of kuhl networks differ in two watersheds adjacent to the Neugal. In the Awah watershed, the pattern of multikuhl networks is relatively dense and so, like the Neugal pattern, provides a template of physical interconnectedness that could be the basis for various interdependent, interkuhl relations. In contrast, the kuhl network of the Mand watershed is much less dense. There, truncated networks created by the interaction of local topography and the technical constraints of gravity-flow irrigation limit the extent to which interkuhl exchange and coordination are possible.

The embeddedness of kuhl regimes within "ongoing structures of social relations" (Granovetter 1985), in addition to the physical template of kuhl interconnectedness, helps to explain the transformation over time of asymmetrical dependence into mutual dependence. The embeddedness argument emphasizes the ways in which networks of personal relations that link individuals, rather than institutional arrangements or moral sentiments, foster trust and minimize "malfeasance." Mark Granovetter has argued that interpersonal trust is directly related to the density of the network of social relations between individuals, and malfeasance is inversely related to it.[11] In areas of high network density, farmers often cultivate

(One inch = 3.6 miles)

FIG. 30. The Neugal watershed, showing *mauza* ("revenue village") boundaries and primary kuhl channels. Source: *Riwaj-i-Abpashi* 1918.

(One inch = 3.4 miles)

FIG. 31. Two watersheds in Kangra Valley, showing primary kuhl channels and mauza boundaries. Left: Awah Khad watershed; right: Mand Khad watershed. Source: *Riwaj-i-Abpashi* 1918.

fields that are irrigated by different kuhls. They reside in the same or immediately adjacent hamlets. They share the same community of residence and almost always are members of the same panchayat. This facilitates interkuhl coordination because in such cases kin relationships, local institutions, cooperative agriculture and forest societies, and collective activities such as religious festivals and practices link irrigators in myriad ways. Often the desire to maintain the integrity of this web of social relations facilitates interkuhl coordination. It helps to explain the phrase most often used to describe the basis of interkuhl coordination, especially water-sharing arrangements—*bhai bundi se* ("through brotherhood"), referring to the importance of maintaining good relations with one's neighbor.

The embeddedness argument helps to explain why the diversion structures shared by Mahang and Loharal Kuhls and by Taruhl and Chamruhl Kuhls have persisted, whereas that shared by Ghran and Dewan Chand Kuhls did not. The irrigators of the first two pairs of kuhls are engaged in denser networks of social relations than are those of Ghran and Dewan Chand Kuhls. The two pairs of kuhl regimes that share diversion structures have relatively equal command areas, each pair has one kohli who manages both kuhls, most irrigators have plots irrigated by both kuhls of the pair and hence participate in the maintenance of both, and most irrigators of all four kuhls reside in the same or adjacent hamlets, so norms of reciprocity that exist in social arenas other than irrigation bind them together.

Conversely, Ghran Kuhl is much smaller than Dewan Chand Kuhl. It carries water 3 miles and irrigates 60 hectares in Gaddi-dominated hamlets. Dewan Chand Kuhl transports water more than 15 miles to irrigate 185 hectares in a Rajput-dominated area. The kuhls have separate kohlis and are managed independently. Furthermore, shared allegiances such as marital alliances and material exchange networks do not link the two groups. The lack of shared interest, in combination with the asymmetries between the irrigators of these two kuhls, suggests that in contrast to the other two pairs, they are not engaged in a dense network of shared social relations. Consistent with the embeddedness argument, interkuhl coordination between Gran and Dewan Chand Kuhls did not last, whereas it did for the other two pairs of kuhls. Following the 1905 earthquake, irrigators again constructed separate dangas for Ghran and Dewan Chand Kuhls. Taruhl and Chamruhl and Mahang and Loharal Kuhls continue to manage their shared dangas jointly.

Normative and cognitive frameworks also contribute to the coherence of interkuhl exchange networks. The influence of norms and values on interorganizational coordination is a common theme in much of the literature on interorganizational relations (Aldrich 1976; Selznick 1957). Some argue that over time, mutually beneficial patterns of interorganizational behavior assume the character of general norms, which "take on the character of autonomous social forces, directing and regulating collective action" and thus structure relations within symbiotic networks (Astly and Van de Ven 1983:263).

In Kangra, norms of diffuse reciprocity are institutionalized within demarcated social spheres. In chapter 2 we saw that reciprocal relations are particularly strong among members of a subclan living in the same house cluster. Sharing water between kuhls "bhai bundi se" is also rooted in the notion that the merit achieved through gift giving accrues only when nothing is received in return.[12] A striking example of unilateral exchange in Kangri culture is the tradition of *kanya dan* ("the gift of a virgin"). Although prevalent across all castes, this mode of exchange is most highly developed in the tradition of hypergamy among the hierarchically structured Rajput clans. Social prestige and religious merit accrue to the wife givers only when the family receives no material compensation from the wife takers (Parry 1979:208).[13] Although the tradition of kanya dan is a more extreme example of unreciprocated exchange than that which occurs between kuhl regimes, it does indicate the centrality of asymmetrical reciprocity to social relations in Kangra and thus helps explain the cultural basis for the coherence of interkuhl exchange networks.

The ritualistic elements of kuhl management that puja embodies also strengthen and reproduce the group of irrigators as a community. The two main objectives of kuhl rituals in Kangra are to ensure that adequate water flows into the kuhl during the dry season and to protect the kuhl from destructive floods during the monsoon. As described in chapter 2, irrigators propitiate the feminine deity of the kuhl to ensure adequate flow and worship Quaja Pir to ward off floods. Both rituals involve giving prasaad (a food offering) to the deity and then distributing the blessed offering among all the irrigators present, who consume it together. Sharing and consuming the offering simultaneously marks, makes, and strengthens the community of irrigators. The production of community continues as the kohli, while walking home after performing the puja, shares prasaad with neighbors and others whom he meets on the way.

The symbols, actions, and relationships employed in kuhl puja are repeated in daily domestic rituals, at every trip to a shrine or temple, and at all life-cycle ceremonies. The constitutive aspect of puja exemplifies the point made by the new sociological institutionalists (Meyer, Boli, and Thomas 1994; Meyer and Rowan 1977; Powell and DiMaggio 1991; Scott 1983, 1994; Zucker 1987) that institutions reflect and embody cognitive as well as normative elements of their environments. W. Richard Scott (1994:81) argued that "cognitive elements include widely held beliefs and taken-for-granted assumptions that provide a framework for everyday routines." The cognitive elements embodied in kuhl puja contribute to the social construction of actors as community members, and the various components of kuhl puja are (re)enactments of broader "institutional scripts" (Meyer, Boli, and Thomas 1994:10) that play out in a variety of everyday contexts and thus serve to increase the institutionalization of kuhls.[14]

The coherence of interkuhl networks can therefore be attributed to the presence of an ecologically and technologically enabled template of physical interconnectedness embedded in broader networks of social relations and grounded in mutually reinforcing cognitive and normative structures of identity and reciprocity. Actions or policies that weaken the basis for interkuhl coordination reduce the resiliency of the irrigation network. The Irrigation and Public Health Department of Himachal Pradesh manages the kuhl regimes under its authority on a kuhl-by-kuhl basis. Managing each kuhl as an autonomous unit without considering the network of interkuhl relations in which it was previously embedded has reduced interkuhl coordination between department- and village-managed kuhls and has eliminated it among department-managed kuhls. While this may make little difference to the persistence of these regimes during periods that are relatively free of stress, when environmental shocks do occur, the weakened basis for interkuhl coordination reduces the network's ability to buffer the effects of the earthquake, flood, or drought. With fewer possibilities for interkuhl water exchanges after a destructive flood or earthquake, kuhls that sustain severe damage are less likely to be rebuilt, and they become increasingly dependent on state resources for their repair and maintenance.

Does network density affect the ability of kuhl regimes to maintain their integrity despite periodic shocks such as earthquakes and floods? The answer, not surprisingly, is "sometimes." Networks provide resources such as water, water management skills, and labor for repair and reconstruction. Network density is particularly important for kuhl regimes that depend on the pulses of resources that networks provide, especially when alternative sources of them are unavailable. If a kuhl regime is not embedded in a dense network, and if it experiences a sudden need for the resources such a network can provide, then it may cease to function.

For example, a flood destroyed Masanol Kuhl (which has a low interlinkage measure) in the 1970s, and it remained defunct for many years. Not until the current kohli organized a kuhl committee and successfully solicited financial assistance from the local member of the Legislative Assembly was the kuhl reconstructed and again used for irrigation. Had

Masanol Kuhl been part of a dense network of interkuhl relations, its irrigators might have been able to draw immediately on network resources such as water and labor for irrigation and kuhl reconstruction. Other isolated kuhls have also gone defunct. In the headwater region of the Neugal watershed, signs of abandoned kuhls that previously irrigated riparian areas are visible across the boulder-strewn floodplain. It is likely that at some point in the past, floods destroyed these isolated kuhls and they were never reconstructed.

Network density seems to be particularly important for kuhls that experience pulses of intensive resource demands, particularly for water and labor, following destructive shocks. A dense network provides opportunities for regimes to meet short-duration but intensive resource requirements that cannot be met from within the regime itself. In the absence of alternative sources for those resources, interkuhl coordination may play a crucial role in preserving the integrity of individual regimes and, by extension, the network itself.

Clearly, interkuhl networks offer the possibility for kuhl regimes to coordinate among themselves, thus acquiring resources otherwise unavailable. Under some conditions, however, interconnectedness can lead to interkuhl conflict. Under conditions of water scarcity, networks of interconnected kuhl channels make possible interkuhl water transfers, but the same networks can also become the basis for quarrels between kuhl regimes over water distribution. One of the few references to the direct involvement of the colonial government in kuhl management in Kangra Valley concerns the intervention of the district collector during a drought in 1914 to supervise the distribution of water between the densely interconnected upstream and downstream kuhls of Baner Khad, so that the downstream kuhls would receive a specific volume of water. In this case, interkuhl conflicts based on inadequate water supplies required the colonial administration to intervene.

Norms of reciprocity, based on kinship relations and residence in the same hamlet, do contribute to network coherence. On the other hand, intraclan and familial conflicts, often over access to land, can be among the most contentious in the region and can affect the management of kuhls. For example, the July 7, 1987, meeting minutes for Sonia Kuhl describe the committee's attempts to adjudicate a conflict between a father and son in which the son, who owned land upstream of his father, was blocking the flow of water into his father's fields. Although the committee determined that the father had a valid right to the kuhl water, the son still refused to release it. This conflict concerned water distribution within a single kuhl, but such conflicts can extend to interkuhl relations as well. This is perhaps exemplified most dramatically by the murder of downstream Girth farmers, whose clan had constructed Sapruhl Kuhl, by upstream Rajputs who wanted to claim the kuhl for themselves.

Some adjacent kuhls do share and jointly manage diversion structures, as described earlier for Mahang, Loharal, Chamruhl, and Taruhl Kuhls. But in some instances, adjacency leads to conflict, not coordination. For example, a flood in 1977 washed out the diversion structure and upstream channel section of Rai Kuhl, a 12-mile-long kuhl that irrigates 820 hectares in 28 hamlets. Its construction had been sponsored by the precolonial state in 1775. Since the 1970s, the IPHD has managed the kuhl. It did not reconstruct the portion of the kuhl destroyed in 1977; instead, IPHD workers draw water through pipes placed, without permission, in the portion of Pathan Kuhl just upstream of Rai Kuhl. During the late 1980s, the kohli for Pathan kuhl, Dyan Singh, wrote numerous letters protesting this action, both to the IPHD and to his panchayat pradhan. He described how the siphoning of water from Pathan to Rai Kuhl created water shortages for the irrigators of Pathan Kuhl from May 15 until the monsoon arrived. Not until 1993 did the IPHD finally reconstruct the damaged upstream portion of Rai Kuhl and remove the pipes from Pathan Kuhl.

In general, the assumption by the Irrigation and Public Health Department of management authority over some of the kuhls in the Neugal watershed has weakened the integrity and coherence of interkuhl networks. The imposition of state authority on the management of these kuhls has disrupted the common vulnerability to environmental shocks that previously all kuhls in the watershed shared. IPHD-managed kuhls, no longer so vulnerable because funds can always be sanctioned for repairs, no longer depend on the web of interkuhl relations to buffer themselves from such shocks. The junior engineers and daily wage water tenders who work for the state government and manage these kuhls perceive themselves as government employees, not as irrigators subject to capricious environmental shocks that threaten the food supply. Consequently, they have little or no incentive to share water and other resources with adjacent, community-managed kuhl regimes. The vulnerability of the adjacent, community-managed kuhls to environmental emergencies persists, yet because IPHD-managed kuhls are effectively cut out of the web of interkuhl relations, fewer network partners are available to function as buffers against such shocks. As the resiliency previously provided by dense kuhl networks diminishes, vulnerability to environmental perturbations will increase. Unless the functions these neighboring kuhls previously played are replaced by other elements such as access to government grants for kuhl channel repair, it is likely that the overall viability of the interkuhl network will diminish.

Negotiated exchange relations between kuhl irrigation systems for coordinated water management can reduce the risks and uncertainties associated with recurring environmental shocks. Interconnectedness between kuhls is not a problem to be managed or a liability to be controlled but rather a resource that can facilitate kuhl persistence by buffering kuhl regimes from destructive environmental shocks. When interconnectedness between common property resource management regimes leads to coordinated resource management strategies, it may reduce the vulnerability associated with environmental risk and uncertainty and thus contribute to the resiliency of these systems.

This formulation of the relationship between interdependence, coordinated exchange through networks, and reductions in risk and vulnerability differs from others that emphasize the role of collective action in risk reduction and management. For example, Robert Wade (1988) and others have explained the emergence and stability of community-level collective action institutions in terms of the degree of risk with which villagers must contend. In contrast, I have tried to shift the focus away from individual common property resource management regimes to the nature and effects of relations among them. Implicit in this approach is the assumption that important factors that influence the effectiveness of common property resource management regimes may lie outside of the regimes themselves. Thus, two common property resource management regimes may be similar in their internal formal and informal structures, rules, norms, sanctions, and risks, yet because of different relations of interdependency with other regimes, have quite different capacities to absorb the destructive impacts of environmental shocks. This approach also suggests that in some cases, the dependence of a regime on state support is inversely proportional to the density of its potential exchange relations with other regimes. That is, under conditions of environmental vulnerability, a solitary, independent regime will be more dependent on state resources after a destructive flood, earthquake, or other environmental calamity than a regime that is embedded in a dense network of horizontal exchange relations that, through coordinated resource management strategies and the joint mobilization of labor and other resources, provide the regime the resources it needs to absorb the environmental shock.[15]

6
DYNAMIC REGIMES, ENDURING FLOWS

THROUGHOUT THIS BOOK I HAVE ATTEMPTED TO DEVELOP AN EXPLANA-
tion for the durability of the kuhls of Kangra under conditions of persistent
long-term stress and recurring short-term shocks that common property
resource theory suggests should lead to their demise. The quest for a robust,
inductive framework that could account for this apparent anomaly began
with a consideration of the contributions and limitations of theories of
common property resource management. Because of their roots in rational
choice theory and their relatively narrow focus on regime attributes, these
theories were unable to account for the remarkable persistence of the kuhls
of Kangra and, presumably, other common property resource regimes. This
finding led to a far-reaching investigation, rooted in inductive reasoning
based on data from fieldwork and archival research, aimed at elucidating
just what has enabled the kuhls to endure. The investigation revealed a
diverse array of processes and factors that, when integrated into an analytical
framework drawn from a variety of intellectual domains, provided a
coherent account of the kuhls of Kangra. Networks of resiliency, historical
and contemporary statemaking interventions, and culturally constituted
notions of place—all heavily conditioned by patterns of regionalization
and social and ecological heterogeneity in space and time—made up the
warp and weft of the explanatory tapestry developed in the preceding
chapters to explain the durability of the kuhls.

These processes and the framework that integrates them illuminate the
nature and outcomes of regime-specific encounters with and responses to
forces of change and environmental disturbance. The nature and outcomes

of these encounters vary dramatically among kuhl regimes; they are shaped by the imprint of regionality as well as by microlevel social and ecological heterogeneity. At the watershed level, new patterns of authority and organization for water management have emerged. Currently in the Neugal watershed, most farmers on the left bank receive water from a government-managed kuhl for their larh landholdings, contribute to the management of a multivillage kuhl with a committee to irrigate some of their har holdings, and, along with their house cluster neighbors, informally manage another kuhl to irrigate har plots in a third location. On the right bank, the scenario differs only in that instead of receiving water from a government managed kuhl for larh holdings, farmers have switched to rain-fed maize production.[1]

The resulting web of multijurisdictional, interconnected kuhls appears resilient at the watershed level because each kuhl regime has established its own unique management structure and mix of state and local authority, given a particular type and rate of environmental shock or economic change and its own configuration of social and ecological attributes. The existing watershed-level pattern of authority and organization for water management suggests that although specific organizational forms, operations, and scales of regime management have not persisted, in the sense of remaining unchanged, the overall pattern of kuhl networks in the watershed has maintained its coherence.

The inductively derived framework that renders coherent the patterns of persistence and change among the kuhls of Kangra offers us numerous footholds for considering issues concerning the durability of common property resource management regimes. It also speaks to broader themes related to the distribution of authority for natural resource management between state and local entities, the importance of regional-scale processes for understanding the effects of global-local and national-local dynamics, and the widespread trends in resource management toward decentralization and devolution. By exploring the key explanatory strands of the story of the kuhls, we can begin to see the broader implications for common property regimes and community-based natural resource management.

THE SALIENCE OF REGIONALITY

A variety of cultural, political, economic, institutional, and environmental processes and relations "stretched out" over space (Allen, Massey, and Cochrane 1998; Massey 1994) and combined in unique ways together define

Kangra's regionality and simultaneously link it with the rest of the Indian subcontinent and beyond. The articulation of these processes constitutes the unique and dynamic "Kangri way of life," which includes the particularities of irrigated agriculture and the agrarian economy. This relational approach enables us to conceptualize Kangra as a region and draws attention to the social networks and flows that define Kangra's regionality. Although many of the important spatialized social relations that constitute Kangra as a region extend beyond to the Punjab plains, the Indian nation-state, and international arenas, there nevertheless remains a specific constellation of political, institutional, cultural, and environmental processes that constitutes the form and content of Kangra's regionality.[2]

Considering Kangra's regionality in light of the central concerns of this book brings into focus a variety of factors that together have influenced the durability and transformations of kuhl regimes. These factors include the everyday practices of place-making and social reproduction, the ways in which dominant groups preserve their privileged status and subordinate groups assert their own interests, the mechanisms through which extralocal political authority is established and strengthened, and the material and environmental constraints on and opportunities for livelihood in Kangra. A focus on regionality also illuminates the nature of the social relations and ideological and material traffic that simultaneously link Kangra to progressively larger regions and contribute to Kangra's regionality. Thus this perspective draws attention to the ideological underpinnings of British settlement policies in Kangra and their material effects, historical and contemporary patterns of migration out of Kangra, and the region-specific ways in which the modern Indian nation-state has pursued development objectives in Kangra.

These unique features and relationships—part of Kangra's regionality— together constitute the parameters within which kuhl regimes initially developed and have subsequently persisted. Though not foreclosing possible trajectories of change or preordaining responses to stress, these regional parameters heavily condition patterns of persistence and change among kuhl regimes. The ecological and geographical attributes of Kangra delineate both the environmental opportunities and the challenges of gravity-flow irrigation in the region. The regional cultural and institutional complexes provide many of the core social practices that are enacted within regimes. Kuhl regimes can be sites for reproducing those core practices or for resisting and reconfiguring them. Though not determining the specific organizational forms that kuhl regimes assume as they undergo institutional formalization, these features strongly influence the scales at which different types of kuhl regimes can function as viable resource management entities. Last, the relationships that link kuhl regimes to broader political, social, and economic formations beyond Kangra Valley also influence the context of irrigation management in important ways. Thus, regionality can be understood both as the crucible within which kuhl regimes have developed and as the complex of social relations that kuhl regimes, through their persistence, can strengthen, modify, or contest.

One key feature of Kangra's regionality is its ecological and landscape form. The extent of arable land and the potential scope for irrigated agriculture in Kangra is unusually large for a mountainous region. The broad alluvial valleys at the base of the Dhaula Dhar range, the snowmelt that is available for irrigation during the dry season, and the temperate climate create opportunities for irrigated agriculture on a scale virtually unknown in the rest of the Himalayan region. On the other hand, the same topography has prevented the construction of large-scale, state-financed and -managed canal irrigation systems of the sort prevalent on the relatively flat plains to the south, and the lack of significant groundwater reserves has foreclosed the potential for the privately controlled tube-well irrigation technology that is so pervasive in other parts of the subcontinent.

This ecologically based restriction on the scale and method of irrigation in Kangra has constrained the nature and extent of state intervention for promoting irrigated agriculture as well as opportunities for private investment in (and profit from) tube wells. In Kangra, geography rendered mute the threat of large-scale, state-financed irrigation systems to preexisting, locally managed regimes and trumped the state simplifications (Scott 1998) of agriculture, irrigation, and empire that reigned on the plains to the south. On the plains, as in many other parts of the world, the state simplifications associated with large-scale irrigation development were intimately associated with the state power and state science that are the hallmarks of the statemaking enterprise (Sivaramakrishnan 1999). The realization of the goals of this enterprise invariably brought state entities into conflict with preexisting irrigation systems and institutions—although the outcomes of these conflicts varied widely and were influenced by many region-specific factors (Gelles 2000; Lansing 1991; Siy 1982).

By contrast, in Kangra, because of the ecological constraints that foreclosed the possibility of other viable technologies and scales of irrigation, the statemaking-through-irrigation urge had to be expressed through engagement with the technology and institutions associated with kuhl irrigation. In a perhaps analogous fashion, the lack of potential for tube-well irrigation in Kangra Valley eliminated the possibility of investing private wealth for private gain in tube-well irrigation and instead compelled the private agricultural investment urge to be expressed through the sponsorship, construction, and improvement of kuhl infrastructure. In this manner, geographical features of the Kangra region effectively channeled both statemaking energies and private investment flows in ways that supported kuhl regimes.

Ecology and physical geography have influenced the story of Kangra kuhls in other ways as well. Microscale differences in soil types, recognized and given meaning through the local differentiation of har from larh soils, play important roles in farmers' labor allocation and crop choice decisions. The spatial distribution of these soil types—the more fertile har soils generally adjacent to perennial streams and the less fertile larh soils farther away from sources of irrigation water—amplifies these differences. With the expansion of nonfarm employment and concomitant increasing opportunity costs of labor, the differences in soil types, combined with their topographic distribution, spatialized the effects and consequences of increasing labor scarcity on kuhl regimes. Because of the differences in returns to labor, labor was selectively withdrawn from the longer kuhls that irrigated primarily larh areas and concentrated on kuhls that irrigated har areas. The extreme spatial heterogeneity of these interactions between ecology, topography, and farmers' decisions partially accounts for the tremendous variation in the degree of regime formalization and state involvement in kuhl irrigation, both historically and in the contemporary period. Thus, while regional-scale geographical attributes of Kangra channeled statemaking-through-irrigation impulses toward engagement with kuhls, the specific content, structure, and function of that engagement has varied across kuhl regimes and reflects these heterogeneous landscape patterns. Many of these and other microscale variations among kuhl regimes are accounted for by the "reliance-differentiation" framework presented in chapter 4.

Hydrological features of Kangra constitute a second ecological attribute that is common to the region and yet produces highly localized, unpredictable disturbances that are destructive to kuhl regimes. The Dhaula Dhar massif that towers over Kangra Valley effectively traps moisture-laden monsoon clouds and often generates intense rainfall. The steep upper watersheds and headwater canyons are vulnerable to destructive landslides and flooding. Destructive earthquakes, related to the seismic and geological instability of the region, are a second recurring environmental shock. The destructive effects on individual kuhl regimes of these environmental shocks are relatively random, both spatially and temporally. Networks of interkuhl coordination and exchange reduce the vulnerability of individual regimes to these perturbations, thereby enhancing the resilience of the overall network.

Several of the institutional and cultural complexes that help define Kangra's regionality and that condition kuhl regimes in important ways are regionally inflected modifications of complexes prevalent throughout large portions of the Indian subcontinent. These widespread complexes include social hierarchies based on ascribed status; village-level positions of authority that are inherited rights; notions of political authority, statemaking, and territorial sovereignty rooted in idioms of exchange and reciprocity; and the role played by ritual in constituting and strengthening community identity. Locally, these elements are heavily imbued with a distinctly Kangri flavor. For example, although social hierarchies based on caste status are prevalent in Kangra, the extremely skewed distributions of land and resources that exist in other regions of the subcontinent are muted. The relatively egalitarian pattern of landownership in Kangra precluded the emergence of a wealthy, noncultivating, landed elite—in stark contrast to regions such as south Bihar and parts of Tamil Nadu, where statemaking undermined this dominant class and consequently weakened the irrigation institutions and systems that the elite group had previously supported. In Kangra, the differentiation of social interests in agriculture and irrigation was not so great, and the broad-based common interest in contributing to the collective provision of irrigation water has been sustained.

Kuhl regimes articulate with other cultural and institutional complexes that constitute Kangra's regionality. For example, the institutionalization of village-level positions that are inherited rights and the notion of ascribed status in Kangra inform the development and persistence of the role of kohli. Many aspects of the position of kohli resonate with a wide variety of other village-level positions that are inherited and for which remuneration is paid in kind at harvest time. Like positions of ascribed status and authority elsewhere in India that have been weakened or supplanted by more contractual forms of authority, so has the position of kohli lost some of its authority and prestige. Although the status of being kohli has declined, however, it has not imploded because of caste-based conflicts rooted in inequalities, as has happened to such positions in other parts of India. Ritual aspects of kuhl management play an important role in constructing and strengthening notions of community, and they resonate closely with themes and motifs from the rest of the subcontinent. Yet they, too, are thoroughly marked as Kangri in terms of the stories they encode, the deities that are propitiated, and the specific forms the ritual itself assumes.

The traffic in social and cultural norms that links Kangra with the larger region in which it is embedded is complemented by flows of people and markets. Both of these flows have had important ramifications for kuhl irrigation. Historically, people, mostly men, have left the region in search of employment. During the precolonial period this migration was primarily seasonal, and men often served as mercenaries in armies on the plains. Subsequently, this flow expanded to include more permanent and diverse kinds of employment. In the last 30 years, the process has accelerated at a historically unprecedented rate. Now, the extent of nonfarm employment and the size of the remittance economy are defining features of the regional economy.

The second flow, that of markets, has brought to the region a combination of relatively inexpensive green revolution grains from the plains, which reduces the potential viability of market-oriented grain production in Kangra, and a flood of consumer durables along with an associated emphasis on consumerism and consumption. These flows of people, money, and markets make up some of the defining features of the regional political and economic landscape in which kuhls are currently situated. They represent challenges as well as opportunities for the durability of kuhl regimes. The challenges derive primarily from the increased differentiation of social interest in agriculture and kuhl irrigation water, which undermines the common incentive to contribute to the tasks associated with kuhl management. The opportunities arise from the possibility of exploiting the comparative advantages of agriculture in the hills relative to other regions. Whereas other districts of Himachal Pradesh have developed reputations for cultivating specialty crops that thrive in the hills, such as off-season vegetables, stone fruits, apples, seed potatoes, and vegetable seeds, in Kangra such advances have so far been relatively few, except for the expansion of lichee orchards in larh areas and a relatively short-lived spate of cut flower production. Clearly, kuhl-irrigated grain production will never compete with green revolution rice and wheat imported from the Punjab. However, the continuing strength of the grain self-sufficiency ethic (which derives from complex notions related to a deeply rooted sense of place and home, fondness for consuming one's own grain, and associations between health and the consumption of local grain), combined with the possibility of further realizing the potential for exploiting the comparative advantages of hill agriculture and horticulture, provides at least some of the incentive necessary for the continued persistence of the kuhls.

If we are not cognizant of the myriad ways in which kuhl regimes articulate with the cultural, political, institutional, and environmental processes that together constitute Kangra's regionality, any attempt to explicate historical and contemporary patterns of change and continuity in kuhl regimes will fail. In short, it is impossible to understand the spatial and temporal heterogeneity of kuhl regime responses to environmental perturbations or to regional socioeconomic changes without analyzing the salience of regionality to these processes. Indeed, it is perhaps germane to reflect on the impossibility of understanding patterns of change and persistence in kuhl regimes, or in any other common property resource management regime, without undertaking a full examination of the effects and consequences of regionality for the common property regime in question. By understanding the internal collective action challenges associated with managing a common property resource, we satisfy a necessary but not sufficient condition for understanding the likelihood that it will endure. The story of the kuhls demonstrates the necessity of expanding our conceptual approach to address the specific ways in which common property regimes articulate with the various cultural, political, and institutional complexes that together make up the regional processes— the stretched out social relations—that carve places out of spaces.

ACCOUNTING FOR MICROSCALE
HETEROGENEITY OF REGIME STRUCTURE

Studies of common property regimes tend to equate the attributes of formal organizations, such as written rules, fines and sanctions, elected positions, and written records, with the regime's ability to manage a natural resource. Consequently, it is assumed that a regime without the attributes of formal organizations is less able to resolve conflicts and mobilize resources than is a more formalized regime. The formality of organizational structure may be associated with resource mobilization requirements (Martin 1986:219). However, when temporal rather than spatial comparisons are made across a set of common property regimes such as kuhls, it appears that the degree of organizational formality and the process of regime formalization are related to other factors in addition to the regime's resource mobilization needs. As we have seen, some kuhl regimes whose resource mobilization needs have not changed over time have nevertheless gradually adopted more formalized organizational structures. What accounts for these microscale differences in organizational structure among adjacent kuhl regimes?

The process of regime formalization is extremely heterogeneous, even among the kuhl regimes that share water from the Neugal River. The "reliance-differentiation" framework developed in chapter 4 accounts for much of the spatial and temporal heterogeneity of kuhl regime structure. It suggests that in Kangra, regime formalization is a response to the rising internal stress and conflict resulting from increased participation in the nonfarm employment sector as well as to the organizational models embraced by development policies in the modern Indian nation-state. These stresses and the extent of interaction with developmentalist state policies and programs vary nonrandomly among the kuhls of Kangra.

In kuhl regimes characterized by high reliance on kuhl water for irrigation and by low social differentiation among irrigators, the reproduction of core cultural constructs such as reciprocity and the regimes' embeddedness in broader networks of kinship relations enables effective water management without formal organization. These kuhl regimes generally have no kohli, do not maintain kuhl management records, and do not use rules to determine the distribution of responsibility for system maintenance and repair among kuhl members. Among these regimes, the absence of explicit, formal rules indicates not a failure of collective action but rather that informal social relations between farmers and mutual dependence on kuhl water provide adequate incentives for farmers to coordinate in the repair, maintenance, and management of the kuhl whose water they share.

K. Sivaramakrishnan and Arun Agrawal (2003:20) note in their discussion of institutions and power that if institutions are conceived of as "social mechanisms that structure future expectations of actors, it may not even be possible to know where institutions begin and their social context shades off." In the light of this argument, it appears that the broader social and cultural constructs in Kangra provide secure institutional moorings for kuhl regimes whose members share high reliance and low differentiation. In such instances there is no need to formalize a specific irrigation organization, because the institutional landscape of the social context adequately guides social expectations and actions. Some common property regimes that are embedded in regional formations may be able to operate effectively without elaborate formal organizational structures; the lack of such structures does not necessarily imply an inability to mobilize resources for collective action, resolve disputes, or manage a common property resource.

Kuhl regimes in Kangra that are not characterized by high reliance and low differentiation experience greater tension and conflict associated with increasing nonfarm employment. They also tend to interact more frequently with state entities and are therefore subject to the prevailing hegemonic models of bureaucratic organization sanctioned by the state. Most kuhls in this category have consequently created managing committees whose formal structure conforms closely to state-sanctioned rational bureaucratic organization. Although most of these regimes previously had kohlis, the adoption of the committee structure has been associated with the development of more formalized rules regarding the distribution of responsibility for system maintenance and repair and the introduction of systems of fines and sanctions to enforce the rules. Clearly, for these kuhl regimes, the stresses associated with increasing nonfarm employment and increasing interaction with state entities, combined with their resource mobilization requirements, led to the development of more formalized institutional structures. For these regimes, social context alone provided inadequate social capital for addressing the challenges associated with their management.

For some kuhls—generally those characterized by low reliance and high social differentiation—regime formalization proved inadequate to manage the stresses and conflicts associated with increasing nonfarm employment. The resulting rising opportunity costs of labor exceeded the regimes' conflict resolution capacities. Kuhl regimes in this category show signs of internal stress such as contracting command areas, shifts in cropping patterns due to increasing water scarcity, ineffective kuhl committees, and high levels of conflict. The management of some has been taken over by the Irrigation and Public Health Department.

Choices regarding regime management structures seem to respond to two imperatives: the need to balance organizational complexity against the scale and scope of coordination required for regime management and the hegemonic influences of state-sanctioned models of bureaucratic organization. As the scale and scope of coordination challenges increase, institutions embedded in the broader social context must be complemented by specific features of irrigation organization, such as the development of the position of kohli. As rates of environmental change increase—for example, the rate of nonfarm employment—the effectiveness of different organizational arrangements for kuhl management decreases. The stresses caused by rising nonfarm employment weaken the capacity of informally institutionalized practices and relations to structure behavior, and they challenge the ability of the kohli to effectively manage the kuhl. As the capacity for internal resource mobilization diminishes, state support becomes increasingly imperative, but at the cost of conforming to state-sanctioned bureaucratic models. Creating kuhl committees and formalizing rules are mechanisms for increasing the conflict resolution and resource mobilization capacities of kuhl regimes in response to these stresses and challenges.

The choice of effective and equitable organizational structures that strengthen community-level institutional arrangements for common property resource management involves consideration of a multiplicity of diverse models. Even within one relatively small watershed and under conditions of state support and legitimation for one form of formal organizational structure, a diverse array of organizational forms and modes of state engagement has flourished. There is no one size that fits all. Issues of scale, the degree of conflict within the regime, the extent to which certain organizational arrangements are institutionalized, the rate of change in the regional political economy, and the regime's resource mobilization and coordination requirements all influence the process of determining the most effective regime structure for a particular common property resource. The blueprints commonly employed as part of government efforts to promote community-based resource management—for example, village forest committees and water users' associations—rarely, if ever, encompass the organizational diversity that this study of kuhl regimes suggests is necessary to accommodate microscale social and ecological heterogeneity. Although homogeneity of common property regimes satisfies the bureaucratic urge for standardized, simplified, and comparable structures of governance, a rigid adherence to one organizational design virtually guarantees the inability of regimes situated in a socially and ecologically differentiated landscape to effectively respond to the kinds of conditions discussed in this section.

NETWORKS OF COORDINATION AND EXCHANGE

Vulnerability to environmental shocks as well as concomitant risk and uncertainty challenge the integrity of many common property regimes. Indeed, some researchers have argued that common property regimes themselves can be explained as risk reducing strategies (Wade 1988). In the kuhls of Kangra we see the potential role of networks in enhancing the resilience of common property regimes and thereby facilitating their ability to endure, especially under conditions of environmental risk and uncertainty. Kuhl regimes utilize networks of interdependence to help reduce environmental vulnerability and risk. We can see the broader applicability of this insight for other common property regimes when we acknowledge the ubiquity of risk and vulnerability across many fields of common property resource management. Although networks may be latent most of the time, as is the case with kuhl regimes, their periodic utility in buffering unpredictable disturbances may contribute in important ways to the regime's endurance.

Networks composed of interlinked kuhls provide opportunities for pooling labor, sharing water, and coordinating management tasks among kuhls. These networks provide short-term pulses of resources such as labor, water, and expertise during moments of crisis following destructive floods or earthquakes or during droughts. Networks reduce the vulnerability of individual kuhl regimes to environmental shocks by providing redundant sources of key inputs; when a kuhl is temporarily damaged or water scarcity threatens, networks can provide alternative, short-term, but crucial pulses of resources. Not surprisingly, the frequency of interkuhl water exchanges and coordinated water management is positively correlated with network density. Where networks linking kuhls are sparse or nonexistent, often because of topographical and landscape features, individual kuhl regimes are denied access to the resource reserves that networks provide. Without this buffer, during times of crisis these regimes must either mobilize resources from within the regime, negotiate with state entities to provide support, or temporarily or permanently cease functioning.

As discussed in chapter 5, although extensive coordination and exchange between kuhl regimes still occurs in Kangra Valley, the advent of government management of some kuhl regimes, particularly the longest and largest ones, has changed the pattern of authority for kuhl management at the watershed level and weakened the capacity of networks to provide resources during times of crisis. Network density (and consequently, capacity to provide resource pulses) has diminished because the Irrigation and Public Health Department does not participate in interkuhl water or labor exchanges or coordinated water management strategies. Government-managed kuhls have been excised from the networks in which they were previously embedded. The state government's willingness to provide financial support for the operation of government-managed kuhls and, upon request, to provide grants to community-managed kuhls for repairing flood- and earthquake-related damage has, to some extent, mitigated the negative consequences of weakened interkuhl networks. In essence, the state has partially substituted its own resources for those that networks used to provide.

However, the substitution of state resources for network resources has not been a seamless process. Weakened network capacities to provide resources during moments of environmental vulnerability have not been entirely supplanted by state resources, thus increasing the vulnerability of individual kuhl regimes to environmental perturbations. For example, the spate of government takeovers in the late 1970s and early 1980s created a serious imbalance, in terms of government investment in kuhl irrigation, between state- and community-managed kuhls. State management of kuhl irrigation constitutes a 100-percent subsidy for farmers; irrigators pay no taxes on the water that government workers deliver to their fields, nor do they contribute to system maintenance and repair. Meanwhile, adjacent community-managed kuhls receive no regular state support and must petition for government grants to repair flood- or earthquake-damaged channels. The resulting inequity in access to government support has prompted members of some community-managed kuhls to request that their kuhls, too, be managed by the IPHD. The department, not surprisingly, has denied all of these requests. In the context of limited state willingness to provide financial inputs for kuhl management, the need for the resources that networks used to provide may increase in the future.

Other studies of locally managed irrigation systems have also addressed the importance of intersystem linkages. Regarding the subak irrigation systems of Bali, Stephen Lansing (1991) described the ways in which decentralized religious authorities effectively coordinated water transfers and planting cycles for numerous individual subaks across large landscapes. The outcome was a sophisticated and efficient system of agricultural production that maximized water-use efficiency and minimized the likelihood of crop pest outbreaks. Similarly, David Mosse's research on the tank irrigation systems of southern Tamil Nadu (1997a) included analysis of intertank linkages, primarily coordinated water sales and transfers.

What are the implications for the study of common property and community-based resource management regimes of expanding the ambit of inquiry to explicitly incorporate the role of networks in accounting for the persistence of kuhl regimes? This perspective draws attention to the possibility that during moments of environmental shock, otherwise latent relations with adjacent resource management regimes and communities may provide the resource pulses necessary to absorb the short-term, crisis-induced stress and minimize vulnerability. But networks that link community-based resource management regimes can also play other important functions. Lansing has demonstrated how intersystem coordination among Balinese subaks is central to the ongoing coordination of interdependent agricultural activities at the landscape scale. Networks can also take on explicit political dimensions related to defending the claims and interests of rural resource managers and users, especially when individual management regimes are linked through federation-type alliances.[3]

KUHL REGIMES AS STATEMAKING ARENAS

The last strand of the explanatory tapestry brings the state into the analysis of common property regimes. Doing so reveals essential and, some might argue, central subplots in the story of the kuhls. It also provides conceptual space for deliberating on the potential roles of government in supporting democratic practice and community-based natural resource management and environmental stewardship. Such deliberation is particularly timely given the proliferation of community-based approaches (both grassroots movements and government programs) for natural resource management around the world. The implications of these approaches for the structure and practice of government have, to date, been only partially understood.

The kuhl regimes of Kangra provide an excellent vehicle for exploring these issues because of the diverse relationships that have developed between kuhl regimes and state entities across three historical periods—precolonial, colonial, and post-independence. Although the underlying rationale for state involvement in kuhls varied across these periods according to the basis of political authority and underlying ideological assumptions about the functions and purpose of government, there has nevertheless been a remarkable continuity of practice in the varieties of state intervention in kuhl regimes. Across all three historical periods, kuhl regimes have been sites through which statemaking projects have been pursued. Whether in the form of a precolonial ruling lineage's sponsoring a kuhl's construction as a type of political patronage, a colonial administrator's perfecting private property rights to promote agrarian investment or overseeing the codification of irrigation customs through the compilation of the *Riwaj-i-Abpashi*, or a contemporary district commissioner's sanctioning a grant for repairing a flood-destroyed kuhl, statemaking concerns run continuously throughout the last several hundred years of extralocal political involvement in kuhls. Because engaging with, rather than undermining or supplanting, kuhl regimes has been perceived as a way to advance statemaking efforts, kuhl regimes—unlike community-based irrigation traditions elsewhere—have not been seen as obstacles to "modern" forms of irrigation and agricultural development. The functions kuhl regimes have performed, and continue to perform, as statemaking arenas have helped to produce a type of negotiated complementarity between local and extralocal interests in kuhls—one that has facilitated their persistence more than it has undermined their viability.

The intersection of statemaking with kuhl management is to a large extent a function of Kangra's regionality, which channeled the statemaking-through-irrigation urge toward constructive engagement with kuhl irrigation. During the precolonial period, Katoch rulers received political support and consolidated their authority by sponsoring the construction of kuhls. The enhancement of political authority through state-sponsored kuhl construction or repair was especially effective when state engagement with kuhls was linked with the support of a local temple. State sponsorship of kuhls also increased the revenue precolonial rulers received, because irrigated land was taxed at a higher rate than unirrigated land.

During the colonial period, the expansion and support of kuhl irrigation systems was consistent with broader colonial policies promoting agricultural expansion during the latter half of the nineteenth century. These policies reflected the interaction between liberal political theory concerning the role of government and material interests in revenue generation. By establishing secure private property rights, encouraging market expansion and transportation links, and codifying irrigation customs, the colonial administration sought to create conditions conducive to agrarian investment, progress, and development. Material benefits followed from these various "arts and rationalities of governing" (Bratich, Packer, and McCarthy 2003:4) because the expansion of kuhl irrigation increased tax revenues through the higher assessments levied on irrigated land and because increased agricultural production contributed to food security, which became an increasingly important policy concern during the late nineteenth century.[4]

India's independence from British rule in 1947 and the ensuing efforts to craft a modern nation-state unleashed a different set of statemaking processes, rooted in democratic practice and conditioned by discourses of modernity and development. These processes restructured the relationship between kuhl regimes and the state. Conditioned by the exigencies of democratic governance and inflected by transnational discourses of modernity and development, state engagement with kuhl regimes has both undermined and enhanced their durability. The contradiction derives primarily from (unintended?) consequences associated with the dynamics of electoral politics, state interest in devolution and control, and the transnational hegemony of modern forms of bureaucratic organization. These dynamics have produced a situation in which the actions of a democratic state undermine preexisting regional and local institutions characterized by civic engagement and participatory processes.

The logic that gives rise to these contradictory processes can be brought into focus by examining the various forms of post-independence state intervention in kuhl regimes. A good starting point is the willingness of the IPHD to assume full management authority for some of the longest and most difficult to maintain kuhls in Kangra in the 1970s. Although the elected village councils within the command areas of these kuhls did request that the state government take over their management, the government's decision to grant the request stemmed from strategic assessments of the short-term electoral gains that would (and did) ensue. As is often the case with decisions driven by short-term electoral pragmatism, the makers of this decision underemphasized its long-term costs. Perhaps the most direct long-term cost is the ongoing government expenditure now required to maintain an irrigation system that farmers had previously maintained. An indirect cost was the total elimination of prior local organization and capacity for managing the kuhl.

The ramifications also extend to adjacent kuhls. They include the weakening of the watershed-level network of interkuhl relations that previously had provided crucial pulses of resources to kuhl regimes damaged by floods and earthquakes or experiencing severe water scarcity. The IPHD, by separating the kuhls it manages from the interkuhl networks in which they were previously embedded, has reduced the resilience of adjacent community-managed kuhl regimes and increased their vulnerability to environmental shocks. Ironically, this increased their dependence on government support to replace the resources that robust networks had once provided. Yet because of the high levels of government investment in IPHD-managed kuhls and the absence of any water tax (due primarily to farmer opposition) to help recoup those investments, IPHD financial support has been unavailable for community-managed kuhls. In recent years, managers of community-managed kuhls have been forced to approach other state entities, such as the Public Works Department, the

Forest Department, the Revenue Department, and the Block Development Office, for relatively small grants to repair flood damage. The concentration of government financial support on IPHD-managed kuhls, in combination with weakened interkuhl networks, has contributed to the difficulties community-managed kuhl regimes face in mobilizing adequate labor and financial resources to maintain the integrity of the kuhl. Meanwhile, the large investments—supplemented by support from international aid agencies—that the IPHD continues to make in the kuhls it manages accentuates the contrast between government support for government-managed kuhl regimes and that for community-managed regimes.

A second contradictory effect of state involvement in kuhl irrigation stems from the ways in which state attempts to support community-managed kuhl regimes through the formalization of their management structures has led to greater state oversight and control of those regimes. Efforts to establish formal cooperative irrigation societies, which date back to the community development programs of the 1950s and have roots in transnational discourses of development and modernity, imposed a bureaucratic organizational template on kuhl regimes. In the Neugal watershed, two kuhl regimes were organized into formal cooperative irrigation societies and registered under the Cooperative Societies Registration Act. Since their formation in the 1950s, other kuhl regimes in the watershed have adopted this organizational model. Although the veneer of a common organizational template masks the quite different social processes that continue in different kuhl regimes, all committees registered under the Cooperative Societies Act are subject to annual audits and reviews by the Department of Cooperative Societies. These audits and reviews continue to this day and constitute microscale sites of government oversight and review.

The bureaucratization of kuhl regimes through the creation of managing committees and increased interaction with state bureaucracies has also influenced local patterns of social power and influence along lines of caste, class, and gender. In general, kuhl committees are dominated by better-educated, high-caste men. Their involvement in kuhl management has tended to undermine the influence and authority of the kohli, who is generally not Rajput or Brahman. Furthermore, the increased interaction with state entities, regarding, for example, grants to repair flood damage to kuhl channels, reinforces gender inequality because of the cultural proscriptions against women's participation in public arenas, the assumptions of many government bureaucrats that farmers are male, and their perception that men, not women, should be interacting with government officials regarding kuhl management decisions.[5] In a related vein, Madhu Sarin and colleagues (2003) have demonstrated how devolution policies associated with community-based forest management in India (e.g., Joint Forest Management and Community Forest Management) have had similar negative effects on gender and caste equity, have provided avenues for the extension of state control into community spaces, and have undermined local democratic decision-making processes.

The ability of government to undermine or strengthen the power of local groups relative to each other and to the state itself has important implications for understanding local patterns of authority and conflict with respect to the control and management of natural resources. We have seen how the colonial land revenue settlements in Kangra, contrary to the stated objective of simply recording the existing array of rights and obligations surrounding land, actually created new forms of community and property. In other areas, such as the Punjab plains, state actions in the nineteenth century simultaneously established new property rights regimes and strengthened the power of elite groups who were granted access to and control over previously uncultivated areas in exchange for their political support. In south Bihar and southern Tamil Nadu, state policies undermined the authority and resource base of the landed gentry, who previously had played key roles in the management of the local gravity-flow irrigation systems. In both regions, the undermining of this class precipitated the collapse of some of these systems. In Kangra, the creation of the *Riwaj-i-Abpashi* not only codified customary irrigation rights and customs but also constituted new arenas for contesting water rights. Indeed, in the 1980s it provided the basis for a community-managed kuhl regime to lodge a successful court case against the IPHD's planned expansion of an upstream IPHD-managed kuhl. Unless the variety of state roles in local natural resource management is teased out, our understanding of them will remain incomplete and our conclusions and policy prescriptions will be fraught with unexpected consequences and unexplained outcomes.

The actions of democratic states can have diverse effects on local democratic practices, on communities, and on regional institutions. One of the central challenges associated with state-sponsored development efforts that entail decentralization and devolution is how to engage with local and regional institutional structures in a way that neither undermines local capacities for democratic practice nor strengthens the power of elite groups. To date, evidence suggests that decentralization efforts in the context of natural resource management have tended to weaken local institutional capacities and have further disenfranchised subordinate groups—thus undermining the very institutional structures and equity objectives these efforts ostensibly seek to advance. Attentiveness to the importance of understanding the historical development and contemporary roles and contributions of regional institutions is part of the process of reframing state intervention in natural resource management regimes to address the unsustainable contradiction whereby democratic states undermine local and regional democratic institutions.[6]

In Kangra, we have seen how state engagement with kuhl regimes has both weakened and strengthened their durability. On one hand, IPHD involvement in kuhl management has undermined the effectiveness of interkuhl networks and is inequitable from a distributional standpoint. On the other hand, different entities within the state government have played, and in some contexts continue to play, a supportive role for kuhl regimes by providing arenas of legitimate authority for resolving conflicts, financial resources to meet short-term resource mobilization needs, technical assistance, and so forth. When these examples of supportive state roles in local resource management regimes converge with a prioritization of equity, defined expansively to include both intertemporal aspects and current social justice concerns, then the broad outlines of an architecture of state and society relations, rooted in historically conditioned patterns of regionality, will emerge that contains the elements necessary for sustained democratic practice and responsible environmental management.

A close reading of statemaking as it developed in Kangra with respect to kuhl irrigation underlines the importance of understanding how the imprint of regionality affects the mutual constitution of state and society. In Kangra, the state is not a rapacious and centralized entity single-mindedly focused on resource extraction and liquidation of natural capital, nor are communities homogeneous, independent entities that, if left alone, would be able to actualize their (presumably) innate conservation ethic. Instead, as we have seen through the lens of kuhl irrigation, state and community are bound together in processes that constitute both statemaking and community-making enterprises. These enterprises, shaped by powerful attributes of regionality in Kangra, produced specific state formations and communities. A close reading of the mutual constitution of state and society, as inflected by regionality and microscale spatial and temporal heterogeneities, provides the key to identifying the points in space and moments in time when statemaking and community-making will converge in a way that either strengthens local democratic practice or undermines it.

Appendix 1

A NOTE ON METHODS

ALMOST INVARIABLY, THE PEOPLE I MET IN KANGRA DURING FIELDWORK appreciated this research project—a reflection, perhaps, of the place that kuhls occupy in Kangri culture. It made good sense, people thought, for someone from the United States to come and learn about kuhls and to carry those lessons back home. This general support for the study did not, however, translate into unfettered access to anyone with whom I wished to speak about the kuhls. My status as a white male foreigner who could speak Hindi but not the local mountain dialect (Pahari) positioned me in specific ways—it helped secure access to some social arenas but blocked me from engagement with others.

In general, the privileges of my status granted me relatively easy access to other men and traditionally male spaces. These included, for example, male farmers, kohlis, and members of kuhl committees (most but not all of whom were men), as well as government offices, record rooms, and bureaucrats. On the other hand, my status made it difficult for me to interact with women farmers. To a lesser extent, caste and class divisions further molded the contours of my social interactions with people in Kangra, although my somewhat liminal outsider status enabled some degree of fluidity in this regard. Thus, my own positionality necessarily influenced my view of the kuhl regimes and has affected the way in which I have presented their story. Although I am confident that the primary outline of the story of the kuhls would remain the same even if viewed from a different vantage point, I am also sure that a different observation point would lead to modifications of subplots and nuances of interpretation that might vary from those presented here.

I was drawn to Kangra, which I had first visited in 1981, as a study site because of my interest in employing a watershed perspective to examine social relations structured around water and forest management. The existence of sharply delineated watersheds, the extensive kuhl irrigation systems, and the cooperative village forest societies in Kangra were an attractive combination. Although I had initially hoped to examine interactions between water and forest management, it soon became evident that focusing only on the kuhl irrigation systems would be challenge enough. In Kangra Valley, more than 3,000 kuhls irrigate approximately 32,000 hectares, quite likely more than in any other region in the western Himalaya. Within Kangra Valley, I chose one river basin, that of the Neugal River, and the kuhls that diverted water from it, for collecting primary data. I chose a small river basin as the unit for primary data collection in order to facilitate examination of interkuhl relations and their possible role in explaining the persistence of kuhl regimes. I chose the Neugal river basin because it had the highest density of kuhl networks in the valley.

During the fieldwork period, I employed a wide variety of research methods. These included extensive participant observation, three different formal surveys and one informal survey, and informal interviews and group discussions with farmers, kohlis, elder men, officials in the Irrigation and Public Health Department, and district officials. I also made extensive use of colonial documents kept in the District Commissioner's Library and the Revenue Department. Other secondary data included village-level records regarding kuhl management, government records of some of the kuhls presently under their management, and studies published by the Himachal Pradesh Agricultural University in Palampur that provided comparative and background information about local agricultural and resource management systems.

After settling on the Neugal River watershed as the study site, I had to find a way of introducing myself and the research project to the watermasters of the 39 kuhls that drew water from the Neugal. At the suggestion of Anil Gupta at the Indian Institute of Management, Ahmedabad (my faculty advisor for part of the research), I invited the kohlis of all these kuhls to a midday meal in the district town of Palampur. More than 30 kohlis attended, including a few who managed kuhls for the Irrigation and Public Health Department. This initial meeting gave me an opportunity to introduce myself and the purpose of the study, as well as to facilitate discussion among the kohlis regarding some of the current issues in kuhl management. This general meeting set a precedent for the smaller group meetings I organized periodically throughout the fieldwork to generate group discussion among those present, to present my thoughts about what I had been finding, and to elicit feedback on my work. These meetings proved to be valuable opportunities to test local responses to my own thinking and to exchange information between kuhl regimes about management strategies and solutions to common problems.

Throughout the fieldwork I used participant observation to familiarize myself with local agricultural and water management practices. This included plowing with a pair of bullocks and planting, cultivating, and harvesting paddy on a plot of land on loan from a friend, participating in the annual maintenance and repair activities of several kuhls, accompanying kohlis on their nightly patrols of the kuhl's channels to guard against water stealing and watch for channel breaches, attending kuhl committee meetings, and participating in the annual religious ceremonies associated with kuhl management. Participating in these events provided the familiarization with both water management and agricultural practices requisite for my more formal inquiries.

Before conducting semistructured surveys, and with the help of Kim Berry, I made rough sketch maps of all the kuhl regimes in the Neugal basin, and we measured their flows during the dry season, when dependence on kuhl irrigation water was greatest. I stratified all the kuhls in the watershed by flow, length, command area, and number of villages irrigated and then classified them into three groups: small, medium, and large. I chose two kuhl regimes from each size class for intensive fieldwork, along with two kuhls managed by the Irrigation and Public Health Department. For each kuhl regime I developed three survey questionnaires: a farmer survey, a kohli survey, and a survey for members of the kuhl committee, if any. With the help of my research assistant, Mr. Rajesh Thakur, who had recently completed a Master of Science degree in agricultural economics at the Himachal Pradesh Agricultural University at Palampur, I surveyed farmers randomly selected from the head, middle, and tail sections of each of the six chosen kuhls, as well as the kohlis and, where present, the elected officers of the kuhl committee. Most surveys ended with a period of general, open-ended discussion that often provided useful, qualitative insights into kuhl management. Throughout the survey period, informal group meetings with farmers were also held. These provided an important forum for further investigating questions that arose during the surveying and for checking the accuracy of the perceptions we formed during the survey period.

During the second year of fieldwork I spent several months collecting and analyzing government records in order to construct two time series. The first consisted of primary census data from the 1951 decennial census up to and including the 1991 census for all of the more than 300 tikas (hamlets) that lie within the Neugal River watershed. I used this information to track the changing ratio of the agricultural and nonagricultural labor sectors as an indicator of the expanding nonfarm employment sector. The second time series consisted of tika-level information about cultivated area from 1851 through 1991, also aggregated at the watershed level. I collected this information from various settlement and assessment reports in district archives of the Revenue Department and the District Commissioner's Library. The declines in cultivated area, in combination with expanding wage labor markets and increasing population, speak to the dramatic changes in the socioeconomic context of kuhl management.

Throughout the second year of fieldwork I continued to collect relevant secondary information, including the various records that kohlis and kuhl committee members maintained regarding kuhl management. During this time I began to write between periodic visits to the field. This iterative writing process provided a valuable opportunity to discuss my developing ideas with kohlis and others knowledgeable about kuhls and to solicit their feedback and responses. During the writing, it became apparent that the analysis of kuhl regime responses to changing socioeconomic conditions would be strengthened if I used information about all the kuhl regimes in the Neugal basin. Accordingly, with the able assistance of Mr. Jugal Kishore for much of the time, I conducted interviews with kohlis, elders, and other key informants for kuhls in the Neugal watershed that I had not surveyed earlier.

Appendix 2

TWO KUHL STORIES

Recounted by Shyam Lal Sharma

"BRAHMANS DON'T DO *BEGAR*"

Precolonial hill state rulers relied on begar, or compulsory labor service, to accomplish a variety of tasks. These included transporting loads of timber, stone, and other materials required for public works, carrying letters and parcels, and providing wood and grass for the camps of government officers on field tours. The distribution of liability for different kinds of begar reflected the stratification of society by caste rank. Brahmans were exempted from all forms of begar. This story describes the consequences of violating the caste-based proscriptions against Brahmans doing begar for the construction of Kirpal Chand Kuhl. In doing so, it serves as an instrument for inscribing caste-based privilege on the regional landscape.—JMB

Kirpal Chand, brother of Raja Bhim Chand who ruled Kangra State from 1690 to 1697, built the kuhl that memorialized his name. Originating in the headwaters of the Neugal River, Kirpal Chand Kuhl meanders southward through verdant valleys and along pine-clad ridgetops for over 30 kilometers. Along its way, the kuhl irrigates hundreds of hectares of prime agricultural land within the boundaries of more than 60 hamlets. The construction of the kuhl's main channel was particularly difficult at the place known as Garh, below Village Daroh. There, the kuhl had to pass across two ridges. The only way to convey the kuhl's water between the two ridges was to construct a massive stone and earth embankment that equaled the height of the ridges and over which the kuhl's water could flow. It took 12 years of continuous work to construct the embankment. Near the end of that period, the raja's officer approached two Brahman brothers who lived in Garh and asked them to come for begar the next day.

The next day the brothers arose and did their usual lengthy morning prayers and ablutions. After finishing their spiritual practices, each brother uprooted a large tree and fashioned it into a massive forked implement. Using the uprooted tree trunks as a type of broom, they started to roll two huge boulders, each the size of a two-story house, toward the construction site in the same way one might sweep the dust off the floor. The raja's officer chanced to come upon this sight and immediately recognized their great spiritual powers. He promptly forgave both brothers their begar duties and asked them to please return home. The two boulders were left at that spot and can be seen there to this day.

"NEVER ARGUE WITH THE *KOHLI*"

The ability of the kohli to influence natural forces is renowned and is celebrated in more than one Kangri story. This one illustrates the power of the kohli and the consequences of questioning his authority. It serves as a vehicle for naturalizing the kohli's power and for claiming divine sanction for his authority.—JMB

On the left bank of the Neugal Khad, across from Bhagotla village, dangas divert water into the four kuhls, Loharal, Mahang, Taruhl, and Chamruhl, that irrigate the villages of Sidhpur Rani and Sidhpur Sarkari. Because the kuhls are of medium length and irrigate the same villages, only one kohli has traditionally been responsible for managing these kuhls. The right to be kohli is a warisi, an inherited right passed down within a family or clan from one generation to the next. The current rightholder's great great-grandfather, Gurdyal Kohli, is remembered as a kohli of great distinction and power. He had a long flowing beard, and many considered him almost a saint. During the months of May and June, when water is scarce and demand for it is high, Gurdyal Kohli used to position himself on a knoll that afforded a view of all four kuhls. On a *charpoy* [wood frame cot], he stayed there day and night directing the distribution of water through the tups of each kuhl. Neighbors and family members brought him food so that he could remain at that location until the monsoon rains began.

Once, in an altercation over water distribution, a farmer struck Gurdyal Kohli. In dignified silence Gurdyal Kohli turned from the farmer and went straight to the kuhl's danga. There, he struck his head three times against the sacred rock where for generations his ancestors had worshipped the kuhl's deity. At the same time he cried, "Mata-ji, insaaf karo" [Mother, do justice]. Suddenly, from the narrow canyon where the Neugal Khad issues forth, a deafening roar was heard. A massive wall of water came thundering and raging down the canyon. Flames and sparks leapt up from the water. Huge boulders tumbled against each other as if they were mere marbles. The destructive might of the flood washed away the dangas of all four kuhls and obliterated the upper portions of the channels that clung to the riverine cliffs. Despite years of work to repair the damage, the four kuhls never again flowed with as much water as before the farmer struck Gurdyal Kohli.

Appendix 3

SUMMARY CHARACTERISTICS OF KUHL REGIMES
OF THE NEUGAL WATERSHED

TABLE 13. Characteristics of Kuhl Regimes of the Neugal Watershed,
Right Bank, Upstream to Downstream

Kuhl	IPHD or Communal	Command Area (ha)	Channel Length (km)	No. Tikas Irrigated	Interlinkage Measure[1]
Bhradi	C	67.0	3.5	4	2.0 (H)
Chanogi	C	90.0	3.0	4	2.0 (H)
Bhagotla	C	15.0	2.5	2	1.0 (L)
Kathul	C	70.0	7.5	3	1.5 (M)
Sapruhl	C	70.0	15.0	3	2.0 (H)
Pathan	C	45.0	5.0	2	2.5 (H)
Rai	IPHD	820.0	20.0	28	1.7 (M)
Makruhl	C	20.0	3.5	2	4.0 (H)
Samruhl	C	15.0	1.0	1	5.0 (H)
Pangwan	C	60.0	1.0	1	5.0 (H)
Sonia	C	25.0	1.5	1	5.0 (H)
Gagruhl	C	27.0	3.0	2	3.0 (H)
Majettli	C	5.0	0.5	1	1.0 (L)
Bal	C	23.0	1.0	1	1.0 (L)
Natyrya	C	0.5	0.5	1	1.0 (L)

1. The interlinkage measure for a kuhl is the ratio of the number of other kuhls that irrigate each of the villages it irrigates to the number of villages the kuhl itself irrigates. When the ratio (y) is less than or equal to 1, interlinkage is low (L); when $1 < y < 2$, interlinkage is medium (M); and when $y \geq 2$, interlinkage is high (H).

2. The har/larh ratio is the number of villages whose har areas a kuhl irrigates relative to the number of villages whose larh areas it irrigates.

3. Core (C), periphery (P), or core and periphery (C/P): when larh = 0, then C; when larh = 1, then C/P; when larh > 1, then P.

Har/Larh[2]	Core or Periphery[3]	Alternative Water	No. Kohlis	Kuhl Committee	Single or Multicaste
1/0	C	N	1	Y	S
1/0	C	N	1	N	S
1/0	C	N	1	Y	S
0/2	P	Y	1	Y	M
1/2	P	Y	1	Y	M
2/0	C	N	2	Y	M
4/3	P	N	—	—	M
2/0	C	N	1	Y	M
1/0	C	N	1	Y	M
1/0	C	N	1	Y	M
1/0	C	N	1	Y	M
2/0	C	N	1	Y	M
1/0	C	N	0	N	S
1/0	C	N	0	N	S
1/0	C	N	0	N	S

TABLE 14. Characteristics of Kuhl Regimes of the Neugal Watershed,
Left Bank, Upstream to Downstream

Kuhl	IPHD or Communal	Command Area (ha)	Channel Length (km)	No. Tikas Irrigated	Interlinkage Measure[1]
Ghran	IPHD	?	5.0	9	1.0 (L)
Dewan C.	IPHD	185	25.0	24	3.2 (H)
Mia Fateh	IPHD	256	20.0	23	2.7 (H)
Dai	IPHD	257	25.0	22	3.0 (H)
Ghughrul	IPHD	128	5.0	5	4.0 (H)
Kirpal C.	IPHD	1,713	33.0	62	2.6 (H)
Raniya	C	545	12.0	10	4.3 (H)
Mahang	C	?	?	8	4.2 (H)
Loharal	C	?	?	6	6.0 (H)
Taruhl	C	65	6.0	7	5.0 (H)
Chamruhl	C	65	6.0	7	5.0 (H)
Patnuhl	IPHD	526	11.0	25	3.7 (H)
Menjha	C	140	8.0	3	5.0 (H)
Sangar C.	IPHD	324	26.0	16	2.5 (H)
Masanol	C	40	4.0	4	0.5 (L)
Spein	C	15	1.5	1	1.0 (L)
Sulah	C	4	1.0	1	1.0 (L)
Saldian	C	2	1.0	1	1.0 (L)
Machlena	C	15	1.0	1	1.0 (L)
Karni	C	4	0.5	1	1.0 (L)
Rein	C	40	2.0	1	1.0 (L)
Bouru	C	9	0.5	1	1.0 (L)
Upperli	C	?	?	18	1.5 (M)
Buhli	C	300	10	17	2.5 (H)

1. The interlinkage measure for a kuhl is the ratio of the number of other kuhls that irrigate each of the villages it irrigates to the number of villages the kuhl itself irrigates. When the ratio (y) is less than or equal to 1, interlinkage is low (L); when $1 < y < 2$, interlinkage is medium (M); and when $y \geq 2$, interlinkage is high (H).

2. The har/larh ratio is the number of villages whose har areas a kuhl irrigates relative to the number of villages whose larh areas it irrigates.

3. Core (C), periphery (P), or core and periphery (C/P): when larh = 0, then C; when larh = 1, then C/P; when larh < 1, then P.

4. An asterisk (*) indicates that alternative water sources are available for a portion of the kuhl's command area but not for the whole command area.

Har/Larh[2]	Core or Periphery[3]	Alternative Water[4]	No. Kohlis	Kuhl Committee	Single or Multicaste
1/0	C	N	—	—	S
3/2	P	Y*	—	—	M
5/6	P	Y*	—	—	M
4/1	C/P	Y*	—	—	M
2/0	C	N	—	—	M
5/5	P	Y*	—	—	M
3/1	C/P	Y	2	Y	M
4/1	C/P	N	1	N	M
2/0	C	N	1	N	M
3/0	C	N	1	Y	M
3/0	C	N	1	Y	M
5/2	P	Y*	—	—	M
1/1	C/P	N	1	Y	M
5/1	C/P	Y	—	—	M
2/0	C	N	1	Y	M
1/0	C	N	0	N	S
1/0	C	N	0	N	S
1/0	C	N	0	N	S
1/0	C	N	0	N	S
1/0	C	N	0	N	S
1/0	C	N	0	N	S
1/0	C	N	0	N	S
2/0	C	Y	1	N	M
2/0	C	Y	1	N	M

NOTES

INTRODUCTION

1. Chief Secretary to the Government of the Punjab to Secretary to the Government of India, Home Department, telegrams no. 239 and 240, 23 April 1905. Delhi: National Archives.

2. See Agarwal and Chak 1991 for a discussion of landslide dams in the Himalaya, including their frequency and large contribution to overall erosion and sediment loads.

3. In contrast to the igneous and metamorphic Dhaula Dhar range, the Sivalik Hills are composed of a highly erosive sedimentary conglomerate. This area is known as the Changar, which means "dry." In the Changar, streams and rivers erode deep gorges through the hills, eliminating the possibility of gravity-flow irrigation. Cultivation is restricted to the steep, dry hillsides. Where cultivation is possible, the primary food grains are maize and wheat, often intercropped with pulses.

4. Irrigation as a common property resource differs significantly from other commonly managed resources such as grazing land and forests. Grazing land and forests are essentially reservoirs of solar energy. The key management challenge concerns how to distribute the benefits of that stored energy to the community of rights holders while preserving the productive capacity of the resource. With irrigation, there is no prior reservoir of resource benefits to distribute. Until collective action has been undertaken to provide water for irrigation and other purposes, there is no possibility of anyone's benefiting from it. This contrasts with the possibility of an individual's cutting trees from a forest or grazing her animals on uncultivated land. The possibility of irrigation presupposes the existence of collective action. Although the free rider challenge does exist in the context of irrigation, rather than threatening the productivity of the resource base itself—as it can in the context of forests, pastures, and fisheries—it reduces the water available to other users without necessarily threatening the future biophysical viability of the resource.

5. Some of the many important contributions to the field of common property resource theory include Agrawal 1996, Berkes 1986, Bromley 1992, McCay and Acheson 1990, McKean 1992, Ostrom 1990, Ostrom, Gardner, and Walker 1994, Seabright 1993, and Wade 1988. See Mosse 1997b for a thoughtful critique of the institutional-economic modeling approach of common property resource theory.

6. These exclusionary effects have current relevance. For example, only households whose ancestors' names appear on the list of proprietors included in Alexander Anderson's 1894 Kullu forest settlement are considered valid rights holders and thus eligible for compensatory remuneration in exchange for the annulment of their rights as part of the establishment and management of the Great Himalaya National Park in Kullu District, Himachal Pradesh. Descendants of families whose names do not appear on the list (most likely woman-headed households, nonagriculturalists, and lower-caste households) qualify for no compensation or government subsidies, even though from a usufructuary standpoint, both they and their ancestors could have been as intimately engaged in the management and utilization of resources currently within the park boundaries as those whose family names appear in Anderson's settlement (Saberwal and Chhatre 2003).

7. Not surprisingly, in this agrarian environment grazing land was quite scarce. Before harvest time, grazing was confined to the uncultivated areas adjacent to hamlets. After harvest, the stubble-covered fields became temporary grazing land let out to nomadic pastoralists, or Gaddis, to graze their herds of sheep and goats— a practice that continues to this day. Groups of Gaddis organize their seasonal migrations between the high alpine meadows of the Dhaula Dhar and the low Sivalik Hills to coincide with the availability of vegetation for grazing. As Gaddi herders and their flocks of goats and sheep pass through cultivated areas that have been harvested, they receive payments in kind (food and cooking fuel) in exchange for penning their flocks on the harvested fields and leaving behind valuable manure (Saberwal 1999).

1 / AN EXPLANATORY TAPESTRY

1. Not all common property resource problems conform to the structure of the prisoners' dilemma game. Some translate into other games, such as "chicken" and "assurance" (Bardhan 1993b; Ostrom 1990).

2. See Williamson 1975 and 1981 for transactions-cost analysis and Coase 1984 for its roots in institutional economics.

3. In order to explore the emergence of collective action, Ostrom, Gardner, and Walker (1994) developed formal models based on game theory to examine the conditions under which rational, utility-maximizing individuals would collaborate with others for the provision of a collective good. Acknowledging the constraining

and somewhat unrealistic assumptions associated with one-shot game theoretic models of human behavior, they modeled behavior (both experimentally in the laboratory and in field settings) using theories of repeated, competitive, n-person games in which the players operate under conditions of bounded rationality and are able to communicate with one another. These games are embedded in a broader institutional framework that specifies the structure of incentives and penalties and costs and benefits that individual actors face. Using this approach, Ostrom and colleagues demonstrated that cooperative strategies do exist as an equilibrium outcome of these types of games.

4. Ostrom, Gardner, and Walker (1994) do note that other researchers, such as Isaac and Walker (1988, 1991) and Hackett, Schlager, and Walker (1993), have observed similar positive effects on payoffs and efficiency enhancement resulting from face-to-face communication. However, explanations for why such communication is important have been harder to come by. On the basis of their empirical research, Ostrom and colleagues (1994:199) suggest that the positive effects of face-to-face communication derive from the fact that communication affords individuals opportunities to develop an agreement that approximates the group's maximum payoff and to coordinate a strategy for implementing that agreement.

5. The uneven application and enforcement of rules also creates space for the preferential treatment of the more powerful individuals within a community. Thus Agrawal (2001) has demonstrated how the village forest councils in the hills of Kumaon, India, selectively enforce rules governing forest use in a manner that reflects the local power asymmetries of caste and gender. In this case, the proportion of rule violators who pay the fines levied against them is far greater among women and low-caste men then it is among upper-caste persons (2001:30).

6. These rules may operate at the constitutional, the collective choice, or the operational level (Ostrom 1990). Ciriacy-Wantrup and Bishop (1975) also distinguished three levels of decision-making rules within an organization. The lowest, "operating level," rules refer to the day-to-day decisions that organizations make regarding inputs, outputs, and similar operational activities. Middle-level, or "institutional level," rules regulate decision-making on the operational level. Rules affecting the structures of institutions are made at the highest "policy level." These include laws or acts specifying how people can create a legitimate, chartered organization that has standing vis-à-vis government authorities. In this conception of a nested cluster of decision-making levels, decisions made at a higher level affect those at the next lower level. Higher-level rules constitute the context of change for lower-level rules.

7. In contexts where important factors are not monetized, changing opportunity costs convey the same meaning as changes in relative prices.

8. Fritz Scharpf (1978:355) extended this line of reasoning to create a two-by-two table with resource substitutability and resource importance as the two axes. He argued that an organization's relationship to an element in its environment

would be one of high dependence when substitutability was low and importance was high, one of low dependence when substitutability and importance were both low or both high, and one of independence when substitutability was high and importance low.

9. The distinction between material and exchange resources builds on a distinction made earlier by Jerald Hage (1978) between the environment as a resource provider and the environment as a network of organizational relations.

10. This statement is true for all kuhls during the hot, dry, pre-monsoon season. In some areas, however, ephemeral streams that flow during the rainy season are diverted into kuhl channels, thus reducing dependence on the perennial water source. Using Scharpf's two-by-two table, this suggests that although the importance of water for kuhls remains high throughout the year, the substitutability of perennial stream water varies depending on the presence of nearby ephemeral streams.

11. Roland Warren (1967:404–6) differentiated organizational fields into four categories based on (1) the degree to which goals were shared among units, (2) the degree to which interunit decision-making was centralized, (3) the level at which decision-making authority resided, (4) the extent to which the units were autonomously structured, (5) the level of commitment to interunit leadership relative to unit leadership, and (6) the degree of "collectivity orientation." Of the four types of interorganizational field contexts (unitary, federative, coalitional, and social-choice), the "coalitional context" best describes the field of interkuhl relations. Individual kuhls coordinate their interactions in an ad hoc manner when and to the extent that their goals overlap; there is no formal organization for interkuhl decision-making; authority for interkuhl coordination rests within each kuhl, primarily with the watermaster; most kuhls are autonomous from each other but they do coordinate their labor inputs for joint efforts; although norms govern the relationship between watermasters, there is no commitment to a joint form of leadership or management structure; and there is a minimal level of "collectivity orientation" among the irrigators of different kuhls.

12. The social relations that generate trust and cooperation can also create the conditions for conflict and "enormous malfeasance" (Granovetter 1985:491–93). Networks of interdependence can generate interorganizational competition as well as cooperation (Hage 1978:121). Within kuhls this is exemplified by the fact that some of the fiercest conflicts over water can occur between members of the same clan, especially when control over water is related to fraternal conflicts over the partition, ownership, and cultivation of previously joint landholdings.

13. Another way of expressing the essentialness variable is in terms of the value of the benefit that the regime provides. High-value benefits, whether measured according to monetary or other measuring scales, are "essential," whereas low-value benefits would be considered "inessential."

14. Symbolic capital is the capital of "honor and prestige," which can be accumulated in various ways, including the conversion of material capital (Bourdieu

1990 [1980]:118). Accumulated stocks of symbolic capital can be used for mobilizing resources such as labor (through corvée) and political support during times of need. Symbolic and material capital circulate within a common economy; people, states, and other agents act in ways that maintain and augment both.

2 / THE DYNAMIC LANDSCAPE OF KUHL IRRIGATION

1. At major life-cycle rituals, communal work parties are organized to fell, split, and transport the wood required to cook food for the meals at which large numbers of guests are fed over three to five days. Those who contribute labor during these events receive a free meal and, most importantly, the right to call upon communal labor at some unspecified future time.

2. After the British defeated the Sikhs in 1846, thousands of men who had served in the Sikh army, now unemployed, returned to their homes in the low hills of what is now Himachal Pradesh, including Kangra Valley. The earnings these soldiers had previously brought home had been used to help meet government revenue demands and for other large household expenses, such as the purchase of draft animals. Barnes remarked that not only did the presence of these unemployed soldiers at home represent a significant reduction in household income, but also, being trained as soldiers, they were not particularly skilled or interested in agricultural pursuits. The elimination of this source of income was one of the reasons he recommended a reduction in revenue demands for these areas at the time of the first settlement (Barnes 1855:53).

3. Although planters "threatened to import labor on a large scale" because the local supply of labor was so "uncertain and irregular," this appears not to have occurred. Note regarding Kangra tea written in 1892 by R. A. Ballard, honorary secretary to the Kangra Valley Tea Planters' Association (Punjab District Gazetteer 1909:120–23).

4. To track these changes at the local level, I compiled information on the area cultivated and the proportion of agricultural to nonagricultural male workers for all the tikas in the Neugal Khad watershed. I used information from the tika level because, despite numerous changes in the boundaries of the larger units of administration—that is, mauza, *taluka, patwar* circle, tehsil, and district—the area within each tika has remained constant since the first regular settlement in 1850. In the rare instances in which two tikas had been amalgamated or their names changed, I confirmed the changes with the concerned *patwari* (village-level Revenue Department official) and adjusted the data accordingly. This permitted the comparison of cultivated area over time within individual tikas. To compile the time series data for the area cultivated in the Neugal watershed, I first identified the 24 mauzas within the watershed and the more than 300 tikas that compose them. I excluded mauzas downstream of the kuhl-irrigated areas, where the Neugal

River enters the dry, hilly Changar region. Taluka-level assessment reports provided tika-level cultivated area information for the 1851, 1871, 1889, and 1915 settlements. The next available information sources were the 1971, 1981, and 1990 censuses. Prior censuses did not include the area cultivated, and 2001 census data for cultivated area were not released before this book went to press. After compiling tika-level time series data on cultivated area for the dates mentioned, I aggregated the information first at the mauza level and then at the watershed level. Although the tika-level cultivated area from the 2001 census was unavailable, my observation of the watershed during the fieldwork period leads me to conclude that the overall pattern and extent of cultivation have changed little since the early 1990s.

5. I also began tracking agricultural and nonagricultural employment trends for women. However, wildly fluctuating ratios of agricultural to nonagricultural women workers, and even fluctuations in the total number of women workers, rendered the data suspect and unusable. For example, the 1961 census reported 6,594 female agricultural workers in the irrigated portion of the Neugal watershed. Ten years later, this figure had inexplicably plummeted to 944, and the number of nonagricultural female workers had also declined—despite a total population increase from 32,728 to 39,768. In effect, several thousand women workers had simply disappeared from the census records during a period when increased nonfarm employment for males was shifting the burden of agricultural work to women (Sarin 1989). These fluctuations were most likely due to inconsistencies in the ways census enumerators phrased questions about women's employment and the bias among most households toward not admitting that women worked in the fields. The ability to withdraw female labor from agricultural work is a strong and public indicator of a household's class status. Households that cannot afford to do so are reluctant to tell census enumerators that women in the household are agricultural workers.

6. The 1953 Himachal Pradesh Consolidation of Land Holdings Act and the Himachal Pradesh Holding Consolidation and Prevention of Fragmentation Act of 1971 provide legal leverage for consolidating landholdings, which in 1977 averaged 13 different parcels (Mehta and Kumari 1990:74). Consolidation, contingent upon the request of a majority of farmers, has been most successful in the flatter portions of the state (below 2,500 feet in elevation), which border the Punjab plains. Although consolidation is supported by academics, policymakers, and government officials, farmers themselves generally prefer a dispersed rather than a concentrated pattern of landownership, in order to distribute risk across a variety of elevational gradients, soil types, and other microclimate variables (Greenberg 1997:94–95). With respect to labor obligations for kuhl-irrigated parcels, consolidation has minimal impact, because labor contributions are generally calculated as a proportion of irrigated land, regardless of its degree of dispersal or concentration.

7. In Uttar Pradesh, *guhl* is the local name for gravity-flow irrigation systems.

8. A major kuhl has a perennial water source and irrigates two or more villages. The estimate of the number of kuhls in Kangra Valley comes from the *Riwaj-i-Abpashi* (Irrigation Customs), which was revised as part of the 1915 settlement of Kangra District. The area irrigated by kuhls is drawn from *Statistical Outline of Himachal Pradesh* (1990).

9. In general, the lower terraces (har) receive a more assured supply of water and are more fertile than the upper areas (larh). Most hamlets are located in larh areas in order to maximize productive use of the lower terraces and because high ridgelines are more defensible. During periods of peak agricultural activity, draft animals are kept in simple sheds in the har, and often farmers sleep there to prevent illicit water use, especially during times of water scarcity.

10. Among the kuhls of Kangra, there is no simple association of one kohli to one kuhl. The relationship between kohlis and kuhls is scale dependent. The largest kuhls are managed by three to five kohlis, each responsible for one of the main channels of the kuhl. Smaller kuhls are managed by a single kohli, and in some instances one kohli may be responsible for managing a small group of two or three adjacent kuhls. The smallest kuhls are managed informally with no kohli.

11. Whereas farmers' dependence on kuhl water for irrigation is seasonal, others depended on it year-round and hence had interests in maintaining year-round flows. Kuhl hydropower was previously used to power small mills (*graths*) to grind all the wheat, corn, and other grains and pulses of the area. In exchange for grinding 15 kilograms of grain, the owner of the grath would keep one kilogram of flour. Every kuhl had at least one or two graths along their channel. The larger kuhls had as many as 15 to 25 graths. Grath owners had a strong vested interest in maintaining water flow in the kuhl. They would regularly walk the length of the channel, clearing debris, repairing leaks, and performing other tasks necessary to maintain the flow required for their mills. Often they fashioned wooden screens to prevent the waterwheel from picking up leaves and twigs. These actions helped provide clean water flows throughout the year. With electrification, most graths have been replaced by electrically powered mills, despite people's stated preference for grath-ground flour.

12. Similarly, Edward Martin (1986:317) reported that in the farmer-managed irrigation systems he studied in Nepal, the structure of the organization for irrigation management was directly related to the amount of labor required to maintain the system.

13. I do not have complete information regarding the number of woman-headed households in the kuhl-irrigated portion of the Neugal watershed. However, casual observation suggests that they make up no more than 10 percent of all households. The attendance register for Pangwan Kuhl shows that 7 of the 75 households that use Pangwan Kuhl water are woman headed. All but two of these women have sons who participate in khana; those two are excused from khana but still receive irrigation water. The proportion of woman-headed households is much higher in the nonirrigable Changar region bordering the southern edge of Kangra Valley.

There, the majority of households are woman-headed for substantial periods because of male out-migration.

14. The 13 kuhls are Bhradi, Chanogi, Raniya, Bhagotla, Katuhl, Sapruhl, Pathan, Masanol, Makruhl, Pangwan, Sonia, Upperli, and Buhli.

15. The six kuhls are Mahang, Loharal, Taruhl, Chamruhl, Menjha, and Gagruhl.

16. The eight kuhls are Menjha, Sapruhl, Masanol, Makruhl, Sonia, Gagruhl, Upperli, and Buhli.

17. The five kuhls are Mahang, Loharal, Taruhl, Chamruhl, and Pangwan.

18. John Ambler (1989:358) described a similar system he observed in the Tampo River in western Sumatra in which local custom (*adat*) forbade the use of mud or straw in the headworks of upstream irrigation systems, in order to ensure water flow for downstream systems.

19. The risk of damage to the ripening crop from autumn and spring hailstorms has implications for the timing of crops, varieties sown, and method of sowing. The advantage of mach is that the paddy crop gets a head start several weeks before the rains and therefore can be harvested sooner than paddy sown by battar. This reduces the likelihood of damage by an autumn hailstorm. Varieties of paddy that have longer growing cycles and whose stalks are easily broken cannot be sown in the middle to upper reaches of the watershed. The risk of hail damage to them is too great. An early wheat harvest is preferred because it enables early sowing of the paddy crop. Therefore, the sooner the wheat can be sowed following the paddy harvest, the less likely that hail will damage the next season's paddy.

20. The finger is the smallest unit of measure for water. The kohli also measures flow using the following cross-sectional areas: *bilroo,* the mouth of an earthen vessel used to carry and store water; *gala,* the space created by touching the thumbs and forefingers of both hands; *seer,* the space created by touching the thumb and forefinger of one hand; *nakhod,* the equivalent of two galas; and *nala,* the equivalent of four nakhods.

21. A thimbi is a local volumetric measure, previously made of a hollowed piece of wood, now metal, that holds approximately two kilograms of threshed, unhusked rice. Traditionally, harvest time was also when members of the other service and artisan castes, such as the carpenter (*tarkhan*), blacksmith (*lohar*), potter (*kumhar*), and basketmaker (*dhoumna*), received payment in kind for rendering their services during the previous agricultural season. Except for in-kind payments made to the kohli, cash payments made at the time of service have replaced many of these other in-kind, harvest-time payments.

22. Field preparation for potato sowing entails plowing, breaking remaining clods, removing the kharif crop residue, leveling, and furrowing. Farmers dig a long furrow (12 inches deep) through the middle of the longitudinal axis of the field. Shallow furrows (6 inches deep, 18 inches apart) are dug at right angles to it as far as the field bund. They then plant seed potatoes in the raised rows between the shallow furrows.

3 / STATEMAKING AND IRRIGATION IN KANGRA

1. Alliances between elements within the state and dominant social groups that may be mutually beneficial often work to the detriment of other social groups, as in the case of the nomadic graziers whom the canal colonies displaced. In some instances groups displaced by one set of policies may seek redress through strategic alliances with other elements of the state, as Saberwal (1999) documented with regard to Gaddi–Revenue Department alliances in Kangra.

2. When the state chooses to exercise its monopoly over the legitimate use of force against local communities and groups, the metaphor of negotiation fails and the situation becomes analogous to what Nancy Peluso (1993) called "coercive conservation."

3. This should not be taken to imply that state-society and state-economy distinctions are unimportant. To the contrary, these taken-for-granted distinctions are historical products of the evolution of institutions of modern government that mask the blurred boundaries and interpenetration of state, society, and economy. The common illusion of separateness is an effect of statemaking processes "that create the appearance of a world fundamentally divided into state and society and state and economy" (Mitchell 1999:95). Analysis of these processes reveals the interlinkages among these elements and is central to understanding the appearance of the modern state.

4. Early state regimes in Kangra conformed to Ludden's definition of medieval kingdoms as "networks of transactions rather than bureaucratic institutions," the latter being more characteristic of state regimes in Kangra just before the onset of colonial rule in 1846.

5. Stanley Wolpert (1982:108) noted that the major Rajput dynasties themselves originated in Central Asia.

6. According to local legend, the first raja of the Katoch lineage, Bhum Chand, sprang from the perspiration of the goddess in the temple at Kangra. Two hundred and thirty-four generations later, his descendant Susarma-Chand fought on the side of the Kauravas in the great war of the Mahabharata. Tracing dynastic lineages back to their mythological origins is another "technology of power" used to legitimate political authority that developed during the sixth and seventh centuries in South Asia (Ludden 1999:77).

7. Members of the Katoch lineage founded the principalities of Jaswan, Guler, Siba, and Datarpur. Two separate Rajput clans to the west and southeast of the old Kangra State also claim descent from the Katoch lineage (Hutchison and Vogel 1933).

8. Upon his return to Ghazni, Mahmud displayed the vast amounts of gold, silver, and precious gems he had taken from the fort and the nearby goddess temple. Because it is doubtful that the rajas of Kangra could have accumulated such vast

wealth, Sir Alexander Cunningham and other historians have argued that the Hindu rajas of Kabul had placed much of their wealth, including their genealogical tree, in Kangra for safekeeping. Anand Pal Shahi of Kabul had organized a confederacy of his vassals and fellow rulers to protect Peshawar and his trans-Indus dominions against the Muslim invaders. The hill rajas of Kangra and neighboring states were part of this confederacy and had left their own states unprotected while serving with Anand Pal Shahi. Because the hill rajas of Kangra were part of the Kabul confederacy, some of the confederacy's wealth might well have been stored in the fort at Kangra (Hutchison and Vogel 1933:115–120).

9. Trade between Kabul and Kangra continued throughout the period of British rule. Residents of Kabul reportedly prized Kangra green tea, introduced by the British, through the middle of the twentieth century.

10. Akbar's interest in Kangra was stimulated by the things for which it was famous, including its strong fort, basmati rice, the treatment of eye diseases, and the manufacture of new noses. New noses were in demand because it was not an uncommon punishment for criminals, especially those accused of sexual offenses, to have their noses cut off. The practice continued into British rule, and at least one early European traveler in Kangra described the technique (Hutchison and Vogel 1933:148; Punjab District Gazetteer 1926:61).

11. Twenty-two arched doorways lead into the great audience hall Sansar Chand constructed at Tira-Sujanpur. Sansar Chand reportedly assigned each doorway to one of the conquered hill chiefs (Hutchison and Vogel 1933).

12. Describing the conditions that prevailed during the Gurkha occupation of Kangra, Barnes (1855:10) noted that "in the fertile valleys of Kangra not a blade of cultivation was to be seen; grasses grew up in the towns, and tigresses whelped in the streets of Nadoun." In 1820, 11 years after the end of the Gurkha occupation, the English traveler William Moorcroft, passing through the once bustling commercial center of Nadoun, observed that although the local population had begun to return, "the bazaar which was formally crowded by bustling traders, is . . . frequented by only a few fakirs and pilgrims" (1841:78).

13. In 1820, Moorcroft, during an extended stay with Sansar Chand at Alampur while waiting for permission from Ranjit Singh to continue onward to Ladakh, noted that "the loss of territory, and falling off of his dependencies, have so much reduced the revenues of Katoch, that . . . he has but 70,000 rupees a year for the expenses of himself and his family after paying his troops" (1841:130).

14. Tax-farming is an arrangement (generally short term) whereby the government grants an individual the responsibility for paying it a fixed amount of annual revenue from a multivillage region or area. In exchange, that person is entitled to retain the difference between what he is able to collect and what is paid to the government. This system of contracting out revenue collection responsibilities encourages the maximization of short-term profit and was associated with rack renting (the charging of excessive rents) and disinvestment in the agrarian economy.

15. See Neale 1969 for a good discussion of the meaning of land control in precolonial India as a source and instrument of political power, in contrast to British conceptualizations of land as an input in an economic system whose internal logic was profit maximization. Further analyses of the political and social functions of land in precolonial India are found in Embree 1969, Dirks 1985 and 1992, and Cohn 1987.

16. During the reign of Aurangzeb (1658–1707), for example, the raja of Nurpur (a hill state to the west of Kangra), in exchange for controlling the frontier outposts of Bamian and Ghowrband on the western frontier northwest of Kabul, was given an official rank (*mansab*) and a jagir (Barnes 1855:9). Habib (1963:258) argued that members of the governing class in the Mughal empire were primarily compensated by jagirs of this sort.

17. These grants of land were known as *inam*. The Mughal ruler Jehangir recognized the importance of support from the religious institutions and the class of people given inam to the legitimacy of the Mughal regime. He is reported to have said that they were as important to the empire as the real army (Habib 1963:310).

18. This pattern of exchange of land for political support also prevailed in cities and urban areas. Describing urban political relations in north India during the decline of the Mughal empire, Bayly (1983:125) noted that "regional rulers . . . needed to mollify the suburban gentry by appointing members to local public office . . . or by enhancing their grants of revenue-free land."

19. Although I use here the system of classification of land grants employed in the first settlement report for Kangra District, I am aware of the pitfalls of allowing the language of historical source material to become the language of analysis— against which Dirks warned (1985:128). Indeed, the separate classification of political and religious grants in the settlement report masks the inherently political functions that "religious" grants also played.

20. For this reason, jagirs and, to a lesser extent, inam were classified by the amount of revenue they produced rather than by the extent of cultivated area they contained.

21. For example, interests in—that is, claims to—the produce of a field were distributed among the cultivator, village artisans such as the potter, basketmaker, ironsmith, and watermaster (who received a portion of the harvest as compensation for the services they provided), the person who might hold the hereditary right to cultivate the field but who engaged with another for the field's actual cultivation, and the man who claimed the right to the revenue from the field, whether that be the *jagirdar*, the *inamdar*, or the representative of the state. None of these claimants, including the state, possessed the hallmark of a proprietary right—the right to alienate the field.

22. In addition to payment in kind, the raja received monetary rent on these tenancies. Lyall (1874:29) gave an example of a village's revenue papers, which

enumerated the taxes that Gaddi shepherds paid for grazing rights, a Katoch Rajput paid for setting ridgetop falcon nets, and mill operators paid for the right to operate water-powered mills. Although this suggests that the raja's proprietary claims to these resources were enforced, the degree of state control over other customary use rights of a more general nature is difficult to determine.

23. Ten other state-sponsored kuhls are undated because I was unable to determine when the named sponsor lived.

24. I base this statement on circumstantial evidence. The story of the origin of Sapruhl Kuhl states that the individual who sponsored its construction used one quintal (100 kg) of *hing* (asafetida) in the *dhal* made to feed the workers. Hing, a local product, is used sparingly to flavor dhal. Rural daily wage laborers are generally fed the midday meal. This is also done during communal labor exchanges.

25. A *seer* was a unit of weight equaling just over two pounds.

26. Interestingly, the settlement records do not corroborate the use of corvée for kuhl construction even though they describe many other aspects of begar, including the purposes it was used for and who had to do it. This may be because the last state-sponsored kuhls were built at the beginning of the nineteenth century, 50 years before the first regular settlement took place.

27. Although various Sikh leaders controlled Kangra District for approximately 20 years prior to British rule, they had relatively little effect on land tenure and kuhl management. The *Riwaj-i-Abpashi* notes that new kuhls were constructed during the period of Sikh rule, but the Sikhs did not alter the tenure of land; many areas were under their management for only a short time, and some tracts never were (Lyall, 1874:23).

28. Shares were allotted on the basis of the productive capacities of individuals and were subject to periodic reallotment as those capabilities changed over time (Smith 1996:33).

29. Smith (1996:47) noted that "in the ideal conception now, a village community was defined by descent from a village founder. . . . Having a share in common property was considered the sign of superior status in a village, as a member of the ancestral core of proprietors whose genealogy and history were now matters of official record." Similarly: "A village community is a body of proprietors who now or formerly owned a part of the village lands in common, and who are jointly responsible for the payment of the revenue" (Douie 1985 [1899]:61).

30. Because the settlement had established a fixed rate of revenue assessment for at least 20 years, rising grain prices throughout the British period meant that by 1920 the share of the harvest paid as revenue had declined to as little as 8 percent of the total value of the output in some parts of the district (Raj 1933:54).

31. Under certain conditions, land transfers also took place during the precolonial period. Land could be transferred by gift if the pattah holder had no heirs. Similarly, a proprietor in arrears of taxes could mortgage his land to another individual, who would then be responsible for paying the tax and in exchange would

receive half of the harvest from the former proprietor-cultivator. In some cases, if the arrangement became long term or if there was an "error at [the] first settlement," the former proprietor's claim to the land was reduced to that of a tenant and the mortgage holder became the proprietor (Lyall 1874:66). Although these forms of land transfers did occur, the hereditary right to cultivate land was not bought and sold as a commodity prior to the first regular settlement (Barnes 1855).

32. Whether or not these fears were well founded is unclear. Relying on empirical analysis of reports published between 1878 and 1885, Cohn (1987) showed how the extensive transfer of land in the Banaras region, much of it to urban-based "new men" who had acquired wealth because of the conditions created by British rule, did not hinder the flow of investment into agriculture and how agricultural investment actually increased during this period. Indeed, Cohn argued (1987:412) that the combination of a fixed revenue demand and dramatic increases in the value of agriculture more than compensated for the flow of wealth to urban areas and that despite extensive shifts in landownership from rural to urban areas, "nothing happened" to the economic well-being of the former zamindars and tenants in the rural hinterlands of the Benaras region. In Kangra, too, the prices of agricultural products increased significantly during this period. However, unlike in the Benaras region, there was little or no scope for the production of valuable cash crops such as sugarcane. Thus the actual social and economic effects of the land sales and mortgages in Kangra are still conjectural.

33. This transfer of property held many implications. It nullified the rights of landless households to forest resources collected from unenclosed, uncultivated areas. Revenue from these areas, previously paid to the ruler, was now collected by the *lambedar* (village tax collector) and distributed to all landholders in proportion to the amount of tax each paid. And now landholders, rather than the state, had the authority to grant permission to an individual to reclaim and cultivate an uncultivated tract.

34. During the precolonial period, taxes were assessed on the basis of cultivated area per family holding, not by village, as in the plains. This reflects the severalty model of tenure known as *raiyatwari* (Baden-Powell 1892, 2:537) that existed in Kangra prior to British rule. In this system, holdings were separate and not part of a joint estate, there was no joint responsibility for tax payment, and there were no joint shares in the commons that could be partitioned accordingly.

35. See Smith 1996, chapters 1 and 2, for an insightful discussion of the distinction between the colonial definition of *shamilat* and the precolonial nature and extent of rights in the commons in the Punjab plains.

36. Prior to land reform legislation in the 1970s, 25 of the 58 holdings greater than 10 acres belonged to Mahajans, 18 were owned by Brahmans, and 9 by Rajput families (Parry 1979:56).

37. The *Riwaj-i-Abpashi* register created at this time is still kept today in the

Revenue Department offices in Kangra and Palampur Tehsils, where it is used as the basis for deciding contemporary water disputes in court.

38. The conservative bias inherent in any process that seeks to codify custom formed the basis for the opposition of liberal utilitarians in Great Britain to rule by custom, as opposed to rule by universal principles of law. Utilitarian positivists in the tradition of Jeremy Bentham and John Stuart Mill railed against the codification of custom as the basis of colonial rule and rightly linked it with the ruling conservative and paternalist ideology in Great Britain, which was adamantly opposed to liberal reform. Instead, they argued, law should be founded upon the principles of Reason and Utility (Battacharya 1996:24).

39. One *nala* equals eight *gala*, and one gála equals the volume of water that can pass through an opening of the size created by joining the thumbs and index fingers of both hands.

4 / PATTERNS OF CHANGE

1. For most other forms of agricultural work, however, the increased participation of men in the nonfarm employment sector has dramatically increased the responsibilities and workloads of women (Sarin 1989).

2. Bhradi Kuhl and Raniya Kuhl are the two kuhl regimes whose committees do not maintain attendance records. The former has none because the kuhl's irrigators formed the committee primarily to fight a court case against the Irrigation and Public Health Department over water rights, not in response to internal stress; attendance registers were irrelevant for this purpose. Raniya Kuhl has one of the older kuhl committees but no attendance records, primarily because of elite domination of the committee and caste-based antagonisms within the regime.

3. The relatively equal distribution of land in Paror and Kharot (relative to that of Raniya Kuhl's irrigators, for example) and their caste homogeneity suggest that inequalities between households, based on either caste or class, are not extreme and that inequality does not account for the declining cooperation for khana and danga construction in the Kathul Kuhl regime.

4. Kishori Lal noted that although sending a young boy technically satisfies the requirement that a household contribute labor for khana, boys cannot do as much work in a day as men. Similarly, Dhyan Singh, kohli of Pathan Kuhl, noted in his attendance records whether a household sent only a young boy. Dhyan Singh maintained the most finely graded attendance rosters I saw. Whereas most kohlis noted only whether a farmer was present or absent, Dhyan Singh assessed the performance of those present with modifiers such as "lazy," "good," "came late," "came empty-handed" (i.e., without shovel or pick), or "boy."

5. Each kuhl highlights a different process. The dynamics revealed—declining

dependence, the pull of nonfarm employment, and the push of inequality—probably exist in most kuhl regimes but to different degrees. The different meanings of declining participation among kuhls results from the relative strength of these elements.

6. This incident is the topic of one of the songs that members of the Doumna (basketmaker) caste sing during the month of Chaitre, the first month of the Hindu calendar. See Narayan 1996 for a complete analysis.

7. As discussed in chapter 3, long-term declines in the kohli's authority are related to the codification of irrigation customs in the *Riwaj-i-Abpashi* and the statemaking efforts linked to its creation. The discussion here focuses on the more recent transformations in this position.

8. Unlike in the tank irrigation systems of southern Tamil Nadu, where water distributors have challenged their low-caste hereditary positions and the tradition of in-kind payments (Mosse 1997a:32), in Kangri kuhl regimes, the roles, responsibilities, and remuneration of kohlis have not been so contentious. The reasons for the differences are illuminating. First, and perhaps most importantly, the position of kohli, although hereditary, is not restricted to a specific caste; kohlis of kuhls in the Neugal watershed come from different castes, high and low. The position of kohli was historically a desirable hereditary right awarded to a family or clan in recognition of its contribution to the construction or reconstruction of the kuhl. Contrary to the situation in southern Tamil Nadu, in which the hereditary nature of the *nirppacci* water distributors was linked to their servile, low-caste status, the hereditary nature of the position of kohli ensured that the privilege of being kohli stayed with the original family or clan that had been awarded that warisi (hereditary right). Interestingly, all kohlis, regardless of caste, perform the annual puja at the kuhl's diversion structure. This ritual often includes higher-caste farmers than the kohli himself. Thus the position of kohli is unusual in its ability to float between castes. Second, though dissension occurs over the rate of remuneration of the kohli, the fact that the payment is in kind rather than in cash does not represent a social stigma, nor does it reflect an undesirable, caste-based status marker.

9. As Greenberg (1997) pointed out, fallowing in Kangra has been and continues to be an extremely small proportion of total land use. Currently, fallow land in Kangra makes up approximately 1 to 2 percent of the total cultivated area (Swarup and Sikka 1986:12, quoted in Greenberg 1997:205). Thus the decision to engage in social fallowing due to a combination of scarce labor and fodder supplies also performs important ecological functions.

10. The Himachal Pradesh Minor Canals Act of 1976 authorized the Himachal Pradesh Irrigation and Public Health Department to "assume the control and/or management of any canal [kuhl] if the owner[s] of the canal consents thereto." The authority to manage the kuhl can be returned to the owners upon their request at any time. After six years of government management, the owners may ask the government to acquire the kuhl under the provisions of the Land Acquisition Act of 1894. Doing so grants the government authority to "exercise all powers of control,

management and direction for the efficient maintenance and working of such canal or for the due distribution of the water thereof." It also grants the government authority to levy a tax for the use of kuhl water, "keeping due regard to the maintenance and operation charges for the system and the cost of collection of water rates" (Minor Canals Act 1976:sections 9, 28, 34–36). This water tax is separate from, and in addition to, the tax assessed on irrigated land.

11. The annual audit of registered kuhl committees ensures "proper" accounting of money the kuhl committee receives through government grants, membership fees, contributions for puja, and fines. Additionally, many farmers feel that a registered kuhl committee has better standing with the district administration when applying for grants than an unregistered committee.

12. The only example I observed of panchayat involvement in water management and conflict resolution was for the jointly managed Mahang and Loharal Kuhls, which have no kuhl committee. The panchayat appoints the kohli (since the family holding the warisi to be kohli no longer claims the right) and resolves water conflicts when they arise. Panchayats generally do not assume the role of kuhl committee because panchayat boundaries are rarely coterminous with a kuhl's command area, because the politics of panchayat elections incorporate different forms of authority and interests than kuhl committee elections, and because the motivations and benefits associated with being a panchayat member do not overlap with those associated with serving on a kuhl committee. I heard of only one example of a conflict being taken to the SDM or police station. This concerned an organized protest of several hundred farmers in the 1970s against the proposed IPHD construction of a cement diversion structure at the head of the Neugal watershed. The proposal violated prohibitions against making a permanent structure and also threatened downstream water supply. Despite the protest, a permanent diversion structure was constructed.

13. Hicks and Peña (2003:143) also noted the lack of congruence between the imposed bureaucratic model of acequia organization and preexisting customary rules and operating procedures, as well as the tensions and conflicts that arose from this incongruence.

14. Berry's (2003) primary concern was to explain the origin and development of the "scientific housewife" in the United States and the ways in which this model (and the politics of gender, class, race, and sexuality that it cloaked) and associated conceptions of agricultural development and modernity were imported to India in the 1950s, where they were hybridized with elite gender ideologies and contributed to the development of a distinct Indian modernity.

15. In the Neugal watershed, there are no low reliance–low differentiation kuhl regimes. By definition, a kuhl long enough to reach a less fertile, upland larh area (low reliance) passes through multiple villages and has multicaste irrigator groups (and therefore high differentiation). Regardless, the reliance and differentiation framework does not make a strong prediction about the outcome for kuhl regimes

characterized by low reliance and low differentiation under conditions of increasing nonfarm employment. Low reliance suggests that because of the low productivity of the land the kuhl irrigates, the availability of alternative water sources, or both, farmers are less likely to contribute to the maintenance and repair of the kuhl. The regime's low differentiation, however, suggests that the organizational requirements for managing the kuhl and the potential for conflict among farmers are minimal. Therefore, some members may contribute adequate labor and other resources to maintain and repair the kuhl. Site-specific factors not encompassed within the variables reliance and differentiation will determine the effects of increasing nonfarm employment on these kuhl regimes.

5 / NETWORKS OF INTERDEPENDENCE

1. Todd LaPorte (1995) uses the terms "net (knot) rider" and "net thrower" to describe two vantage points from which to understand organizational networks. The "knot rider" perspective is that of an individual node in an organization or network. It is an organization-centric view—in the Kangri case, the perspective of Mr. Ohri regarding the potential opportunities and liabilities the network represents for Sonia Kuhl. In contrast, the perspective of the "net thrower," located above the level of individual network nodes, is a higher-order vantage point that reveals the overall structure of the network. In the case of kuhl networks, this view reveals the relative density or sparseness of links between individual network nodes (kuhls).

2. This perspective on the positive value of redundancy draws from and is consistent with the recent work of Bobbi Low and colleagues (2003) in which they examine the role of redundancy in reducing risk and uncertainty in a wide variety of social and ecological systems. They note that redundancy is especially important under heterogeneous spatial conditions such as obtain in the Neugal watershed (Low et al. 2003:106).

3. At the watershed level, the pattern of overlapping kuhl networks conforms closely to James Thompson's (1967:54) concept of sequential interdependence, in which the parts of an organization are serially related to each other. He further defined sequential interdependence as a set of conditions in which the parts are not symmetrically interdependent and the order of their interdependence can be determined. Thompson predicted that sequential interdependence gives rise to coordination "by plan," which involves "the establishment of schedules for the interdependent units by which their actions may then be governed" (1967:56). The informality of these "schedules" matches the kinds of interkuhl coordination shown in Table 12 and discussed later.

4. In other words, a village with only lower fields will be engaged with only one kuhl, whereas a village with both lower and higher fields will be engaged with multiple kuhls.

5. This definition of interdependence is consistent with and follows from Karen Cook's definition of exchange, which emphasizes resource transfers through voluntary transactions by two or more actors (1977:64). It is more restrictive than Sol Levine and Paul White's definition of exchange, which encompasses "any voluntary activity between two organizations" (1961:120).

6. In order for past actions to affect present interkuhl exchanges and for present exchanges to affect the possibility of future coordination, a long-term, collective memory of the past is necessary. Such a collective memory is more likely in settings of stable communities and populations than in other organizational settings with less historical continuity. Within kuhl regimes, the institutionalization of the position of kohli increases the likelihood that past events will influence present decisions and that future ramifications, even if subsequent to an individual's tenure as kohli, will influence present choices.

7. See Ostrom, Anderies, and Janssen 2003 for other possible functions that large-scale units can provide for smaller units within multilevel social-ecological systems.

8. I am grateful to Vinay Gidwani for pointing out that rational choice theory would lead us to expect that interkuhl sharing arrangements should "unravel from the top down" because the most upstream kuhl regime can never directly benefit from such an arrangement.

9. Regarding the Pareto improvements associated with networks, Uzzi (1996:56) remarked that "contrary to Adam Smith's quip that individuals do best for others by doing selfishly for themselves, the above evidence suggests that firms that act in the interest of others (and against their short-term interests) may do more for the collective economy and society than if they had followed purely selfish pursuits." Others have also noted the shortcomings of rational choice assumptions of self-interested behavior and the ways they underemphasize the influence of social structure. For example, John Padgett and Chris Ansell, in their analysis of fifteenth-century Medici trading networks, showed that self-interest was less an attribute of persons and more a characteristic of the structure in which those persons were embedded (1993:1308, cited in Uzzi 1996:38).

10. One *topa* equals 50 *thimbi*. A thimbi is a volumetric measure of grain equivalent to approximately two kilograms of threshed, unhusked rice.

11. Similarly, Howard Aldrich and David Whetten (1981:391) argued that the "ultimate predictor" of network stability was the presence of multiple linkages between network members, which reduced the probability that any link would fail. These multiplex organizational relations included "exchanging multiple resources, communication between multiple boundary spanners, friendship or kinship ties, and overlapping boards of directors."

12. Watermasters and farmers invariably used the phrase *bhai bundi se* ("through brotherhood") in discussions of informal interkuhl water-sharing arrangements. The term implies that there is no expectation of direct reciprocity or even an assurance

of compensation in the future. It implies a sense of community, "brotherhood," that binds those engaged in water sharing within a common ethical order.

13. The ideology of *kanya dan* extends the obligation to give to the wife-taking family without receiving any material compensation not only to the natal households of the wife and mother but also to those of the father's mother's brother and mother's mother's brother. The asymmetrical flow of gifts from the wife giver's family to the wife taker's family often continues for three generations. The belief that receiving any form of compensation will cancel the merit accrued by giving the gift prevents the wife giver from ever accepting food in the wife taker's house and, at the top of the Rajput hierarchy, has resulted in the forbidding of other forms of marriage exchange that do not conform to this "unilateral ideal" (Parry 1979:209). Although the practice of kanya dan tends to be more rigidly adhered to among higher castes, as ideology it is all pervasive. See Bodeman (1988:208) for an analogous example from southern Italy in which familism operates primarily within upper-class families but is nevertheless an important ideological construct across all classes.

14. Hicks and Peña (2003) also remark on the relationship between ritual and community among the users of acequias in the American Southwest. In this regard, they note that "the annual spring ditch cleaning is an occasion defined by ritual and festival. The assertion of these commitments is significant as a foundation of community solidarity . . . reaffirming commitment to *acequiadad* (acequiahood) and the community of labor that sustains it" (2003:131).

15. Physical networks connecting individual community-managed irrigation systems can provide other benefits besides helping individual regimes rebound from environmental disturbances. In addition to risk reduction functions, networks make possible water sales and water transfers from one system to another, thus increasing the overall profitability and social benefits of water (Mosse 1997a). Intersystem irrigation networks can also provide the means for achieving finely tuned, watershed-level irrigation coordination regarding landscape-level timing and sequencing of agricultural activities. In some cases this has important implications for water consumption efficiency, pest control, and overall agricultural productivity (Ambler 1989; Lansing 1991).

6 / DYNAMIC REGIMES, ENDURING FLOWS

1. Except for the institutional stickiness associated with bureaucratic change, this multijurisdictional pattern of kuhl management could conceivably flip-flop if the value of an agricultural product well suited for larh conditions should dramatically increase. If this happened, farmers' incentives for controlling water deliveries to larh areas might provide adequate motivation for them to assume responsibility for managing kuhls with low har-to-larh ratios that are currently

under government management. State intervention in general might recede in kuhls with high larh command areas.

2. This formulation of regionality draws from and is consistent with the notion of region and regional modernity presented in Sivaramakrishnan and Agrawal 2003.

3. Examples of such community-based networks and federations include the Colorado Acequia Association (Hicks and Peña 2003), the Federation of Community Forestry Users in Nepal (Britt 2001), and Community Forest Management federations in Orissa, India (Sarin et al. 2003).

4. The colonial expressions of governmentality in Kangra had significant social ramifications, some of them bearing directly on kuhl regimes. These were enumerated in chapter 3.

5. See Meinzen-Dick and Zwarteveen 2001 for a review of gender issues in community-based irrigation management in South Asia.

6. See Edmunds and Wollenberg 2003 for a discussion of the possibilities for refocusing devolution policies so that they support social justice and local democratic practice.

GLOSSARY

amin. An itinerant field surveyor employed by the colonial administration in north India during the land settlement process.

bartan. Usufruct (e.g., the right to collect thorns for fencing, graze livestock, cut grass) in uncultivated areas used in common in Kangra.

battar. The method of paddy sowing in which only one flood irrigation is provided before dry rice seeds are sown. Monsoon rains provide subsequent water.

begar. Unpaid labor extracted by precolonial hill state rulers for tasks such as transporting materials for public works projects, carrying letters and parcels, and providing wood and grass to government officials on field tours.

bhai bundi se. "Through brotherhood," a principle invoked by farmers to explain interkuhl water-sharing arrangements and coordination.

bhataan. A long-handled, malletlike wooden implement used mainly by women farmers to break up heavy clods of soil following *ghuhar.*

bilroo. The volume of water that can flow through an opening equivalent in size to the neck of an earthen water-carrying pot.

chadre, choli. The clothing women in Kangra wore prior to adopting the Punjabi *salwar kamiz.* Cloth for chadre and choli is offered to a kuhl's feminine deity during the kuhl *puja.*

chakotli. Stones placed at a *tup* to regulate water flow.

chanu. A cut in a terrace bund to allow water to flow to the next lower terrace.

cheb. Sod used for plugging leaks in kuhl channels, for *danga* repair, and for packing around *thellu.*

danga. A kuhl's diversion structure.

dharma. Duty, usually in the context of one's roles and responsibilities in life.

dol. A form of water allocation in which most of a kuhl's flow is diverted for a fixed number of days to a village that otherwise has no rights to the kuhl's water.

drati. A curved, multipurpose sickle.

gala. The volume of water that can flow through the area formed by joining one's forefingers and thumbs.

ghagra. A type of skirt that women in Kangra wore prior to adopting the Punjabi *salwar kamiz*.

ghuhar. Heavy plowing following *rabi* harvest.

grath. A mill for grinding grain, powered by kuhl water.

har. The fertile, low-lying fields adjacent to the perennial streams that flow from the Dhaula Dhar mountain range.

honda. Patrolling the kuhl to guard against water theft and identify leaks.

inam. A Mughal term referring to tax-exempt grants of land given by a ruler, often to temples and Brahmans. The holder of an *inam* is an *inamdar*.

iqrar-nama, wajib-ul-arz. Persian terms referring to the village-level record of rights prepared as part of the colonial land settlement process.

izzat. Honor.

jagir. A Mughal term referring to the right to collect and retain the assessed tax from a particular area, granted by a ruler as a form of compensation for services rendered, for political support, and so forth. The holder of a *jagir* is a *jagirdar*.

jel. Light plowing following *ghuhar*.

kanal. An area of land equivalent to 0.16 hectares.

khad. Perennial or annual mountain torrent or river in Kangra.

khana. The annual cleaning and repair of kuhl channels and the *danga*.

kharif. The summer (monsoon) agricultural season.

kudal. A short-handled agricultural implement with a blade similar in shape to that of a spade.

larh. The less fertile plateau and ridgetop areas of Kangra Valley.

mach. A method of irrigation (continuous flood) and the sowing of sprouted rice seeds.

mai. Leveling a plowed field by drawing a weighted plank behind two bullocks.

mauza. A "revenue village," the fiscal unit, composed of from one to many *tikas* (hamlets), used during the precolonial and colonial periods as the areal unit by which to assess and collect taxes.

nakhod. The quantity of water equivalent to two *galas*.

nala. The quantity of water equivalent to four *nakhod*.

oor. The method of rice cultivation involving transplanting rice seedlings from nursery areas to fields.

panchayat. An elected village council. The *panchayat pradhan* is the elected head of the *panchayat.*

pattah. A deed or title that spelled out the rights and responsibilities pertaining to a *warisi,* rights to land, and so forth, granted by precolonial rulers.

patwari. Village-level Revenue Department official.

prasaad. An offering of food to a deity. During *puja* to a kuhl's feminine deity, the offering is often a cooked sweet dish made from semolina.

puja. Religious ritual. A temple priest or one who does *puja* is a *pujari.*

Quaja Pir. The entity propitiated during a kuhl's *puja* to ward off and protect the kuhl from destructive floods. A *pir* is also the founder or leader of a Sufi order or shrine.

rabi. The winter agricultural season.

raja. "Ruler," generally used to refer to Hindu rulers and princes.

rani. "Queen," generally used to refer to the female members of ruling Hindu clans and lineages.

Riwaj-i-Abpashi. The colonial codification of irrigation customs in Kangra.

ryot (rai'yat). A Mughal term referring to the person who paid the tax on a plot of land; generally defined by the British as tenant or peasant.

sag battar. The provision of a single irrigation to dry fields. It is followed by plowing and sowing dry rice seeds.

salwar kamiz. Loose-fitting pants and knee-length blouse worn by women in north India.

seer. A unit of weight just over two pounds, roughly equivalent to one kilogram.

settlement. A term used by the British colonial administration to refer to the process of assessing revenue (tax) rates on agricultural land and the agreements made with groups or individuals for paying a fixed revenue to the colonial government.

shamilat. Village common property.

sothan. Similar to long trousers, worn by women in Kangra prior to adopting the Punjabi *salwar.*

subedar. Mughal administrative position loosely equivalent to "military commander."

taluka. A Mughal term referring to a district subdivision.

thellu. Bamboo water measuring device.

thimbi. The volume equivalent to approximately two kilograms of threshed, unhusked rice.

tika. A hamlet consisting of clusters of single- or multicaste houses.

topa. Fifty *thimbi.*

tup. A diversion point where an irrigation channel divides into two or more smaller channels.

warisi. A hereditary right derived from a ruler as a separate, taxable tenancy.

wazir, kardar. Mughal terms for administrative officers with revenue and governance responsibilities.

zamindar. A noncultivating elite landlord; one who collects revenue (often from the *ryot*) and remits it to the government; "landholder."

REFERENCES

Agarwal, Anil, and Ajit Chak. 1991. *State of India's Environment: Floods, Flood Plains and Environmental Myths.* New Delhi: Centre for Science and Environment.

Agrawal, Arun. 1996. The Community vs. the Market and the State: Forest Use in Uttarakhand in the Indian Himalayas. *Journal of Agricultural and Environmental Ethics* 9(1):1–15.

———. 2001. State Formation in Community Spaces? Decentralization of Control over Forests in the Kumaon Himalaya, India. *Journal of Asian Studies* 60(1):9–40.

Akerloff, George. 1984. A Theory of Social Custom, of Which Unemployment May Be One Consequence. In *An Economic Theorist's Book of Tales*, by George Akerloff, pp. 69–99. Cambridge: Cambridge University Press.

Aldrich, Howard. 1976. Resource Dependence and Interorganizational Relations: Local Employment Service Offices and Social Services Sector Organizations. *Administration and Society* 7:419–54.

Aldrich, Howard, and David Whetten. 1981. Organization-Sets, Action-Sets, and Networks: Making the Most of Simplicity. In *Handbook of Organizational Design*, edited by P. C. Nystrom and W. H. Starbuck, pp. 385–408. Oxford: Oxford University Press.

Allen, John, Doreen Massey, and Allan Cochrane. 1998. *Rethinking the Region.* New York: Routledge.

Ambler, John S. 1989. *Adat* and Aid: Management of Small-Scale Irrigation in West Sumatra, Indonesia. Ph.D. dissertation, Cornell University, Ithaca, N.Y.

Ambraseys, Nicholas, and Roger Bilham. 2000. A Note on the Kangra M_s = 7.8 Earthquake of 4 April 1905. *Current Science* 79(1):45–50.

Anderson, Alexander. 1897. *Final Report of the Revised Settlement of Kangra Proper.* Lahore: Civil and Military Gazette Press.

Appadurai, Arjun. 1996. *Modernity at Large: Cultural Dimensions of Globalization.* Minneapolis: University of Minnesota Press.

Astley, W. Graham, and Andrew H. Van de Ven. 1983. Central Perspectives and Debates in Organization Theory. *Administrative Science Quarterly* 28:245–73.

Axelrod, Robert. 1986. An Evolutionary Approach to Norms. *American Political Science Review* 80(4):1095–1112.

Baden-Powell, Baden Henry. 1892. *The Land Systems of British India,* vols. 1–3. Oxford: Clarendon Press.

Baker, J. Mark. 1998. The Effect of Community Structure on Social Forestry Outcomes: Insights from Chota Nagpur, India. *Mountain Research and Development* 18(1):51–62.

———. 2000. Mistaken Rights: The Effects of Colonial Redefinitions of Property and Community in Kangra on Agricultural and Forest Resources. In *Agrarian Environments: Resources, Representations, and Rule in India,* edited by A. Agrawal and K. Sivaramakrishnan, pp. 47–67. Durham, N.C.: Duke University Press.

Bardhan, Pranab. 1993a. Symposium on Management of Local Commons. *Journal of Economic Perspectives* 7(4):87–92.

———. 1993b. Analytics of the Institutions of Informal Cooperation in Rural Development. *World Development* 21:663–739.

Barnes, George C. 1855. *Report of the Land Revenue Settlement of the Kangra District, Punjab.* Lahore: Civil and Military Gazette Press.

———. n.d. *Canal Irrigation of Valleys: Notes on the System of Irrigation Prevailing in the Upper Valleys of the Kangra District.* Selections from the Public Correspondence no. 37.

Battacharya, Neeladri. 1996. Remaking Custom: The Discourse and Practice of Colonial Codification. In *Tradition, Dissent, and Ideology: Essays in Honor of Romila Thapar,* edited by R. Champakalakshmi and S. Gopal, pp. 20–51. Delhi: Oxford University Press.

Bayly, Christopher A. 1983. *Rulers, Townsmen and Bazaars: North Indian Society in the Age of British Expansion, 1770–1870.* Cambridge: Cambridge University Press.

Benson, J. Kenneth. 1975. The Interorganizational Network as a Political Economy. *Administrative Science Quarterly* 20:229–49.

Berkes, Fikret. 1986. Marine Inshore Fishery Management in Turkey. In *Proceedings of the Conference on Common Property Resource Management,* National Research Council, pp. 63–84. Washington, D.C.: National Academy Press.

Berry, Kim. 2003. Lakshmi and the Scientific Housewife: A Transnational Account of Indian Women's Development and Production of an Indian Modernity. *Economic and Political Weekly* 38(11):1055–68.

Bicchieri, Cristina. 1990. Norms of Cooperation. *Ethics* 100(4):838–61.

Bodeman, Y. M. 1988. Relations of Production and Class Rule: The Hidden Basis of Patron-Clientage. In *Social Structures: A Network Approach,* edited by B. Wellman and S. D. Berkowitz, pp. 198–220. Cambridge: Cambridge University Press.

Bourdieu, Pierre. 1977 [1972]. *Outline of a Theory of Practice*. Cambridge: Cambridge University Press.

———. 1990 [1980]. *The Logic of Practice*. Stanford, Calif.: Stanford University Press.

Bratich, Jack, Jeremy Packer, and Cameron McCarthy. 2003. Governing the Present. In *Foucault, Cultural Studies, and Governmentality*, edited by J. Bratich, J. Packer, and C. McCarthy, pp. 3–22. Albany: State University of New York Press.

Britt, Charla. 2001. Mixed Signals and Government Orders: The Problem of On-Again Off-Again Community Forestry Policy. *Forests, Trees and People Newsletter* 45:29–33.

Bromley, Daniel W. 1992. *Making the Commons Work: Theory, Practice, and Policy*. San Francisco: ICS Press.

Burchell, Graham. 1991. Peculiar Interests: Civil Society and Governing "the System of Natural Liberty." In *The Foucault Effect: Studies in Governmentality*, edited by G. Burchell, C. Gordon, and P. Miller, pp. 119–50. Chicago: University of Chicago Press.

Chakravarty-Kaul, Minoti. 1996. *Common Lands and Customary Law: Institutional Change in North India over the Past Two Centuries*. Delhi: Oxford University Press.

Charak, Sukhdev Singh. 1978. *History and Culture of Himalayan States*, vol. 1. New Delhi: Light and Life Publishers.

Ciriacy-Wantrup, Siegfried V. 1969. Natural Resources in Economic Growth: The Role of Institutions and Policies. *American Journal of Agricultural Economics* 51:1314–24.

Ciriacy-Wantrup, Siegfried V., and Richard C. Bishop. 1975. "Common Property" as a Concept in Natural Resource Policy. *Natural Resources Journal* 15(4):713–27.

Coase, Ronald H. 1984. The New Institutional Economics. *Journal of Theoretical and Institutional Economics* 140(1):229–31.

Cohn, Bernard S. 1987. *An Anthropologist among the Historians and Other Essays*. Delhi: Oxford University Press.

Connolly, V. 1911. *Preliminary Assessment Report of the Dehra and Hamirpur Tahsils of the Kangra District*. Lahore: Punjab Government Press.

Cook, Karen S. 1977. Exchange and Power in Interorganizational Relations. *Sociological Quarterly* 18:62–82.

Coward, E. Walter Jr. 1990. Property Rights and Network Order: The Case of Irrigation Works in the Western Himalayas. *Human Organization* 49(1):78–88.

de los Reyes, Romana P. 1980. *Managing Communal Gravity Systems: Farmer's Approaches and Implications for Program Planning*. Quezon City: Institute of Philippine Culture.

Dirks, Nicholas B. 1985. Terminology and Taxonomy, Discourse and Domination: From Old Regime to Colonial Regime in South India. In *Studies of South India:*

An Anthology of Recent Research and Scholoarship, edited by R. Frykenberg and P. Kolenda, pp. 127–50. Madras: New Era Publications.

———. 1992. From Little King to Landlord: Colonial Discourse and Colonial Rule. In *Colonialism and Culture*, edited by N. B. Dirks, pp. 175–208. Ann Arbor: University of Michigan Press.

Douglas, Mary. 1986. *How Institutions Think*. Syracuse, N.Y.: Syracuse University Press.

Douie, James McCrone. 1985 [1899]. *Punjab Settlement Manual*. Delhi: Daya Publishing House.

Dubash, Navroz. 2002. *Tubewell Capitalism: Groundwater Development and Agrarian Change in Gujarat*. Delhi: Oxford University Press.

Duncan, James. 1990. *The City as Text: The Politics of Landscape Interpretation in the Kandyan Kingdom*. Cambridge: Cambridge University Press.

Edmunds, David, and Eva Wollenberg, eds. 2003. *Local Forest Management: The Impacts of Devolution Policies*. London: Earthscan.

Embree, Ainslie T. 1969. Landholding in India and British Institutions. In *Land Control and Social Structure in Indian History*, edited by R. E. Frykenberg, pp. 33–52. Madison: University of Wisconsin Press.

Emerson, Richard M. 1962. Power-Dependence Relations. *American Sociological Review* 27:31–40.

Ensminger, Jean, and Andrew Rutten. 1991. The Political Economy of Changing Property Rights: Dismantling a Pastoral Commons. *American Ethnologist* 18:683–99.

Evans, P. B., D. Rueschemeyer, and T. Skocpol, eds. 1985. *Bringing the State Back In*. Cambridge: Cambridge University Press.

Feeny, David, Fikret Berkes, Bonnie McCay, and James Acheson. 1990. The Tragedy of the Commons: Twenty-Two Years Later. *Human Ecology* 18(1):1–19.

Foucault, Michel. 1991. Governmentality. In *The Foucault Effect: Studies in Governmentality*, edited by G. Burchell, C. Gordon, and P. Miller, pp. 87–104. Chicago: University of Chicago Press.

Galaskiewicz, Joseph. 1985. Interorganizational Relations. *Annual Review of Sociology* 11:281–304.

Geertz, Clifford. 1980. Organization of the Balinese Subak. In *Irrigation and Agricultural Development in Asia: Perspectives from the Social Sciences*, edited by E. W. Coward, pp. 70–90. Ithaca, N.Y.: Cornell University Press.

Gelles, Paul. 2000. *Water and Power in Highland Peru: The Cultural Politics of Irrigation and Development*. New Brunswick, N.J.: Rutgers University Press.

Giddens, Anthony. 1976. *The New Rules of the Sociological Method*. New York: Basic Books.

———. 1984. *The Constitution of Society*. Berkeley: University of California Press.

———. 1986. *The Nation-State and Violence*. Berkeley: University of California Press.

Gilmartin, David. 1994. Scientific Empire and Imperial Science: Colonialism and Irrigation Technology in the Indus Basin. *Journal of Asian Studies* 53:1127–49.

Gordon, Stewart. 1994. *Marathas, Marauders, and State Formation in Eighteenth-Century India.* Delhi: Oxford University Press.

Government of Himachal Pradesh (GOHP). 1979. *Agricultural Census in Himachal Pradesh.* Shimla: Directorate of Land Records.

———. 1990. *Statistical Outline of Himachal Pradesh.* Shimla: Directorate of Economics and Statistics.

Government of India. 1951, 1961, 1971, 1981, 1991, 2001. *Census of India, Himachal Pradesh, District Kangra Village and Township Directory.*

———. 1982. *Report of the Indian Council of Agricultural Research (ICAR) Research Review Committee.* New Delhi: ICAR.

Gramsci, Antonio. 1971. *Selections from the Prison Notebooks.* Edited and translated by Quentin Hoare and Geoffrey Nowell-Smith. London: Lawrence and Wishart.

Granovetter, Mark. 1985. Economic Action and Social Structure: The Problem of Embeddedness. *American Journal of Sociology* 91:481–510.

Greenberg, Brian. 1997. An Ecology of "Harm" and "Healing": Agricultural Intensification and Landscape Transformation in the Western Himalayas. Ph.D. dissertation, University of Chicago.

Grover, Ruhi. 1997. Rhythms of the Timber Trade: Forests in the Himalayan Punjab, 1850–1925. Ph.D. dissertation, University of Virginia.

Guha, Ramachandra. 1989. *The Unquiet Woods: Ecological Change and Peasant Resistance in the Himalaya.* Berkeley: University of California Press.

Guha, Ranajit. 1981 [1963]. *A Rule of Property for Bengal: An Essay on the Idea of Permanent Settlement.* Durham, N.C.: Duke University Press.

Gupta, Akhil. 1998. *Postcolonial Developments: Agriculture in the Making of Modern India.* Durham, N.C.: Duke University Press.

Gururani, Shubhra. 2000. Regimes of Control, Strategies of Access: Politics of Forest Use in the Uttarakhand Himalaya, India. In *Agrarian Environments: Resources, Representations, and Rule in India,* edited by A. Agrawal and K. Sivaramakrishnan, pp. 170–90. Durham, N.C.: Duke University Press.

Habib, Irfan. 1963. *The Agrarian System of Mughal India.* New York: Asia Publishing House.

Hackett, Steven, Edella Schlager, and James Walker. 1993. The Role of Communication in Resolving Commons Dilemmas: Experimental Evidence with Heterogeneous Appropriators. *Journal of Environmental Economics and Management* 27(2):99–126.

Hage, Jerald. 1978. Toward a Synthesis of the Dialectic between Historical-Specific and Sociological-General Models of the Environment. In *Organization and Environment: Theory, Issues, and Reality,* edited by L. Karpik, pp. 103–45. Beverly Hills, Calif.: Sage.

Hanf, Kenneth, and Laurence J. O'Toole Jr. 1992. Revisiting Old Friends: Networks,

Implementation Structures and the Management of Inter-organizational Relations. *European Journal of Political Research* 21:163–80.

Hardiman, David. 1995. Small Dam Systems of the Sahyadris. In *Nature, Culture, Colonialism: Essays on the Environmental History of South Asia,* edited by D. Arnold and R. Guha, pp. 185–209. Delhi: Oxford University Press.

Hardin, Garrett. 1968. The Tragedy of the Commons. *Science* 162:1243–48.

Hicks, Gregory, and Devon Peña. 2003. Community *Acequias* in Colorado's Rio Culebra Watershed: A Customary Commons in the Domain of Prior Appropriation. *University of Colorado Law Review* 74(2):101–52.

Hirschman, Albert O. 1970. *Exit, Voice and Loyalty: Responses to Decline in Firms, Organizations, and States.* Cambridge, Mass.: Harvard University Press.

Holling, C. S., and Lance H. Gunderson. 2002. Resilience and Adaptive Cycles. In *Panarchy: Understanding Transformations in Human and Natural Systems,* edited by L. Gunderson and C. S. Holling, pp. 25–62. Washington, D.C.: Island Press.

Hunt, Robert C., and Eva Hunt. 1976. Canal Irrigation and Local Social Organization. *Current Anthropology* 17(3):389–411.

Hutchison, J., and J. Vogel. 1933. *History of the Punjab Hill States.* Lahore: Government Printing.

Isaac, Mark, and James Walker. 1988. Communication and Free-Riding Behavior: The Voluntary Contribution Mechanism. *Economic Inquiry* 26:585–608.

———. 1991. Costly Communication: An Experiment in a Nested Public Goods Problem. In *Laboratory Research in Political Economy,* edited by T. Palfrey, pp. 269–86. Ann Arbor: University of Michigan Press.

Jepperson, Ronald L. 1991. Institutions, Institutional Effects, and Institutionalism. In *The New Institutionalism in Organizational Analysis,* edited by W. W. Powell and P. J. DiMaggio, pp. 143–63. Chicago: University of Chicago Press.

Jodha, Narpat S. 1985. Market Forces and the Erosion of Common Property Resources. In *Agricultural Markets in the Semi-arid Tropics,* pp. 263–77. Proceedings of an international workshop, October 24–28, 1983. Patancheru, India: ICRISAT.

Kessinger, Tom. 1974. *Vilayatpur 1848–1968: Social and Economic Change in a North Indian Village.* Berkeley: University of California Press.

Lansing, J. Stephen. 1991. *Priests and Programmers: Technologies of Power in the Engineered Landscape of Bali.* Princeton, N.J.: Princeton University Press.

Lansing, J. Stephen, and James N. Kremer. 1993. Emergent Properties of Balinese Water Temple Networks: Coadaptation on a Rugged Fitness Landscape. *American Anthropologist* 95:97–114.

LaPorte, Todd. 1975. Organized Social Complexity: Explication of a Concept. In *Organized Social Complexity: Challenge to Politics and Policy,* edited by T. LaPorte, pp. 3–39. Princeton, N.J.: Princeton University Press.

———. 1995. Shifting Vantage and Conceptual Puzzles in Understanding Public Organizational Networks. *Journal of Public Administration Research and Theory* 6:49–74.

Leach, Edmund. 1961. *Pul Eliya.* Cambridge: Cambridge University Press.

Levine, Sol, and Paul White. 1961. Exchange as a Conceptual Framework for the Study of Interorganizational Relationships. *Administrative Science Quarterly* 5:583–601.

Lewis, Henry. 1971. *Ilocano Rice Farmers: A Comparative Study of Two Philippine Barrios.* Honolulu: University of Hawaii Press.

Low, Bobbi, Elinor Ostrom, Carl Simon, and James Wilson. 2003. Redundancy and Diversity: Do They Influence Optimal Management? In *Navigating Social-Ecological Systems: Building Resilience For Complexity and Change,* edited by F. Berkes, J. Colding, and C. Folke, pp. 83–115. Cambridge: Cambridge University Press.

Ludden, David. 1978. Ecological Zones and the Cultural Economy of Irrigation in Southern Tamilnadu. *South Asia* 1(1):1–13.

———. 1999. *The New Cambridge History of India: An Agrarian History of South Asia.* Cambridge: Cambridge University Press.

Lyall, James B. 1874. *Report of the Land Revenue Settlement of the Kangra District, Punjab.* Lahore: Central Jail Press.

Maass, Arthur, and Raymond Anderson. 1986. *And the Desert Shall Rejoice: Conflict, Growth, and Justice in Arid Environments.* Malabar, Fla.: R. E. Krieger.

Mann, Michael. 1995. Ecological Change in North India: Deforestation and Agrarian Distress in the Ganga-Jamna Doab 1800–1850. *Environment and History* 1: 201–20.

Martin, Edward. 1986. Resource Mobilization, Water Allocation, and Farmer Organization in Hill Irrigation Systems in Nepal. Ph.D. dissertation, Cornell University, Ithaca, N.Y.

Massey, Doreen. 1994. *Space, Place, and Gender.* Minneapolis: University of Minnesota Press.

McCay, Bonnie J., and James M. Acheson, eds. 1990. *The Question of the Commons: The Culture and Ecology of Communal Resources.* Tucson: University of Arizona Press.

McKean, Margaret A. 1992. Success on the Commons: A Comparative Examination of Institutions for Common Property Resource Management. *Journal of Theoretical Politics* 4:247–81.

Mehta, Parkash, and Anjala Kumari. 1990. *Poverty and Farm Size: A Case Study.* New Delhi: Mittal Publications.

Mehta, Uday Singh. 1999. *Liberalism and Empire: A Study in Nineteenth-Century British Liberal Thought.* Chicago: University of Chicago Press.

Meinzen-Dick, Ruth, and Margreet Zwarteveen. 2001. Gender Dimensions of Community Resource Management: The Case of Water Users' Associations in South Asia. In *Community and Environment: Ethnicity, Gender, and the State in Community-Based Conservation,* edited by A. Agrawal and C. Gibson, pp. 63–88. New Brunswick, N.J.: Rutgers University Press.

Meyer, John, John Boli, and George Thomas. 1994. Ontology and Rationalization in the Western Cultural Account. In *Institutional Environments and Organizations: Structural Complexity and Individualism*, edited by W. R. Scott and J. W. Meyer, pp. 9–27. Thousand Oaks, Calif.: Sage.

Meyer, John, and Brian Rowan. 1977. Institutionalized Organizations: Formal Structure as Myth and Ceremony. *American Journal of Sociology* 83:340–63.

Middleton, L. 1919. *Final Report of the Third Revised Land Revenue Settlement of the Palampur, Kangra and Nurpur Tahsils of the Kangra District.* Lahore: Government Printing.

Mitchell, Don. 2000. *Cultural Geography: A Critical Introduction.* Oxford: Blackwell.

Mitchell, Timothy. 1999. Society, Economy, and the State Effect. In *State/Culture: State Formation after the Cultural Turn*, edited by G. Steinmetz, pp. 76–97. Ithaca, N.Y.: Cornell University Press.

Moorcroft, William. 1841. *Travels in the Himalayan Provinces of Hindoostan and the Punjab.* London.

Mosse, David. 1997a. Ecological Zones and the Culture of Collective Action: The History and Social Organization of a Tank Irrigation System in Tamil Nadu. *South Indian Studies* 3:1–88.

———. 1997b. The Symbolic Making of a Common Property Resource: History, Ecology and Locality in a Tank-Irrigated Landscape in South India. *Development and Change* 28:467–504.

Narayan, Kirin. 1996. Kuhl—"The Waterway": A Basketmaker's Ballad from Kangra, Northwest India. In *The Walled-Up Wife: A Casebook*, edited by A. Dundes, pp. 109–20. Madison: University of Wisconsin Press.

Neale, Walter C. 1969. Land Is to Rule. In *Land Control and Social Structure in Indian History*, edited by R. E. Frykenberg, pp. 3–16. Madison: University of Wisconsin Press.

Negi, Jai Deep. 1992. The Begar System in the Shimla Hill States during the British Period. Master of Philosophy dissertation, Himachal Pradesh University, Shimla.

Negi, Yashwant S. 1993. The Conditions for Agroforestry Development on Farms in the Western Himalayas of India. Ph.D. dissertation, University of California, Berkeley.

Netting, Robert McC. 1974. The System Nobody Knows: Village Irrigation in the Swiss Alps. In *Irrigation's Impact on Society*, edited by T. Downing and M. Gibson, pp. 67–76. Tucson: University of Arizona Press.

North, Douglas C. 1986. The New Institutional Economics. *Journal of Institutional and Theoretical Economics* 142:230–37.

Oakerson, Ronald J. 1986. A Model for the Analysis of Common Property Problems. In *Proceedings of the Conference on Common Property Resource Management*, National Research Council, pp. 13–30. Washington, D.C.: National Academy Press.

O'Brien, E. 1889. *Assessment Report of the Palam Ilaqa, Kangra District.* Lahore: Civil and Military Gazette Press.

———. 1890. *Assessment Report of the Palam Taluqa, Palampur Tahsil, Kangra District, 1890.* Lahore: Caxton Printing Works.

———. 1891a. *Assessment Report of the Taluka Rajgiri in the Palampur Tahsil, of the Kangra District.* Lahore: Civil and Military Gazette Press.

———. 1891b. *Assessment Report of the Taluka Banghal, Palampur Tahsil, in the Kangra District.* Lahore: Civil and Military Gazette Press.

Olson, Mancur. 1965. *The Logic of Collective Action: Public Goods and the Theory of Groups.* Cambridge, Mass.: Harvard University Press.

O'Neil, Brian J. 1987. *Social Inequality in a Portuguese Hamlet.* Cambridge: Cambridge University Press.

Ostrom, Elinor. 1990. *Governing the Commons: The Evolution of Institutions for Collective Action.* Cambridge: Cambridge University Press.

Ostrom, Elinor, John Anderies, and Marco Janssen. 2003. The Robustness of Multi-Level Socio-Ecological Systems. Paper presented at the annual meeting of the American Political Science Association, Philadelphia, August 28–31.

Ostrom, Elinor, Roy Gardner, and James Walker. 1994. *Rules, Games, and Common-Pool Resources.* Ann Arbor: University of Michigan Press.

Padgett, John, and Christopher Ansell. 1993. Robust Action and the Rise of the Medici, 1400–1434. *American Journal of Sociology* 98(6):1259–1319.

Pande, U. C. 1991. *Study of State and Farmer Managed Irrigation Systems in District Almora in Uttar Pradesh Hills.* New Delhi: Water and Land Management Institute.

Parry, Jonathan P. 1979. *Caste and Kinship in Kangra.* New Delhi: Vikas Publishing House.

Peluso, Nancy. 1993. Coercing Conservation? The Politics of State Resource Control. *Global Environmental Change* 4(2):199–217.

Pfeffer, Jeffrey, and Gerald Salancik. 1978. *The External Control of Organizations: A Resource Dependence Perspective.* New York: Harper and Row.

Polanyi, Karl. 1944. *The Great Transformation.* Boston: Beacon Press.

Powell, Walter W., and Paul J. DiMaggio, eds. 1991. *The New Institutionalism in Organizational Analysis.* Chicago: University of Chicago Press.

Prakash, Gyan. 1999. *Another Reason: Science and the Imagination of Modern India.* Princeton, N.J.: Princeton University Press.

Punjab District Gazetteer. 1909. Vol. 1, part A, *Kangra District.* Lahore: Government Printing.

———. 1926. Vol. 7, *Kangra District.* Lahore: Government Printing.

Raj, Bhai Mul. 1933. *An Economic Survey of the Haripur and Mangarh Talukas of the Kangra District of the Punjab.* Lahore: Board of Economic Inquiry Punjab.

Rangan, Haripriya. 2000. State Economic Policies and Changing Regional Landscapes in the Garhwal Himalaya, 1818–1947. In *Agrarian Environments: Resources, Representation, and Rule in India,* edited by A. Agrawal and K. Sivaramakrishnan, pp. 3–46. Durham, N.C.: Duke University Press.

Riwaj-i-Abpashi [Irrigation Customs]. 1918. Compiled as part of the 1918 settlement of District Kangra.

Saberwal, Vasant. 1999. *Pastoral Politics: Shepherds, Bureaucrats, and Conservation in the Western Himalaya.* Delhi: Oxford University Press.

Saberwal, Vasant, and Ashwini Chhatre. 2003. The Parvati and the Tragopan: Conservation and Development in the Great Himalayan National Park. *Himalayan Research Bulletin* 21(2):79–88.

Sarin, Madhu. 1989. *Himachali Women: A Situational Analysis.* Jagjit Nagar: SUTRA.

Sarin, Madhu, et al. 2003. Devolution as a Threat to Democratic Decision-Making in Forestry? Findings from Three States in India. In *Local Forest Management: The Impacts of Devolution Policies,* edited by D. Edmunds and E. Wollenberg, pp. 55–126. London: Earthscan Publications.

Scharpf, Fritz. 1978. Interorganizational Policy Studies: Issues, Concepts, and Perspectives. In *Interorganizational Policy Making,* edited by K. Hanf and F. Scharpf, pp. 345–70. Beverly Hills, Calif.: Sage.

Schotter, Andrew, and Barry Sopher. 2003. Social Learning and Coordination Conventions in Intergenerational Games: An Experimental Study. *Journal of Political Economy* 111(3):498–529.

Scott, James C. 1998. *Seeing Like a State: How Certain Schemes to Improve the Human Welfare Have Failed.* New Haven, Conn.: Yale University Press.

Scott, W. Richard. 1983. The Organization of Environments: Network, Cultural, and Historical Elements. In *Organizational Environments,* edited by J. Meyer and W. R. Scott, pp. 155–75. Beverly Hills, Calif.: Sage.

———. 1991. Unpacking Institutional Arguments. In *The New Institutionalism in Organizational Analysis,* edited by W. W. Powell and P. J. DiMaggio, pp. 164–82. Chicago: University of Chicago Press.

———. 1994. Institutional Analysis: Variance and Process Theory Approaches. In *Institutional Environments and Organizations: Structural Complexity and Individualism,* edited by W. R. Scott and J. W. Meyer, pp. 81–99. Thousand Oaks, Calif.: Sage.

Seabright, Paul. 1993. Managing Local Commons: Theoretical Issues in Incentive Design. *Journal of Economic Perspectives* 7(4):113–34.

Selznick, Philip. 1957. *Leadership in Administration.* New York: Harper and Row.

Sengupta, Nirmal. 1980. The Indigenous Irrigation Organization in South Bihar. *Indian Economic and Social History Review* 17(2):157–89.

Shah, Tushaar, and Vishwa Ballabh. 1997. Water Markets in North Bihar: Six Village Studies in Muzaffarpur District. *Economic and Political Weekly* 32(52):A183–90.

Sharma, Ashwani Kumar. 1990. An Economic Analysis of Different Sources of Irrigation in Kangra District of Himachal Pradesh. Ph.D. dissertation, Himachal Pradesh Agricultural University, Palampur.

Sidky, H. 1996. *Irrigation and State Formation in Hunza: The Anthropology of a Hydraulic Kingdom.* Lanham, Md.: University Press of America.

Singh, C. M., et al. 1992. *Strengthening and Establishment of Agrometeorological Observatories in Himachal Pradesh for Estimating Evapotranspiration.* USAID Hill Areas Land and Water Development Project. Palampur: Himachal Pradesh Agricultural University.

Singh, Chattrapati. 1985. *Common Property and Common Poverty.* Delhi: Oxford University Press.

Singh, Chetan. 1998. *Natural Premises: Ecology and Peasant Life in the Western Himalaya, 1800–1950.* Delhi: Oxford University Press.

Singh, Kushwant. 1977. *A History of the Sikhs.* Delhi: Oxford University Press.

Sivaramakrishnan, K. 1999. *Modern Forests: Statemaking and Environmental Change in Colonial Eastern India.* Delhi: Oxford University Press.

Sivaramakrishnan, K., and Arun Agrawal. 2003. *Regional Modernities: The Cultural Politics of Development in India.* Delhi: Oxford University Press.

Siy, Robert Y. Jr. 1982. *Community Resource Management: Lessons from the Zanjera.* Quezon City: University of the Philippines Press.

Skaria, Ajay. 1999. *Hybrid Histories: Forests, Frontiers and Wildness in Western India.* Delhi: Oxford University Press.

Smith, Richard S. 1996. *Rule by Records: Land Registration and Village Custom in Early British Panjab.* Delhi: Oxford University Press.

Someshwar, ShivSharan. 1995. Macro Policies, Local Politics: The Official and the Clandestine Processes of Deforestation in the Western Ghats of South Kanara, India. Ph.D. dissertation, University of California, Los Angeles.

Spooner, Brian. 1974. Irrigation and Society: The Iranian Plateau. In *Irrigation's Impact on Society,* edited by T. Downing and M. Gibson, pp. 43–57. Tucson: University of Arizona Press.

Swarup, R., and B. K. Sikka. 1986. *Agricultural Development in Himachal Pradesh.* Delhi: New Light Publishers.

Tang, Shui Yan. 1992. *Institutions and Collective Action: Self-Governance in Irrigation.* San Francisco: Institute for Contemporary Studies.

Thompson, James D. 1967. *Organizations in Action.* New York: McGraw Hill.

Tolbert, Pamela S., and Lynne G. Zucker. 1983. Institutional Sources of Change in the Formal Structure of Organizations: The Diffusion of Civil Service Reform, 1880–1935. *Administrative Science Quarterly* 28:22–39.

Tucker, Richard P. 1983. The British Colonial System and the Forests of the Western Himalayas, 1815–1914. In *Global Deforestation and the Nineteenth-Century World Economy,* edited by R. Tucker and J. F. Richards. Durham, N.C.: Duke University Press.

Tupper, Charles L. 1881. Some Punjab Survivals. In *Punjab Customary Law.* Calcutta: Office of the Superintendent of Government Printing.

Uphoff, Norman, et al. 1985. *Improving Policies and Programs for Farmer Organization and Participation in Irrigation Water Management.* Water Management Synthesis II Project. Ithaca, N.Y.: Cornell University.

Uzzi, Brian. 1996. The Sources and Consequences of Embeddedness for the Economic Performance of Organizations: The Network Effect. *American Sociological Review* 61(4):674–98.

———. 1997. Social Structure and Competition in Interfirm Networks: The Paradox of Embeddedness. *Administrative Science Quarterly* 42(1):35–67.

Vashishta, L. C. 1951. *Census of India,* vol. 7, part 2-A. Government of India Press.

Wade, Robert. 1988. *Village Republics: Economic Conditions for Collective Action in South India.* Cambridge: Cambridge University Press.

Warren, Roland. 1967. The Interorganizational Field as a Focus for Investigation. *Administrative Science Quarterly* 12:396–419.

Wellman, Barry. 1988. Structural Analysis: From Method and Metaphor to Theory and Substance. In *Social Structures: A Network Approach,* edited by B. Wellman and S. D. Berkowitz, pp. 19–61. Cambridge: Cambridge University Press.

Whitcombe, Elizabeth. 1972. *Agrarian Conditions in Northern India: The United Provinces under British Rule, 1860–1900,* vol. 1. Berkeley: University of California Press.

White, T. Anderson, and C. Ford Runge. 1995. The Emergence and Evolution of Collective Action: Lessons from Watershed Management in Haiti. *World Development* 23:1683–98.

Williamson, Oliver E. 1975. *Markets and Hierarchies: Analysis and Antitrust Implications.* New York: Free Press.

———. 1981. The Economics of Organization: The Transaction Cost Approach. *American Journal of Sociology* 87:548–77.

Wittfogel, Karl A. 1957. *Oriental Despotism: A Comparative Study of Total Power.* New Haven, Conn.: Yale University Press.

Wolpert, Stanley A. 1982. *A New History of India.* New York: Oxford University Press.

Worster, Donald. 1985. *Rivers of Empire: Water Aridity and the Growth of the American West.* New York: Pantheon.

Yoder, Robert D. 1986. The Performance of Farmer-Managed Irrigation Systems in the Hills of Nepal. Ph.D. dissertation, Cornell University, Ithaca, N.Y.

Young, Peyton. 1996. The Economics of Convention. *Journal of Economic Perspectives* 10(2):105–22.

Zucker, Lynne G. 1987. Institutional Theories of Organization. *Annual Review of Sociology* 13:443–64.

———. 1991. The Role of Institutionalization in Cultural Persistence. In *The New Institutionalism in Organizational Analysis,* edited by W. W. Powell and P. J. DiMaggio, pp. 83–107. Chicago: University of Chicago Press.

INDEX

Acequias, 165, 184, 243

Agarwal, Anil, 228n2

Agrawal, Arun, 39, 40, 41, 205, 230n5

Agriculture: cash crops, 66, 203; crop failure, 66; cropping patterns, 63, 152; crop yields, 65(tables); field preparation for potato sowing, 235; field preparation for winter (rabi) crops, 93–94; *har* and *larh* fields, 54(fig), 178–79 (tables); irrigation's effects on cropping patterns and yields, 63–65; monetary returns from, 65; rice cultivation, 83–88; social fallow, 152–53; subsistence orientation and, 66, 203; timing of, 235n19

Akerloff, George, 25

Allen, John, 198

Alluvial plains of Kangra Valley, 6(fig)

Ambler, John, 235n18

Anderies, John, 30

Astley, Graham, 32–33

Awah Khad watershed, 190(fig)

Bardhan, Pranab, 169

Barnes, George C.: description of Kangra Valley, 7; description of settlement pattern, 54–55; extent of cultivation in Kangra, 17–18; first regular settlement, 117–18, 119; kuhl regime ritual, 79; kuhls, 103, 112; land grants, 105, 238; outmigration for military service, 232n2; precolonial hill rulers, 101; precolonial state-sponsored kuhl construction, 109; privatization of *shamilat*, 124. *See also* Land settlement; *Shamilat*

Bartan, 106

Battacharya, Neeladri: and codification of custom, 123, 127, 241; and gender and caste effects of land settlement, 16, 118–19

Bayly, Christopher, 238n18

Begar. See Corvee labor

Berry, Kim, 165, 218, 243n14

Bihar, irrigation, 113–14, 214

Bourdieu, Pierre: habitus, 46–47, 48; relationship among rules, practice, and action, 144; symbolic capital, 43–44, 231–32

Burchell, Graham, 119

Caste: and conflicts over kuhl water, 130,

143, 146–50; and conflicts within kuhl regimes, 167; and corvee labor obligations, 109–10, 220–21; and land ownership patterns, 124–25, 240; and naturalizing analogies, 47; and selective rule enforcement, 230; and settlement patterns, 45, 55–6. *See also* Kohli; Kuhl regimes; Land ownership
Chak, Ajit, 228*n2*
Chakravarty-Kaul, Minoti, 16, 17, 42, 122
Ciriacy-Wantrup, 230*n6*
Civic commons, 184–85. See also *Acequias*
Cochrane, Allan, 198
Cohn, Bernard, 121, 240*n32*
Common property resource management regimes: democratic practice of, 211–15; effects of environmental change on, 11, 36(fig); effects of regionality on, 12, 14, 204; exchanges among, 12; institutionalization of, 47–49; limitations of current theory, 11, 13; networks of, 209–10; and rational choice frameworks, 10, 12, 23; role of state in, 12, 14, 38, 41–42, 97, 207, 214. *See also* Networks; Regionality; Statemaking
Community-making, 133–35, 215; within *acequias*, 246*n14*. *See also* Statemaking
Corvee labor (*begar*), 108–10, 220–21, 239. *See also* Caste
Coward, E. Walter, 112
Cropping patterns, 63–65, 152
Cultural hegemony, 47

Decentralization, x, 214–15
Dhaula Dhar mountains, 6(fig)
Dirks, Nicholas, 106, 238*n19*
Douglas, Mary, 48
Donie, James, 239*n29*
Drought: colonial government response to, 132, 134, 194; interkuhl water

transfers and, 43, 180; networks as buffers against, 175, 176, 193, 208. *See also* Kuhl regimes; Kuhls; Networks
Duncan, James, 52

Earthquakes, 3, 4; and common property regime persistence, 35; government response to, 3, 134, 209; and interkuhl water sharing, 79, 185, 191; networks as buffers against, 193, 196, 202, 208, 212; organizational responses to, 13, 30, 31, 32, 35. *See also* Kuhl regimes; Kuhls; Networks
Edmunds, David, 247*n6*
Environmental shocks. *See* Drought; Earthquakes; Floods

Floods, 53, 66; and common property regime persistence, 35; effects on kuhls, 4, 37, 53, 93, 194; government response to, 102, 110, 134, 209, 213; and interkuhl water transfers, 43, 68, 79, 180; in oral tradition, 222; networks as buffers against, 175, 176, 186, 193, 196, 208, 212; organizational responses to, 4, 13, 30, 31, 32, 35, 172, 180, 182, 185, precipitation patterns and, 8, 53. *See also* Kuhl regimes; Kuhls; Networks
Foucault, Michel, 40, 119
Free riding, 145, 159. *See also* Kuhl regimes

Game theory, 23–25, 29, 229–30; limitations of, 183–85. *See also* Rational choice theory
Gardner, Roy, 24, 230*n4*
Giddens, Anthony, 46
Gidwani, Vinay, 245
Gilmartin, David, 38–39
Governmentality, 40–41, 119–21, 129, 134, 165

Granovetter, Mark, 33, 188
Greenberg, Brian, 242n9
Guha, Ranajit, 117
Gunderson, Lance, 176
Gupta, Anil, 217
Gurkha occupation of Kangra, 103, 237
Gururani, Shubhra, 40

Habib, Irfan, 106, 238n16
Habitus, 46–47, 48. See also Bourdieu,
    Pierre
Hage, Jerald, 231
Hardin, Garrett, 11, 22
Hicks, Gregory, 165, 184, 243n13, 246n14
Himachal Pradesh Irrigation and Public
    Health Department, 76; effects on
    interkuhl networks, 193–96; and
    kuhl management, 153–54, 167, 170–
    74, 212–13; and Minor Canals Act of
    1976, 242–43. See also Kuhl regimes;
    Kuhls
Hirschman, Albert, 169
Holling, C.S., 176
Hunza, Pakistan: and gravity-flow
    irrigation, 114–15. See also
    Statemaking; Technologies of power

Irrigation: as a common property
    resource, 228; flood, 86–87(figs);
    networks, 13; networks in Bali, 209;
    and organizational forms, 9; and
    state-local interactions, 9–10, 214;
    and water transfers in Tamil Nadu,
    209. See also Bihar; Hunza, Pakistan;
    Lansing, Stephen; Mosse, David;
    Statemaking; Tamil Nadu

Janssen, Marco, 30

Kangra: absence of co-parcenary village
    communities, 18; cultivated areas,
    17–18, 58, 64(fig), 122, 124,
125(table); effects of settlement on
    forest rights, 18–19; landholdings,
    61(table), 125(table); population
    trends, 58–59; precolonial political
    history, 99–105; property rights
    regimes in, 51–52, 106–7; regionality
    of, 43, 198–204; social and ecological
    landscape features, 52, 200. See also
    Katoch rulers; Land settlement;
    Regionality
Kangra Valley: description of, 6–7; floods,
    53; location, 2(map), 5; physical
    landscape of, 5, 6(fig), 7, 52–53;
    rainfall, 8, 53; settlement patterns in,
    54–56. See also Kangra
Katoch rulers, 105–15; alliance between
    Kangra and Kabul, 101; and kuhl
    construction, 102–3, 107–12; relations
    with Mughal rulers, 101–2; religious
    patronage and kuhl construction, 110;
    Sansar Chand, 103–4
Kishore, Jugal, 219
Kohli: caste status of, 242; declining
    authority of, 69–70, 150–51; and kuhl
    management responsibilities, 68, 70–
    76, 79, 88–90, 95; legitimacy of, 69; in
    oral tradition, 69, 221–22; origin of
    the right to be, 68–69; renumeration
    of, 68, 93, 95; responsibilities for ritual,
    80–83; and water measurement, 90–
    92, 158–59. See also Kuhl committees;
    Kuhl regimes; Nonfarm employment
Kuhl committees: and bureaucratization,
    163–67, 206; and conflict manage-
    ment, 156–57; and gender inequity,
    213; origins of, 154; reasons for, 154–
    55; and record keeping and rule
    enforcement, 161–62; relationship to
    kohli, 155–57, 166; state involvement
    with, 162–63; and statemaking, 164–
    65. See also Kuhl regimes
Kuhl regimes: and caste-based inequality,

143, 144–46, 220–21; characteristics of, 224–27; colonial government engagement with, 126, 131–33, 194; committees, 141–42, 143–44; as community-making arenas, 44, 82–83; and declining participation within, 139–144; dynamic regional landscape of, 95–96; effects of topography on, 44; and free riding, 159–61, 167; inequality within, 144–46; institutional change, 167–74; interdependence of, 182; and interdisciplinary explanations for, ix–x; institutionalization of, 48–49; interkuhl coordination, 180–81(table), 180–88 passim; and judicial arenas for conflict negotiation, 128, 129, 131; network density and kuhl regime persistence, 193–96; networks of, 32, 67–68, 176–79, 208; organizational variation among, 137–38, 205–7; origin dates of, 108; participation rates, 140–41, 159–61; and rational choice theory, ix; ritual aspects of, 79–83, 147, 192–93; as statemaking arenas, 44, 45–46, 126; water distribution for summer (kharif) crops, 88–93; water distribution for winter (rabi) crops, 94. *See also* Kohli; Kuhl committees; Kuhls; Kuhl water; Land classification, types of; Networks; Nonfarm employment; Rational choice theory

Kuhls: annual cleaning of, 70–76; area irrigated by, 7, 67, 217; constructed by, 8, 112; illicit water use, 89–90; new construction of, during colonial period, 124–25; numbers of, 7, 217; periodic reconstruction of the primary water diversion structure, 77–79, 93; seasonal dependence on, 8; state-sponsored, 108(table); takeover by Irrigation and Public Health Department, 75–76, 206, 209; water measurement, 90–92, 142, 156, 235n20, 241n39. *See also* Himachal Pradesh Irrigation and Public Health Department; Kohli; Kuhl regimes

Kuhl water: for milling grain, 234; uses of, 7. *See also* Agriculture; Kohli; Kuhl regimes; Kuhls

Land alienation, 121–22

Land classification, types of: and changing patterns of authority for kuhl management, 198; *har*, 36–37, 234; and kuhl networks, 67–68, 177; and labor requirements for kuhl regimes, 53–54, 108, 201; *larh*, 36–37, 234; relationship to changing cropping patterns, 152, 171; relationship to dependence on kuhl water, 168–69, 171, 172

Land consolidation, 233

Land holdings: distribution of, 61; changes in, 62

Land ownership: by caste, 125; effects on social interest in irrigation, 63, 202; precolonial transfers of, 239–40

Land reform, 62

Landscape: as site for encoding/contesting social relations, 12, 14, 109–10, 148, 221; and state authority, 110. *See also* Kangra Valley

Land settlement: and community-making, 118–19, 122–23; effects on property rights, 116, 117, 118, 120–21, 123, 214; equity impacts, 119; European roots of, 117, 119, 120; first regular, in Kangra, 115, 116, 117–21; first summary, in Kangra, 115; origin of land use categories, 123; social effects of, 16, 118. *See also* Barnes, George; Battacharya, Neeladri;

Liberal theory of government; Lyall, James; Punjab; *Shamilat*

Lansing, Stephen, 13, 30

LaPorte, Todd, 176, 182, 188, 244*n1*

Leach, Edmund, 44

Liberal theory of government, 119–20, 133

Low, Bobbi, 244*n2*

Ludden, David, 38–39, 99–100, 236*n4*

Lyall, James B., 56, 106, 124, 128; and the codification of irrigation custom, 126, 127

Mand Khad watershed, 190(fig)

Market economy: expansion of, 136

Martin, Edward, 234*n12*

Massey, Doreen, 12, 43, 52, 148, 198

Mehta, Uday, 120

Meinzen-Dick, Ruth, 247*n5*

Methods, research, 218–19

Mill, James, 119

Mill, John Stuart, 119, 241*n38*

Mitchell, Don, 52

Mitchell, Timothy, 38, 236*n3*

Monsoon floods. *See* Floods

Moorcroft, William, 237*n13*

Mosse, David, 30, 38, 44, 113, 146, 151, 209

Mughal rule, 100, 101–2, 103, 110, 238. *See also* Katoch rulers

Narayan, Kirin, 242*n6*

Narbadeshwar temple, 111(fig)

Naturalizing analogies: and kuhls, 46, 48, 49; and habitus, 47; and institutional change, 49

Neale, Walter, 238*n15*

Negi, Yashwant, 62, 152

Networks: benefits of, 246; coherence of among kuhls, 188–93; and common property resource management, 30; and Irrigation and Public Health

Department takeover of kuhls, 208–9, 212–13; and kuhl regime persistence, 35, 175–76, 208; and organization theory, 30–34; and reciprocity, 183; stability of, 245. *See also* Kuhl regimes; Kuhls; Organization theory; Topography

Neugal River watershed, 189(fig); and agricultural and nonagricultural workers, 59(fig); and changes in cultivated area, 17–18, 58(fig); and changes in population, 58–59; cropping patterns, 63–64; and destructive floods, 4; kuhl committees in, 155(table); kuhl regimes in, 224–27(tables); location of, 5(map). See also Kohli; Kuhl committees; Kuhl regimes; Kuhls; Methods, research

Nonfarm employment: and attitudes towards farming, 60; effects on kuhl regimes, 52, 137–53, 167–74, 205–7; historical roots of, 56–57; and labor for kuhl management tasks, 60; as military service, 56–57; nature of, 60, 203; as supplement to subsistence agriculture, 56; trends, 58–60

North, Oliver, 23, 25, 49

O'Neil, Brian, 169

Olson, Mancur, 23

Organization theory: the "collective-action" view, 32; and interorganizational networks, 32–34; resource dependence theory and, 31. *See also* Hage, Jerald; LaPorte, Todd; Networks; Pfeffer, Jeffrey; Scharpf, Fritz; Scott, Richard; Thompson, James; Warren, Roland

Ostrom, Elinor, 30; characteristics of common property resource management (CPRM) regimes, 10; and effects of environmental change on CPRM regimes, 11; game theory and collective action, 23, 24, 230*n4*; and rule changes within CPRM regimes, 25, 27–28, 230

Outmigration: effects on kuhls, 4. *See also* Kuhl regimes

Panchayat: involvement with kuhl management, 75, 153, 156, 157, 243

Pangwan Kuhl, 78(fig), 80–81(figs)

Parry, Jonathan, 55, 57, 61, 121, 240*n36*, 246*n13*

Pathan Kuhl, 141(table)

Pattah, 18, 106–7, 239

Peluso, Nancy, 236*n2*

Pena, Devon, 165, 184, 243*n13*, 246*n14*

Pfeffer, Jeffrey, 32

Physiocratic theory, 117, 119, 120, 133

Place-making, 12, 43; and regionality in Kangra, 199. *See also* Regionality

Prakash, Gyan, 41

Property rights: effects of colonial rule on, 240. *See also* Land ownership; Land settlement; Punjab; *Shamilat*

Punjab: British control over, 117; and changing land use patterns, 15, 18, 122; effects of land settlement on common shares, 118, 123, 240; and green revolution agriculture, 66; involvement with kuhl committees, 154, 164; irrigation in, 39, 42, 119; Land Alienation Act of 1900, 122, 134; social effects of land settlement, 16–17, 97–98, 119, 127–28, 214. *See also* Land settlement

Rangan, Haripriya, 39

Raniya Kuhl, 76–78(figs)

Rational Choice Theory: assumptions of, 22; and common property regime persistence, 34–37; and institutional change within common property

resource management regimes, 25–28; limitations of, 28–29, 183–85, 245; and the prisoner's dilemma, 22. *See also* Game theory; Transactions-cost economics

Redundancy, and ability to absorb environmental shocks, 185–86; and resilience of kuhl regimes, 176; and risk reduction, 244. *See also* Risk; Resilience

Regionality, 12; effects on kuhl regime persistence, 43, 199–200; and institutional change, 49. *See also* Kangra; Statemaking

Resilience: of common property regimes, 208; interkuhl coordination and, 176; and kuhl networks, 177, 193, 198, 202; and vulnerability to flooding, 185

Risk: and collective action, 196; and common property regimes, 13, 196, 207; of crop loss, 146, 235; farmer response to, 84, 152, 233, 235; management of, 21; networks as buffers against, 29, 30, 32–33, 208; organizational response to, 30, 174. *See also* Networks; Redundancy; Resilience

Riwaj-i-Abpashi (Irrigation Customs): and the colonial codification of custom, 127–29; effects of codification on kohli authority, 130–31; as evidence in court, 131; as a legal record of rights, 128–29; preparation of, 126; revision of, 128; social effects of codification, 130; and state sponsored kuhl construction, 108; and water conflict, 128, 129

Saberwal, Vasant, 39, 236*n1*

Salancik, Gerald, 32

Sapruhl Kuhl, 72–73(figs), 147–48(figs)

Sarin, Madhu, 214

Scharpf, Fritz, 183, 230
Scott, James, 19, 200
Scott, W. Richard, 192–93
Sengupta, Nirmal, 113
Shamilat, 240; colonial introduction in Kangra, 123–24; efforts to privatize, 124
Sikh rule in Kangra, 45, 100, 102, 115, 117, 232, 239. *See also* Singh, Ranjit
Singh, Dhyan, 241n4
Singh, Ranjit, 103–5
Sivaramakrishnan, K., 40, 205
Skaria, Ajay, 105
Smith, Richard, 239n29, 240n35
Soil types: effects on kuhls, 44. *See also* Land classification, types of
Someshwar, ShivSharan, 40
Sonia Kuhl, 80(fig), 92(fig)
State: conceptions of, 38, 40; involvement with kuhl regimes, 154; local interactions with, 38–46, 98. *See also* Governmentality; Himachal Pradesh Irrigation and Public Health Department; Kuhl regimes; Statemaking
Statemaking, 40, 200, 202, 236; colonial, in Kangra, 116, 126; and common property resource regimes, 98; and community-making, 133–35; and irrigation in Hunza, Pakistan, 114–15; and kuhl construction, 110–12, 133; and kuhl regimes, 99, 165, 200–201, 210–12, 215; and regionality in Kangra, 211; and water management, 129. *See also* Governmentality; Kuhl committees; Kuhl regimes
State simplifications, 200

Tamil Nadu: and tank irrigation, 113–14, 214, 242. *See also* Mosse, David
Tax-farming, 237
Technologies of power, 99–100, 101; and gift giving, 105; and irrigation in Hunza, Pakistan, 114; and kuhl sponsorship, 102–3, 110–12; and land grants, 99, 104, 105
Thompson, James, 31, 244n3
Tolbert, Pamela, 164
Topography: effects on kuhl management, 45; effects on kuhl networks, 44, 54
Tragedy of the Commons, 11, 22
Transactions-cost economics, 23

Uzzi, Brian, 33–34, 184–85, 245n9

Van de Van, Andrew, 32–33

Wade, Robert, 40, 196. *See also* Risk
Walker, James, 24, 230n4
Warren, Roland, 231n11
Water. *See* Kuhls
Water measurement. *See* Kuhls
Wellman, Barry, 183
Wollenberg, Eva, 247n6
Wolpert, Stanley, 236n5
Women: and agricultural work, 136, 241; bride-price payments, 121; census data on, 233; effects of land settlement on, 16; households headed by, 234; norms barring from communal kuhl management tasks, 73, 138, 160; summer (kharif) season agricultural work, 85; winter (rabi) season agricultural work, 93. *See also* Battacharya, Neeladri; Caste; Kuhl committees; Sarin, Madhu

Young, Peyton, 24

Zwarteveen, Margaret, 247n5
Zucker, Lynn, 164

Library of Congress Cataloging-in-Publication Data

Baker, J. Mark, 1961–
The kuhls of Kangra: community-managed irrigation
in the Western Himalaya / J. Mark Baker.—1st ed.
p. cm.—(Culture, place, and nature)
Includes bibliographical references and index.
ISBN 0-295-98491-0 (hardback: alk. paper)
1. Commons—India—Kåangra (District)
2. Community development—India—Kåangra (District)
3. Land use, Rural—India—Kåangra (District)—Management.
4. Natural resources, Communal—India—Kåangra (District)—Management.
5. Irrigation—India—Kåangra (District)—Management.
I. Title. II. Series
HD1289.I5B35 2005   333.91'3'095452—dc22   2005000291